# INVISIBLE CHAINS

CANADA'S UNDERGROUND WORLD OF HUMAN TRAFFICKING

# INVISIBLE CHAINS

BENJAMIN PERRIN

VIKING
CANADA

VIKING CANADA

Published by the Penguin Group

Penguin Group (Canada), 90 Eglinton Avenue East, Suite 700, Toronto, Ontario, Canada M4P 2Y3
(a division of Pearson Canada Inc.)

Penguin Group (USA) Inc., 375 Hudson Street, New York, New York 10014, U.S.A.
Penguin Books Ltd, 80 Strand, London WC2R 0RL, England
Penguin Ireland, 25 St Stephen's Green, Dublin 2, Ireland (a division of Penguin Books Ltd)
Penguin Group (Australia), 250 Camberwell Road, Camberwell, Victoria 3124, Australia
(a division of Pearson Australia Group Pty Ltd)
Penguin Books India Pvt Ltd, 11 Community Centre, Panchsheel Park, New Delhi – 110 017, India
Penguin Group (NZ), 67 Apollo Drive, Rosedale, North Shore 0632, New Zealand
(a division of Pearson New Zealand Ltd)
Penguin Books (South Africa) (Pty) Ltd, 24 Sturdee Avenue, Rosebank, Johannesburg 2196, South Africa

Penguin Books Ltd, Registered Offices: 80 Strand, London WC2R 0RL, England

First published 2010

2 3 4 5 6 7 8 9 10 (RRD)



A portion of the proceeds of this book will be donated by the author to initiatives
to end human trafficking.

Manufactured in the U.S.A.

Library and Archives Canada Cataloguing in Publication data available upon request to the publisher.

ISBN: 978-0-670-06453-3

Visit the Penguin Group (Canada) website at **www.penguin.ca**

Special and corporate bulk purchase rates available; please see
**www.penguin.ca/corporatesales** or call 1-800-810-3104, ext. 2477 or 2474

*For Sevey and You.*
*You know who you are.*

*Slavery is a weed that grows in any soil.*

—EDMUND BURKE

*Never doubt that a small group of thoughtful,*
*committed citizens can change the world.®*
*Indeed, it's the only thing that ever has.*

—MARGARET MEAD

# CONTENTS

# PREFACE

In the midst of peace and beauty it is unusual to turn your thoughts to images of abuse and ugliness, but that is precisely what happened to some university friends and me late in the summer of 2000. We were staying at a lakeside cottage in Muskoka, Ontario, a region where the lakes are cool and placid, the granite rocks are as Canadian as a Group of Seven painting, and the cry of the loons at dusk can raise the hairs on the back of your neck.

As we watched the sun begin to set on a day that was nearing the end of another cottage season, we joked that it looked just like a beer commercial.

We weren't nostalgic, however. We were eager for the future and, some would say, idealistic. After all, we were on the brink of our professional lives, overflowing with opportunities and plans. I anticipated a career in business, although I had not sharpened my focus any narrower than that. Others were preparing their own vision for the future, some in accounting, some in law or public policy.

As diverse as our goals might have been, our backgrounds were similar—young men and women from middle-class families enjoying the luxury of a beautiful setting to share dreams and laughter, none of us with a serious concern in our own lives worth expressing. All of us on that lakeside patio considered ourselves fortunate. We would enter the "responsible adult" period of our lives with an excellent education and equally good prospects for success. We could expect, with reasonable hard work, to maintain the quality of life we were enjoying at the moment, and in doing so we would represent a small minority of the world's general population.

Instead of talking about our own comfortable futures, however, we took turns reviewing a litany of suffering being experienced around the world—poverty, starvation, war crimes, genocide, HIV/AIDS, child soldiers, and the modern-day slavery of human trafficking....

Slavery? Human trafficking? I was taken aback. These were eighteenth- and nineteenth-century concerns. We had just celebrated the start of the twenty-first century. Surely these issues weren't still in need of attention on a wide scale in foreign regions, let alone our own country.

The idea that people continue to deal in human beings as though they were domestic animals, furniture, or a commodity was impossible for me to imagine. Yet after some discussion and contemplation, I realized that to ignore the issue was equally unconscionable. The well-worn words of Edmund Burke resounded in my head: "All that it takes for evil to prevail is for good people to do nothing." I don't know where I first heard the famous challenge, but it would haunt me for the next decade.

We were aware of evidence that human trafficking persisted around the world. But to what extent? How did it function? Who were its victims? And how could it be addressed and eliminated?

What began as idle chatter developed into a commitment to do something—anything. How could we do nothing and let evil prevail? I suspect that discussions similar to this one occur constantly among people of our age, as a reflection of our idealism if nothing else. This discussion was different, however. This one led to awareness followed by action. It managed, to one extent or another, to alter the lives of everybody who had gathered to relax and enjoy that quiet Muskoka evening more than a decade ago.

We made a pledge to each other. When we got home, we would research the problem and exchange findings, we would raise public awareness of the situation, we would go abroad to help those struggling against this oppression, and we would coalesce our efforts into an organization we named "The Future Group."

We spent the next eight months setting our plan in motion and raising funds to cover our costs. The largest and most immediate expense would be a hundred-day deployment to an area that represented the most critical abuse of people as contemporary slaves, and we soon settled on Cambodia.

Of all the countries in the world, Cambodia should rank among the most peaceful and abundant. Its culture extends back thousands of years, its overriding values are Buddhist, and its people are basically gentle in their approach to others. Yet few countries are as dominated by issues of slavery, owing in large part to the patronizing of the country's sex industry by tourists from Australia, Western Europe, and North America, including untold numbers of Canadian men every year.

If we could document and expose the problem while volunteering with local organizations that assist survivors of sex slavery, warn at-risk youth, and deter would-be child sex offenders from developed countries, we would have made a small but important difference. It was a tall order. Going up against an entrenched industry of sexual exploitation that is sustained through corruption, crime, and violence was a daunting prospect that more than once gave us pause. But we could not ignore the pull we felt to address this problem.

Those were our intentions when, eight months after that summer evening discussion in Muskoka, I and three other members of The Future Group travelled to Cambodia to spend one hundred of the most remarkable days of our lives.

Arriving in the capital, Phnom Penh, felt a little like arriving in a war zone. The city, once a French colonial outpost, consists mostly of crumbling low-rise buildings. Settling into our quarters, we quickly established a routine: Mornings and afternoons were spent volunteering with the local aid organizations, including AFESIP Cambodia—in English, "Acting for Women in Distressing Situations"—a grassroots group dedicated to fighting the trafficking of women and children for sex slavery. Founded by Somaly Mam, a Cambodian survivor of sex trafficking, the group takes an approach that is victim-centred, with long-term goals of achieving successful and permanent rehabilitation and reintegration.

In the evenings, we would discuss ideas to improve the local response to the problem and write emails home to raise money to implement them. Some nights, I and two other male members of the group dressed as tourists to investigate the bars and brothels of the city along with local human rights activists, recording the number of girls, their approximate ages, and any signs of physical abuse we saw. We then returned to our room to prepare our reports for local prosecutors and police.

This first-hand experience powerfully affected all of us. It was clear that the girls spent the daytime hours in brothels and hotels throughout the city and the evenings in the long string of bars spread throughout the red-light districts. In these situations, we recognized that the tragedy encompassed thousands of girls, women, and young boys who clearly wished only to live normal lives. Hearing the accounts of abuse suffered by survivors in the shelters while knowing that so many more were being exploited is difficult to process. A shell of sorts develops as a mechanism that permits you to concentrate on the task at hand and set aside the emotional response to all that is being witnessed.

The shell, however, is not impervious. Not forever.

One Friday evening I returned to my apartment and broke down. If I were back in Canada, I would have been out with friends having drinks and dinner, maybe watching a movie. Yet I had just spent this Friday evening watching young girls face another night of being sold to strangers, over and over again. They did so both to try to avoid beatings, and in the hope that someday they could return to their families.

Each survivor we met represented a tragedy of one kind or another, some more distressing and memorable than others. One of these was Sevey, a dark-haired nine-year-old Cambodian girl whom I met at a recovery centre in northern Phnom Penh. The shelter was protected by twelve-foot walls to keep the traffickers from reclaiming their victims—something that nonetheless happened from time to time. To build trust with young survivors like Sevey, I brought a soccer ball, along with water bottles for goalposts. I still remember her bright smile and jubilant laughter as she scored a goal against "Team Canada." Just months before, Sevey had been sold by her parents and was being sexually exploited by touring pedophiles for the financial benefit of her trafficker.

I asked, through the Khmer translator, what Sevey hoped to do now that she was receiving care and education and was free of the people who had purchased her. Her reaction was a flood of tears. Had I said something wrong, perhaps crossed some cultural barrier?

No, I was assured. Sevey had begun to cry because her future was a scary unknown. She came from a tiny remote village deep in the jungles and rice paddies of rural Cambodia. She had never learned the name of the village, if indeed it had one on a map, nor did she know the last name of her parents or how to find them. Clearly she had no hope of ever going home.

The young girl's experience was tragic but hardly unique. According to a 2000 study by UNICEF, 30 to 35 percent of sex trafficking victims in Cambodia are children, many taken from their homes to major urban centres where they are sold for sex. Vietnamese, Chinese, Thai, Laotian, and Filipina girls have also been brought to the country to be sexually exploited. Our research during our hundred days in Cambodia framed these crude estimates in dreadful detail. The "owners" of sex slaves search for poor, unassuming, disease-free young girls, preferably between thirteen and sixteen—sometimes much younger to satisfy the demand of foreign pedophiles. These girls on the threshold of adolescence are forcibly sold for sex acts to between ten and twenty men per day, seven days a week.

Each of these child sex slaves is maintained by a *mama-san* who exercises control over every detail of her life. If the victims refuse to engage in a sex act, they are brutally beaten. They're often kept malnourished in order to make them more compliant and dependent on their *mama-san.* Meanwhile, parents in distant villages may be unaware their child is being sold for sex, genuinely believing the child is working in a restaurant or selling flowers to tourists—common lies told to unsuspecting parents. In other cases, parents offer up their child either knowing or suspecting that she will be sold for sex—a decision that's difficult to comprehend, even given the abject poverty that is the legacy of the bloody Khmer Rouge period. The parents are often paid up front for the "income" their child will earn in the big city; however, that money is now a debt that the child must repay to her *mama-san.* And the debt increases as the *mama-san* charges everything imaginable back to the victim, including food, the "rent" of the room she is sold in, medical treatment, if it is ever given, and fines if men complain about the girl. The system, in other words, relies on physical and sexual violence, combined with financial coercion, to control its young victims for years at a time. As the victim ages and shows more signs of physical and psychological abuse, she's likely to be sold to a lower-end brothel. There, instead of servicing wealthy Cambodian men, foreign travellers, and expatriates, she will be sold for far less to average local men.

There are really only four ways out for most of the victims exploited in this systematic fashion. First, they may risk escape at an opportune moment, but are rarely successful. Second, they may be among the small minority that are rescued (often because their *mama-san* is not paying enough in bribes to the police). Third, they may be killed for persistent acts of resistance or escape attempts, also serving as an example to other victims of the consequences of disobedience. Or, finally, after years of being sold, they may be discarded because they are too costly to maintain or so psychologically and physically damaged that no one will pay to abuse them anymore.

In Cambodia, my team and I helped implement programs to rehabilitate these victims, deter and prosecute offenders, and identify rural villages targeted by traffickers. On more than one occasion we feared for our safety, based on threats by traffickers and others who profited from the situation. At other times we felt almost too overwhelmed to continue, yet we found ourselves being encouraged by the young survivors whose yearning for freedom inspired us.

My colleagues and I returned from Cambodia shaken by the outrageous conditions we had witnessed and determined to alert others to the need for action, including strategies to help Cambodian grassroots organizations dedicated to ending the exploitation of children as sex slaves.

Having seen affluent male tourists from North America, Western Europe, and Australia audaciously walking hand in hand with underage girls they had rented, I knew that our own nation was tainted in contributing to the tragedy. And yet it was a tragedy confined to distant lands. My naive assumption that sex trafficking was something that couldn't happen in Canada was eventually overturned.

One day in November 2003, I received a telephone call from a reporter with the *Calgary Herald* seeking my comment on a recent human trafficking case discovered through an investigation called "Operation Relaxation." The case had taken place not in Cambodia, Thailand, or Vietnam but in my hometown of Calgary. This was shocking enough, but the actual location where the women were being held had an even more personal impact. It wasn't in some industrial area of the city or in the rougher down-and-out locales frequented by drug dealers, but rather just a few blocks from an old-fashioned burger-and-milkshake restaurant called Peter's Drive-In, where my parents had treated me and my siblings after baseball games as kids. How could I justify addressing sexual slavery only in far-off places when it was occurring practically in the neighbourhood where I grew up?

I couldn't. And I didn't.

Over the next several years I researched human trafficking in Canada, intent on learning how it could happen here and what we as a nation were doing about it. Operation Relaxation was like a thread I began to pull, quickly revealing a vast web of exploitation that reached across Canada and, indeed, around the world. There were hundreds, perhaps thousands, of trafficking victims in Canada, but they weren't all from abroad. On a smaller but no less shameful scale, we were guilty of tolerating systems of exploitation in our country every bit as appalling as those in Cambodia.

The response of our courts and government to the situation, whenever it was drawn to their attention, often has been nothing less than disgraceful. No system existed to help victims: Some foreign victims were even treated as criminals—detained and deported, ineligible to receive even basic medical care or counselling. In contrast, their traffickers rarely were charged and, when charges were pressed and a conviction obtained, the sentences handed out were horrendously inadequate.

Most shocking of all was my discovery of a key reason behind such inadequate punishment against the perpetrators: Until 2005, *there was no* Criminal Code *offence of human trafficking.*

By the time Operation Relaxation was complete and its discoveries made public, I had abandoned my plans for a business career in favour of the law. Working within the legal system appeared to be the most effective method of dealing with modern-day slavery and, perhaps, would afford a means of healing the scars I had acquired from my time in Cambodia.

In 2006, after spending more than a year and a half seeking answers from the federal government about Canada's failure to protect trafficking victims—as it had promised to do in an international treaty—I enlisted the help of some exceptional law students to draft a report evaluating this country's treatment of enslaved individuals. Canada got a failing grade.

Fortunately, our report received a flurry of national and international media attention, prompting Monte Solberg, the new minister of citizenship and immigration, to promise to make the system more responsive to victims. And he did. Just two weeks later I received a telephone call from Ian Todd, his chief of staff, inviting me to join them as a senior policy adviser. Within eight weeks the minister had approved new guidelines for the treatment of trafficking victims. These guidelines granted victims temporary residence permits to remain in Canada to help them recover and access interim federal health care and emergency counselling.

The minister's efforts led to the creation of a basic framework for granting foreign trafficking victims legal immigration status in recognition of their suffering at the hands of others—an important initiative, but only the first step toward shaping an effective government response.

The word that best describes Canada's record in dealing with human trafficking is *lethargic.* The United States, the European Union, and many other countries have been active in protecting victims as well as prosecuting traffickers and travelling sex offenders for at least ten to fifteen years. Scholars and public policy experts have been studying human trafficking in their own countries the world over for more than a decade, but Canada has yet to draft a comprehensive response to it within its own borders. In 2007, when I began the research for this book, *not a single person had been convicted of human trafficking in Canada.* Only a handful of victims had been helped, and only one Canadian pedophile had been convicted under Canadian laws that make it an offence to sexually exploit children overseas.

Yet human traffickers in Victoria, Vancouver, Calgary, Edmonton, Saskatoon, Winnipeg, Toronto, Ottawa, Montreal, Quebec City, Halifax, and numerous smaller cities and towns are preying upon foreign victims and Canadian citizens alike. Many of these cases are described in this book, documented with interviews by those on the front lines, along with evidence from police and government records released under the *Access to Information Act.* Many of these stories are being told publicly for the first time—to educate, to inform, and to inspire action that will address this hidden national tragedy.

Beyond raising awareness, in this book I propose concrete recommendations for how Canada can become an international leader in the abolition of human trafficking—not only at all levels of government and law enforcement, but with the help of non-governmental organizations, communities, companies, and individuals. Together we can defend freedom and end modern-day slavery.

# INVISIBLE CHAINS

# 1

# THE RENAISSANCE OF SLAVERY

On Wednesday, November 5, 2003, immigration officials and armed police officers descended on Cloud 9 Body Care, a massage parlour just a few blocks from Rosedale Elementary and Junior High School in Calgary. The raid was part of a carefully orchestrated law enforcement mission targeting more than a dozen locations across the prairie city that chilly morning.

The Calgary Police Service assigned the code name "Operation Relaxation" to their eighteen-month undercover investigation into massage parlours throughout the city, which began with an anonymous tip that women from Southeast Asia were being forced to sell their bodies to repay inflated debts for their travel to Canada. The women, some of whom had already been ensnared in the sex industry in their home countries, were lured with promises of a better life. A Thai woman who was living illegally in Calgary obtained travel documents from corrupt officials in the victims' home countries, and then secured student or visitor visas enabling the women to enter Canada. Once they'd arrived, the women were forced to hand over their travel documents, which were destroyed to prevent anyone from tracing their identities and whereabouts.

The traffickers covered their tracks by using bogus identification to obtain real driver's licences for the women in British Columbia. For an average of twenty-five hundred dollars, a "Wellness Centre" in Richmond, British Columbia, issued certificates stating that the women were trained massage therapists. The fake certificates were sufficient evidence for local municipal officials to issue massage therapy licences. In Calgary alone, at least forty-three people were granted licences based on the fraudulent Wellness Centre documents.

Once in Canada, the women were sold to massage parlour owners in Vancouver, Calgary, and other cities for between eight and fifteen thousand dollars each—not hired or employed, but instead *sold.*

In the hands of her new "owner," each woman was required to pay off a "contract" of at least forty thousand dollars to the massage parlour operator through sex acts with customers. To generate the amount needed to secure their release, the women had to service numerous men almost every day. Most of the women didn't speak English.

Was Cloud 9 Body Care unique or did it serve as a model for similar ventures in other areas of the city? To determine the answer, Calgary police officers went undercover as men wanting to set up their own massage parlour offering sexual services. Within a short time, they had negotiated the "purchase" of several women, along with advice from the traffickers on how to maximize their profits and minimize their problems in handling the victims.

Any amount of money deemed appropriate, the traffickers suggested, could be imposed on the women as the price for their freedom. "We were looking at an eighty thousand dollar contract per girl before their obligations were concluded," says Detective Cam Brooks of the Calgary Police Service. The traffickers even advised the undercover officers on how to ensure that the women did not attempt to flee or alert authorities to their situation.

"You can't let them go out," the traffickers said. "You have to keep them separated so that they don't start talking among themselves about how they can get out of this before their contract is fulfilled. You must watch their every movement."

Based on secretly taped conversations, police obtained arrest and search warrants to raid massage parlours implicated in the criminal network. The owners and operators of the parlours were arrested, and the women found on the premises taken into custody for questioning.

As the dust settled in Calgary after the raids, questions arose about the fate of the exploited women in the massage parlours and the alleged traffickers.

"We see these women as victims, as anyone in the sex trade is," Staff Sergeant Joe Houben told the media. We now know, however, that the foreign women captured in the dragnet who did not have legal immigration status were detained and deported by federal officials, further traumatizing them and exposing them to the risk of re-trafficking or reprisal. The few women who were legally in Canada were released and soon vanished; police suspect they were sent to other locations in Calgary or moved to Vancouver and Toronto.

More than fifty criminal charges were laid against twenty-eight people as a result of Operation Relaxation, but the outcome of those prosecutions is much less impressive than the number of charges suggests. Anthony Lee, a thirty-six-year-old Chinese-Canadian and the alleged owner of Cloud 9 Body Care, managed to evade police during the initial sweep. Police believed that Lee had links to organized crime in Vancouver. After a forty-one-day manhunt, Lee turned himself in to police, who charged him with a series of offences under the *Criminal Code,* including conspiring to procure a person to enter Canada for prostitution, conspiring to direct or take a person to a common bawdy house (i.e., a brothel), and two counts of keeping a bawdy house and living off the avails of prostitution.

Human trafficking had not yet been made an offence in the *Criminal Code*, so Lee could not be charged with that more serious crime. He spent one evening in custody and the following day was released on bail. Two years later, while Lee's case was still making its way through the justice system, Crown prosecutor David Torske told a Calgary court that an "equipment malfunction" had damaged key wiretap evidence implicating Lee in the sale of the Asian women. And since none of the victims were available as witnesses—they'd either been deported or disappeared—all of the charges against Lee, except one, were dropped.

## When fines are mere business expenses

In March 2006, Lee pleaded guilty to the only remaining charge: keeping a common bawdy house. Prosecutor Torske told the court that Lee was engaged in "a modern form of slavery," yet the sentence handed down by Justice Bob Wilkins was a paltry fine of ten thousand dollars. Moreover, Lee was given two and a half years to come up with the money.

Calgary police estimated that each woman exploited in the massage parlour scheme could bring in up to ten thousand dollars per month. On that basis Lee's punishment was nothing more than a business expense, and a petty one at that. In effect, it was like buying a city permit rather than receiving a proportionate penalty for committing a serious crime.

Lee's accomplice and girlfriend, Noi Saengchanh, was a thirty-three-year-old Thai woman with a sixth-grade education who in October 1998 had entered Canada illegally under a false name. Prostituted in Thailand, she drew on her knowledge of the sex trade, joining the other side of the "business" as a facilitator of human trafficking. In July 2004, Saengchanh pleaded guilty to three prostitution-related offences and was sentenced by Justice Catherine Skene of the Alberta Provincial Court to two years imprisonment. After serving one-third of her sentence, she was released and deported back to her native Thailand.

Operation Relaxation did more than confirm that human trafficking could occur in a typical Canadian neighbourhood. It also demonstrated how Canada was ill-equipped to confront modern-day slavery in its own backyard.

"This was before human trafficking was really on the radar," says Detective Brooks. "We had a great opportunity to further this investigation, going even so far as to get an undercover operator to Thailand. Unfortunately, there was an issue around cost and jurisdiction. We met with the RCMP a bunch of times, trying to facilitate this whole thing. It was frustrating. And it never worked out."

Staff Sergeant Houben tried to describe the scope of the problem, and the challenge of dealing with it, to the media. "This is the tip of the iceberg," he said. "It takes a more determined and broader investigation rather than local police forces. It's very difficult [for us] to focus on federal issues. We concentrate on our own turf."

Traffickers and the men who pay to abuse these victims know all too well about the lack of police coordination in confronting this crime, and they use every means available to exploit the situation. Soon after Operation Relaxation and its achievements became public knowledge, several online discussion boards warned men who frequent massage parlours to avoid them in Calgary for a while, recommending that such patrons "go to Edmonton" instead.

Operation Relaxation opened the eyes of law enforcement officials and the courts to the realization that human trafficking can occur anywhere. It also exposed the renaissance of "new" forms of slavery, more clandestine than the traditional slavery practised in many regions of the world through the eighteenth and nineteenth centuries, but just as loathsome and dehumanizing.

## A slave in wartime Africa and peaceful Canada

The evil of the new slavery can only be fully assessed through the experiences of its victims, one of whom is Thérèse.

For almost half of her life, Thérèse was a slave. She grew up in the Democratic Republic of the Congo during a civil war that various human rights groups have labelled a "war against women." Parties in the conflict perpetuated the war by recruiting young boys as child soldiers and forcing girls to become "bush wives." Sexual violence commonly was used to terrorize the population and destroy families. At fourteen, Thérèse became a casualty of this war when her family sold her to traffickers, and for the next eleven years she was forced to provide sex acts to hordes of men.

"She was basically a commodity, sold from one person to another person through all those years," says Sherilyn Trompetter, assistant executive director of Changing Together, an Edmonton-based non-governmental organization (NGO) that helps immigrant women. "Since she was a young child, she did not have control over any aspect of her life."

Thérèse's trafficker controlled five other women, two of whom he eventually beat to death. At one point, Thérèse became pregnant and gave birth to a baby who, when just three months old, was taken away, never to be seen again.

Thérèse's "owner" eventually realized that he could profit more from her exploitation in North America than in Africa, so at twenty-five she was brought to Canada with two other women to be sold for sex. Ironically, a country that continues to pride itself on its role in supporting the Underground Railroad for freed slaves of African origin in the nineteenth century had, by the early twenty-first century, become an attractive destination for traffickers in slaves from the same continent.

In Thérèse's case, however, the move to Canada proved advantageous. Shortly after arriving here in April 2008, she gathered the courage to escape when her trafficker let her use a public washroom. The other women who were brought to Canada with Thérèse weren't so fortunate—authorities appear unable to find them.

## New versus Old Slavery

The slave trade has been illegal in Canada and the rest of the British Empire since 1807, when the U.K. Parliament passed *An Act for the Abolition of the Slave Trade* after a twenty-year campaign led by William Wilberforce. First elected to Parliament at the age of twenty-one, Wilberforce is the subject of an extraordinary story told two centuries later in the film *Amazing Grace*. The title comes from the hymn written by John Newton, himself a former slave trader who became a passionate proponent of abolishing slavery—an "abolitionist."

Under international law, slavery is defined as "the status or condition of a person over whom any or all of the powers attaching to the right of ownership are exercised." More simply, a person treated as property constitutes a slave to be sold, traded, used, abused, and disposed of. International law takes slavery seriously. A slave trader can be prosecuted anywhere in the world that he or she is apprehended, regardless of where the crime took place.

Treating people as property offends our most deeply held beliefs in human liberty. On that basis alone, ending human trafficking deserves to be a priority for modern governments. Too often, though, advocates for better laws prohibiting the practice and calling for stiff penalties against those convicted of human trafficking are treated as though they are trapped in the eighteenth century.

The cruel reality is that slavery continues to exist, albeit in an evolved form. Author and researcher Kevin Bales has even estimated that more people are in bondage today than during any other period in history. While many factors distinguish these old and new species of slavery, the catastrophic impact on the lives of the victims has changed little.

For example, "Old Slavery" owners paid high costs to acquire their slaves and earned relatively low profits from their labour. In contrast, "New Slavery" owners avoid legal ownership but earn high profits from slaves whose cost is often minimal. During the period of Old Slavery, owners usually provided at least basic necessities for their slaves in hope of reaping profit from their labour over the long term. With New Slavery, the exploitative relationship is comparatively shorter, the slaves are considered disposable, and the care they receive is minimal, if any. Finally, ethnic differences were important to slave owners of yesteryear. Today, ethnic origin is not important—slavery has become an "equal opportunity" form of exploitation.

Despite these distinctions between Old and New Slavery, some fundamental similarities remain: the targeting of disadvantaged individuals to reap ill-gotten financial rewards, the resistance of profiteers to exposing these systems of exploitation, the complicity of governments either through corruption or inaction, and the crucial role of individuals and civil society in championing its abolition.

Shock and outrage are often the first reactions from people in Canada and throughout much of the rest of the world who bear witness to human trafficking. Arousing a sense of determination and effective action to address human trafficking is more challenging. In some cases, as in Canada until very recently, no law specifically identified human trafficking as a criminal offence. To deal with the problem, some jurisdictions dusted off old anti-slavery laws as a means of convicting contemporary traffickers, proving, among other things, that our society is generally uninformed about the scope and nature of the problem.

Human trafficking is an affront to our most fundamental rights and freedoms. It destroys lives, undermines democracy, and fuels criminality. Literally a man-made disaster, it affects millions of victims worldwide, funding a lucrative global criminal enterprise.

Most people in Canada, including me initially, assume that trafficking in humans, while it may occur within our borders, exclusively exploits newcomers whose primary objective is to make a new life in Canadian society. However, criminal investigations, including multiple cases documented in this book, are proving this assumption to be hopelessly naive. Human trafficking does not require an international border to be crossed, nor does it necessarily involve movement or transfer of the victim. *Human trafficking in Canada involves the sexual exploitation and forced labour of a diverse array of victims: Canadian citizens and newcomers, adults and children, women and men.*

While film and television often portray "extreme" forms of human trafficking, they rarely reveal the more insidious methods employed by traffickers, who often resort to controlling their victims by means ranging from psychological manipulation and deception to threats of violence and physical assaults. Yet some trafficked persons do not necessarily consider themselves to be victims. Not all of them are kidnapped, beaten, and forcibly confined. Some may have known about the exploitation they would be expected to endure but were unable to leave owing to deception, psychological manipulation, coercion, debt bondage, and threats. Physical violence may be used as a last resort, or routinely. However, the most sophisticated traffickers never use physical violence because they do not have to. No two cases are identical, but all share the core elements of human trafficking recognized by the international community.

## The *Palermo Protocol*: Defining the methods of outrageous evil

In 2000 a United Nations conference in Palermo, Italy, established a common definition of human trafficking in the *Protocol to Prevent, Suppress and Punish Trafficking in Persons.* The *Palermo Protocol* has widespread international support, with 117 signatories, including Canada. All the signatory nations agreed upon a multi-layered definition of the crime and committed to *preventing* human trafficking, *protecting* and assisting victims, and *prosecuting* the traffickers (the "3 *Ps*").

Under the Protocol, human trafficking occurs when

1 an individual recruits, transports, transfers, harbours or receives people
2 by means of deception, fraud, coercion, abuse of power, payment to others in control of the victim, threats of force, use of force or abduction
3 for the purpose of sexual exploitation, forced labour/services, removal of organs, servitude, slavery or practices similar to slavery

If the victim is under eighteen, there is no need to show that any of the "means" have been used to facilitate his or her exploitation. Additionally, under the *Palermo Protocol*, any alleged consent of the victim is irrelevant where any of the means are used. There cannot be free and informed consent when someone has been deceived, defrauded, coerced, controlled by another person, threatened, forced, or abducted.

The women discovered through Operation Relaxation meet this definition of human trafficking. Recruited in Southeast Asia, they were transported to Canada and transferred to massage parlour owners who used fraud and coercion and paid someone in control of the women to sexually exploit them. Another device used to control the women was debt bondage, a practice considered to be similar to slavery. The *United Nations Supplementary Convention on the Abolition of Slavery* defines it as a promise to work as security for a debt where the value of the work is not reasonably applied to pay down the debt. The term *debt bondage* applies, too, if the nature of such work is not defined and its duration is not limited.

Wherever debt bondage is present, human trafficking likely is occurring. For the victims of Operation Relaxation, the actual costs of their travel, accommodations, meals, and personal effects were far less than the amounts demanded by their traffickers, which the victims were told they had to earn to gain their freedom. Moreover, the extent and nature of the sex acts they were expected to provide were not defined—and the amounts paid were not reasonably applied against the supposed debt. Simply put, traffickers use debt bondage to exert a form of financial coercion, often enforced with threats and physical violence, to add another layer of control over their victims.

Citizenship and Immigration Canada acknowledges that it knows of no country that is immune to human trafficking. The outrageous crime assumes many forms and has different names in different societies. In some cases the labels diminish the impact of the exploitation, reducing calls for action to eradicate it.

In Cambodia, a *mama-san* is a trafficker who brokers the sale of young girls and women for sex acts in brothels. In India, a "bonded labour holder" is a trafficker who preys on impoverished families by offering loans in return for the servitude of their children. In Ghana, "fishing masters" are traffickers who force young children to do the dangerous work of retrieving nets underwater, deceiving their families into believing their children are being educated and taught a useful trade. In Canada and the United States, pimps are traffickers who use violence to profit from the sale of teenage girls and women for sex. While each of these countries has its own label for these diverse exploitative practices, all of them fall under the agreed international definition of human trafficking. The importance of the *Palermo Protocol* is its reflection of a broad commitment to end modern-day slavery, to identify its countless manifestations by a single name, and to work together to eradicate them.

# 2

# TRAVELLING SEX OFFENDERS FUELLING DEMAND ABROAD

Human trafficking in far-off lands may seem removed from the lives of average Canadians. Victims like Srey Mao, however, know all too well that travelling sex offenders from numerous countries, including Canada, have contributed to the demand that has enslaved them.

Srey Mao grew up in Kampong Cham province in central Cambodia, where, as far as we can tell, she enjoyed life in a remote village. It all changed when Srey Mao's mother sold her to a brothel owner in the bustling national capital of Phnom Penh when she was seventeen.

Once the money had changed hands, Srey Mao was taken directly to a hotel room where a foreign "child sex tourist" raped and beat her while another man, likely paid by her owner, guarded the door.

From that day, Srey Mao's life became a chain of sexual abuse by countless men who rented her body from her *mama-san.* After several months, Srey Mao finally managed to escape and, in search of comfort and safety, travelled from Phnom Penh to the home of an aunt. There she encountered rejection, not just from her aunt but from the entire village, which stigmatized her as a prostitute. No one in the village allowed her to stay with them, nor would they feed her. In desperation, hoping her aunt would acknowledge that she wasn't responsible for her fate, Srey Mao slept beneath the window of her aunt's bedroom. Her aunt was unyielding: Srey Mao was labelled a prostitute and deserved no love or support.

It was Srey Mao's mother who found her—and only because she was on her way to Phnom Penh to sell Sarun, Srey Mao's younger sister, to the same *mama-san* who'd purchased Srey Mao. When her mother ignored Srey Mao's pleas not to condemn Sarun to the same hell, Srey Mao offered to take her little sister's place. Her mother agreed, and Srey Mao was sold back to the brothels to save her sister.

Srey Mao's love for her little sister was more powerful than the evil that had ravaged her. Although she'd been shunned and treated worse than an animal, her spirit hadn't been crushed.

Within three hours of agreeing to take her sister's place, Srey Mao had been re-sold and was again forced to accept a steady stream of men, at least fifteen, each night. As before, she attempted to escape. This time, however, she was caught and severely beaten before being forced back into the role her "owners" had paid for her to perform.

For six months, hundreds of local men and foreign tourists raped and sexually abused her. In a courageous moment, Srey Mao attempted another escape, this one successful, and made her way through the countryside of Kampong Cham, hoping this time her family would take her in. Again she was rejected. With no one to turn to, Srey Mao returned to Phnom Penh where, hopeless in the face of people, power, and a system she couldn't escape, she attempted suicide by ingesting a mixture of drugs and collapsed unconscious in the street.

Srey Mao awoke in a hospital bed. Someone—a modern-day Good Samaritan—had found her and brought her there. The man hadn't left his name, but without a doubt he'd saved her life.

After hearing the story, doctors at the hospital pooled their money and gave it to Srey Mao, then helped her obtain a bed at a recovery centre for rescued victims of sex trafficking. It was a safe place, away from the *mama-sans* and other traffickers, landscaped with flowers and trees, and staffed by people who rejected the idea that anyone who'd been treated like Srey Mao should be stigmatized for life. She shared the centre with other girls and young women who'd been sold into sexual slavery to meet the demand from tourists, expatriates, and businessmen from Western countries, as well as local men looking for young bodies to purchase.

When I met Srey Mao at the recovery centre, she was nineteen years old and making plans for her sister to join her. As an at-risk child, Sarun would be safe at the centre and not sold into sex slavery. Srey Mao herself was learning to read and write in the traditional Khmer language of Cambodia and, for the first time in years, beginning to make her own decisions and shape her own future.

To prepare survivors to become self-supporting, the recovery centre offered the young women their choice of three training programs: sewing to make clothes, cooking to start a small restaurant, or haircutting and hairstyling to launch a salon.

Srey Mao chose sewing. She wanted to learn how to make beautiful dresses for girls and young women to wear and help them feel good about themselves.

## Exporting the problem but not the fault

It's not known what proportion of the men who bought the power to abuse Srey Mao were foreigners, and how many were from Canada. Some likely were. Foreign men who leave their own countries in fear of arrest, exposure, and punishment contribute to the demand for young women and girls as commodities.

Purchasers of sex acts with underage girls and boys know the odds: They are more likely to be identified, arrested, and prosecuted in Canada than in many countries that suffer from corruption, poverty, and an ineffective legal system.

To those who can hardly fathom a single act of child sexual abuse, encountering it on a widespread and systematic scale, as I did in Cambodia, produces something between shock and amazement that quickly morphs into disgust.

To help expose the problem, I went undercover with other members of The Future Group in 2001 at the request of a local human rights investigator. On this particular evening, our destination was a "karaoke bar" in Phnom Penh that caters mainly to expatriates or tourists whose sexual preference involves underage girls. Of course, the karaoke bar was merely a front for unspeakable crimes of child sexual abuse. The patrons of this establishment came from Australia, Japan, the United States, various European countries—and Canada. Since we were from Canada, the local investigator asked us to come with him to help *him* gain access more easily. That being a Canadian made entry to the facility effortless caused me to feel ashamed of my nationality for the first time in my life.

When we entered the facility, we were met with a large glass window extending from floor to ceiling. Behind it, seated on small bleachers that you might find in a hockey arena in any small town in Canada, were over a dozen young girls. Bright lights glared down on them, and they wore red or blue tags fastened to their tank tops. Their eyes looked distant, their expressions defeated. They were, I estimated, between the ages of thirteen and sixteen. I felt like I was in a pet store, looking at an aquarium, which was not inaccurate. These girls were for sale.

Individual men or small groups peered into the glass enclosure, told the *mama-san* the number of the girl or girls they wanted, and negotiated a price. They were then escorted to a private room to sexually abuse them. In contrast, we were busy scanning the rows of girls to count them, determine their approximate ages and nationalities, and look for any obvious signs of physical abuse. Unbeknownst to the proprietor, we were investigating the front, hopefully to help any of the girls inside who wanted to escape.

Suddenly, the proprietor sidled up to me and asked which one I wanted.

Stuttering, I replied that I didn't know.

"Blue mean Cambodia girl, red mean Vietnam girl," she explained.

I glanced over at the other researchers, whose expressions deliberately concealed the disgust I, too, was feeling. Then I said, "Maybe we'll just start with a beer and sing some karaoke."

After our group declined to select any girl, we were escorted down a dark hallway with doors on either side and led into our own room. The expressions on the girls' faces remained fixed as we passed by. Inside we found a windowless room with an old fake-leather sofa and a "loveseat." A lamp stood in one corner and a disco light overhead spread its random sparkles throughout the room.

For an hour, we drank Heineken and sang horrible renditions of Céline Dion songs as the *mama-san* began sending some of the young girls into the room. The local human rights investigator with us was fluent in Khmer. He spoke to the young girls while we continued to give performances of songs that would have earned us a swift rejection from *American Idol*. In hushed tones, he confirmed that underage girls were being held and exploited in this karaoke-brothel. They were glad that we were planning to get word to the police about this secret den of exploitation. Yet we were careful not to encourage false hope—better than we, they knew the odds of intervention were extremely low.

Thanks to lack of resources, widespread corruption, and broad acceptance of the sex tourism industry by many officials, the local authorities pursued few cases, even though serious criminal offences were being committed contrary to Cambodian law. In some cases, however, pressure from an international NGO like ours could help. So the next day, we used our reports from that evening to encourage the local prosecutor to launch an official investigation into the karaoke bar–brothel and rescue the underage girls caged there.

Generally, only the most egregious cases involving extremely young victims, such as those under ten, or cases involving severe physical violence would spur recalcitrant police and prosecutors to proceed with a rescue. Whatever local officials think of the practice, sex tourism brings millions of dollars in foreign currency to Cambodia, a country in dire economic straits. What would replace this money stream if the attraction vanished overnight? Compared with neighbouring countries like Thailand, Cambodia has little to attract tourists beyond Angkor Wat, the twelfth-century temple sacred to Hindus and Buddhists, which appears on the country's flag. Cambodia is ranked as the 187th-poorest country on the planet with a per capita weekly income of U.S.$36.50. Yet the average price paid by foreign sex offenders for the virginity of an underage girl is U.S.$300–$700. With that kind of economic incentive for sex trafficking, only the most moral and courageous officials choose to demand an end to the racket, or at least prosecute the most offensive brothel keepers.

Occasionally a case actually moves forward, and we hoped our reports would lead to at least some girls being rescued and given a fresh start at one of the few recovery centres in the city.

We applied as much pressure as possible on authorities, encouraged those who continued to operate the recovery centres, helped improve programs to assist those who were rescued, and, in our own ways, prayed for the girls who remained enslaved.

That was almost ten years ago, and the image of those young girls inside that glass prison continues to disturb me.

## Sexual abuse at home and abroad

Those who travel beyond Canada's borders to pursue their sexual abuse of children and women don't always restrict these repugnant actions to foreign locations. Donald Bakker didn't.

Crab Park was created as an urban oasis for residents of Vancouver's poor and crime-ridden Downtown Eastside. With old railway tracks to the south, commercial shipping ports to the east, and the sea bus terminal to the west, Crab Park may not be the most scenic and inviting public space in Vancouver, but for various reasons it has become a focal point for sexual exploitation issues. A park bench overlooking Burrard Inlet bears a plaque with the names of missing prostituted women. A local newspaper speculated that "some of the missing women may have found temporary respite here from the daily terror of their lives," but the opposite appears to be true. For a time, an isolated forested area of the park had become a convenient and discreet place where drugs and sex were for sale, and it is now known as the place where Canada's first overseas case of child sex tourism was discovered.

On a noon hour in late 2003, a Vancouver city worker having lunch near the waterfront heard a woman's screams from the trees and shrubbery in Crab Park. He called the police, who were present when forty-year-old Donald Bakker emerged from the bushes followed by a visibly upset woman. Officers stopped the two and examined a bag Bakker had been carrying. With evidence that he had sexually abused the woman, the police placed Bakker under arrest and seized the bag and its contents.

Inside the bag, police found a video camera and several videotapes that revealed Bakker torturing and mistreating a series of women. With a warrant to search Bakker's car and home, investigators found more videotapes, including one of Bakker sexually abusing Asian girls between seven and twelve years old.

The police turned to an RCMP officer with international expertise on the sexual exploitation of children in an effort to find these girls: Brian McConaghy, a dedicated officer who now operates a charity in Cambodia that helps to rehabilitate survivors of sex slavery. McConaghy noted that the children on the videotapes were speaking a combination of Vietnamese and Khmer, and that some wore a *kroma,* a checkered scarf common in Cambodia.

Also on the tape was a view of a 2003 Cambodian calendar that indicated the probable year of Bakker's sex tourist visit to Cambodia. Investigators began to visit notorious Cambodian brothels in Svay Pak, a well-known brothel district for foreigners, and found a house that looked strikingly similar to the one on Bakker's videotape. Any doubts were resolved when investigators were able to match smudge marks on the wall with those seen in Bakker's video. This remarkable piece of evidence enabled the officers to identify the girls who had been used as child sex slaves.

A few years earlier, Bakker would have escaped prosecution for such crimes committed abroad, but in 1997, Canada joined a growing

International Airport. Sent from the Philippines, it was addressed to Klassen and labelled "quilts." Hidden inside the quilts were DVDs containing footage of girls between the ages of nine and eighteen being sexually abused by Klassen.

Following an international investigation of more than two and a half years, Klassen was charged with thirty-five counts of child sex crimes against seventeen victims in Cambodia, Colombia, and the Philippines, the incidents having taken place over five years. Among the charges laid were sexual interference, permitting sexual activity as a householder, and soliciting a person to have illicit sexual intercourse with another person.

Klassen's court challenge to Canada's child sex tourism laws failed. On December 19, 2008, the B.C. Supreme Court released its decision upholding Canada's child sex tourism legislation under both Canadian constitutional law and international law. The decision paved the way for more rigorous enforcement of the sex tourism law, and Klassen eventually pleaded guilty to numerous charges in May 2010.

Rather than offending international law, as its detractors claim, Canada's child sex tourism law is supported by both international treaties and the practice of other countries. Every major child sex tourism destination country in the world has joined Canada in signing the *UN Convention on the Rights of the Child*, confirming that all children have the inherent and inalienable right to be free from sexual exploitation and sexual abuse. These countries also have agreed to protect children through appropriate national, bilateral, and multilateral measures.

All known and emerging child sex tourism destination countries (except Russia) are also parties to the *Optional Protocol* to the Convention. This treaty requires signatory countries to criminalize numerous child sex offences, whether their citizens and residents commit the offences domestically or in other countries. The treaty also authorizes countries to establish extraterritorial jurisdiction over child sex offences committed by or against their nationals and residents, which means that countries around the world have agreed to child sex tourism laws that ensure offenders do not escape with impunity.

B.C. Supreme Court Justice Cullen says in the *Klassen* decision: "In the absence of extraterritorial legislation, Canada would become a safer harbour for those who engage in the economic or sexual exploitation of children. The nationality principle reflects Canada's clear interest in taking steps to prevent its own nationals or residents from using the advantages of Canadian nationality and residence to perpetuate the economic and/or sexual exploitation of children in other nations." The *Klassen* decision relied heavily on the Supreme Court of Canada's decision in *R. v. Hape*, with the majority of judges stating that "[c]ooperation between states is imperative if transnational crimes are not to be committed with impunity because they fall through jurisdictional cracks along national borders."

Critics of Canada's child sex tourism law are either grossly misinformed about the international treaties mandating these laws or are deliberately ignoring them for their own purposes. Regardless, their arguments have failed to carry the day.

## The power of the almighty dollar

Child sex tourists disproportionately drive demand for human trafficking by typically paying larger sums of money than local men, usually in much sought-after U.S. currency. In response, some venues in developing countries cater specifically to foreigners seeking such activities.

In recent years, foreigners have demanded ever-younger girls because they believe such victims are less likely to have contracted sexually transmitted diseases (STDs) such as HIV/AIDS. Traffickers have responded by employing more effective means of finding and offering these young victims, knowing they can charge a premium. The expanding exploitation is becoming a pressing concern for the international community—a concern that is well founded, although late to receive attention.

Each year foreign pedophiles target countless children in developing countries. It is difficult to assess the number of children in developing countries who are abused by foreigners due to the clandestine and criminal nature of child sexual exploitation. The U.S. Department of State estimates the figure at two million children worldwide. On a country by country basis, End Child Prostitution, Child Pornography and Trafficking of Children for Sexual Purposes (ECPAT), a leading global NGO, estimates that at any given time 22,500 to 40,000 children are being sold for sex in Thailand, 60,000 to 75,000 in the Philippines, and an estimated 30,000 in Mexico. As well, the U.S. State Department's *Trafficking in Persons Report* (2008) has flagged other havens for travelling sex offenders. They include the following countries:

- *Latin America and the Caribbean:* Argentina, Brazil, Costa Rica, Cuba, Dominican Republic, Ecuador, Guatemala, Honduras, Jamaica, Mexico, Nicaragua, Peru, Venezuela;
- *Asia:* Cambodia, China, India, Indonesia, Laos, Mongolia, Nepal, Philippines, Thailand, Vietnam;
- *Africa:* Benin, The Gambia, Kenya, Madagascar, Mauritius, Morocco, Senegal, South Africa, Togo; and
- *Europe:* Russia.

## Canada's shame: Producing the world's most-wanted pedophile

In 2007, Christopher Paul Neil, a former schoolteacher from British Columbia, became the world's most-wanted pedophile. Neil imposed a digitally constructed swirl over his face to hide his identity in photos that allegedly depicted him sexually abusing young children. He then distributed the images on websites for pedophiles. Investigators in Germany eventually unscrambled more than two hundred digitally altered images to reveal Neil's face.

The global policing agency Interpol took the extraordinary step of launching a worldwide public appeal to identify the man in the photos, resulting in hundreds of tips with five positive identifications of Neil. When Interpol published an international wanted persons notice, the Royal Thai Police followed up immediately, identifying victims and issuing an arrest warrant for Neil. Within a few days, he'd been arrested and placed in custody, a stunning example of global co-operation to combat child sex tourism. Tried in a Thai court for the sexual abuse of two Thai brothers ages thirteen and nine, Neil received fines and a sentence of nine years in prison.

Rosalind Prober, president of Winnipeg-based Beyond Borders and North American representative to the board of ECPAT-International, believes that Canada's reputation as a country of overwhelmingly law-abiding citizens makes it easier for Canadian offenders to travel abroad and sexually abuse children. As a result, countless Canadian men have paid to sexually abuse women and children in poor countries around the world.

One admittedly limited measure of Canadian complicity is the number of men from this country who requested consular assistance in dealing with charges of child sexual abuse and exploitation offences filed against them while abroad. Between 1993 and 2008, the Department of Foreign Affairs provided such assistance to more than 150 Canadian men. Some of the countries where these acts allegedly occurred are predictable—Cambodia, Thailand, Costa Rica, Panama, and Cuba—and a few may surprise, including the United States, Mexico, and China.

These represent only those cases flagrant enough to attract attention and action from local law enforcement officials. NGOs and the media have reported many more cases, and even more Canadians have likely evaded detection entirely.

And let's be open about these men. Typically they are not travellers on short trips for business or pleasure who act on impulse. A number of recent cases involve Canadian expatriates living transient lifestyles over several years. If victims file complaints about them, these sex offenders simply travel on their Canadian passports to neighbouring countries where they can continue their activities. In Southeast Asia, Canadians move easily among Thailand, Cambodia, Vietnam, and Laos.

"They feel almost protected being outside of Canada," says Sabrina Sullivan, managing director of The Future Group, of these offenders. "They feel untouchable."

## Poverty, corruption, and impunity

When a Cambodian judge declared John Keeler a pedophile and sentenced the British headmaster to three years in prison, Keeler screamed "Scum!" at the judge, attempted to throw a chair at the bench, declaring, "I paid $5,400. I am supposed to go free. This isn't justice, this is robbery!" As he was led out of the courtroom sobbing, Keeler reportedly said he was "going to die if they put me back in that hole."

Keeler's 2001 conviction for sexually abusing underage children was a landmark case, one of few instances in Cambodia in which a foreigner was sent to prison for such crimes. Addressing police and judicial corruption remains a challenge—so much so that some local NGOs have launched detailed court monitoring programs to identify judges who routinely dismiss charges in such cases and where bribery has been alleged.

While loathsome and incomprehensible, the action of parents selling their children into slavery must be seen against the harsh reality of three factors mentioned earlier: poverty, corruption, and impunity.

Poverty helps create a supply of vulnerable children for traffickers globally. Income from the sex industry is a major contributor to Southeast Asian economies and within the last decade has accounted for an estimated 2 to 14 percent of the gross domestic product of Indonesia, Malaysia, the Philippines, and Thailand. According to a United Nations report on the sale of children, child prostitution, and child pornography, "Poverty relates to the supply side of the problem. It does not explain the huge global demand, with, in many instances, customers from rich countries circumventing their national laws to exploit children in other countries."

Additionally, travelling sex offenders choose countries with high levels of corruption and poor law enforcement. When Thailand began strict enforcement of its laws against the sexual exploitation of children, pedophiles flocked to neighbouring Cambodia, where they were much less likely to be charged, convicted, and imprisoned. This inadequate law enforcement results from two main factors: the dependency of many governments on revenue produced by child sex tourism and the prevalence of corruption.

Transparency International placed both Cambodia and the Philippines in the top quintile of corrupt countries, where more than 32 percent of citizens had paid a bribe in the last year. In 2005, the Filipino police force was found to be the most corrupt institution in the country. The police in Cambodia are also notoriously crooked, and the country's judges are among the least-trusted government officials. Corruption of this magnitude enables foreign tourists to sexually abuse and exploit vulnerable children with impunity, despite local laws prohibiting such practices.

## Inside the minds of travelling child sex offenders

Psychologists have identified two categories of child sex tourists: preferential and situational abusers. Preferential offenders are predatory, actively seeking out children for illicit sexual activity. Some abusers ruthlessly target the most vulnerable victims.

For example, after the Boxing Day tsunami of 2004, the Queensland Police in Australia identified sixty convicted child sex offenders who left that region to volunteer in tsunami-affected areas. Very likely, the offenders were looking for opportunities to be near children and to use money, food, or gifts, along with flattery, compliments, and affection, to persuade them to engage in sexual activities. If necessary, the pedophiles would employ threats, blackmail, and even physical abuse.

Preferential offenders are more likely to be caught because their actions are frequent and habitual. In a sample of thirty-six offenders, the Protection Project at Johns Hopkins University found that almost half had jobs with responsibilities that placed them in daily contact with children or involved children through some other related activity. Fully two-thirds of American men convicted of committing child sexual abuse abroad have done the same at home; they are repeat offenders who target children wherever they can.

It is not surprising that habitual child sex offenders expand their abuse beyond their own borders to evade criminal prosecutions. Incentives to do so are all around them. For years, the North American Man/Boy Love Association (NAMBLA) has been encouraging pedophiles to visit poor developing countries as a relatively safe means of satisfying perverse sexual urges. The invitation in this excerpt from a NAMBLA newsletter is blatant and direct:

> Weigh the pros and cons of becoming involved yourself in sex tourism overseas. Seek and find love from [boys in your home country] on a platonic, purely emotional level. For sexual satisfaction, travel once or twice yearly overseas. You might get arrested overseas for patronizing a boy prostitute. But the legal consequences of being caught patronizing a boy prostitute in a friendly place overseas will be less severe.

Enticements to pedophiles such as this, along with cheaper international travel, have brought child sex tourists directly to vulnerable children.

In contrast, situational abusers may choose to sexually abuse minors only when opportunities arise. They may also deceive themselves about the true ages of their victims. In most cases, these men either don't know or don't care about the circumstances of the people they're abusing, or that others control the people they've paid for sex.

Whether preferential or situational, these abusers have an identical impact on their victims, and neither group can legitimately claim a moral high ground regardless of where or under what conditions they practise the abuse.

The victims of sexual abuse suffer severe psychological effects, including depression, low self-esteem, post-traumatic stress disorder, and suicide. Trafficked children in developing countries who are victimized by Western sex offenders are deprived of their childhood. Often they cannot attend school, socialize, or engage in other normal developmental activities. Many contract HIV/AIDS and other STDs, and girls who become pregnant are at risk from inadequate (or non-existent) medical care before, during, and after delivery. The fate of their babies represents another sad and harrowing situation.

Any sense of self-worth among child victims vanishes with the knowledge that they have no value beyond the passing pleasures they produce for untold numbers of strange men and the money they generate for their traffickers. Most will never see their traffickers or the men who pay to abuse them brought to justice.

Meanwhile, the sexual tourists return to the comfort and security of their homes in Australia, the United Kingdom, the United States, or, in too many cases, to British Columbia, Alberta, Ontario, Quebec, Nova Scotia …

# 3

# INTERNATIONAL TRAFFICKING TO CANADA

Many Canadians are dismayed but not surprised that some of their own countrymen engage in sexual tourism, often pursuing children or supporting a practice that depends on enslaved women. They are frequently astounded, however, to learn about the extent of the reverse flow of victims brought from abroad to Canada.

Canada has been very slow to recognize its human trafficking problem. The first major report by the RCMP, *Project Surrender* (2004), estimated that approximately six hundred foreign nationals are brought to Canada for sex trafficking every year, with an additional two hundred being brought for forced labour trafficking annually. Obtaining enough reliable data is difficult, and the RCMP no longer cites such estimates so as not to overstate or understate the problem.

In 2010, a "threat assessment" by the RCMP instead sought to identify the criminal organizations and networks involved in human trafficking. While the full report is classified, the RCMP has disclosed that it identified over one hundred and fifty human trafficking cases between 2005 and 2009. This is just a glimpse into the problem. The assessment does not include cases identified by NGOs that were not reported to police. Authorities concede, "[T]he number of victims reporting trafficking-related crimes significantly under-represents the actual incidence of TIP (trafficking in persons)."

The United States–Canada *Bi-national Assessment of Trafficking in Persons* (2006) report noted, "[T]raffickers are often of the same ethnicity as the victims they control. ... In Canada, Asian and Eastern European organized crime groups have been most involved in trafficking women from countries such as China, South Korea, Thailand, Cambodia, the Philippines, Russia and from the region of Latin America."

Canada's relatively open immigration policy and its active support of confirmed refugees inspire pride in many citizens. As well they should—most Canadians are descended from immigrants, and while our record in welcoming them is far from perfect, it serves as a model for many familiar with the often intolerant positions of other countries. However, it also allows for appalling incidents of human trafficking, such as the one that ensnared young Manuela.

Manuela was born in the throes of El Salvador's "high-intensity" civil war, one of the twentieth century's longest-running conflicts in Latin America. By the end of the war, in 1992, an estimated seventy-five thousand Salvadorans had died and over a million refugees and internally displaced people had fled their homes to escape the violence.

In the shaky peace following the armistice, Manuela found herself working as a domestic servant. Life was better than during the war, but political instability, corruption, and rampant crime impeded El Salvador's progress.

The environment was ideal for the kind of mistreatment favoured by Manuela's "employer": He forcibly sold her for sex. Manuela's employer transported her north, first to neighbouring Guatemala and then farther afield to Mexico, where she was introduced to Paulo. In Manuela's words, Paulo was "treating her better than the other guys." One day he promised Manuela that if she came to Canada with him, he'd stop selling her for sex. He'd even arrange all of the immigration papers and she could pursue a life unavailable to a girl of her status in El Salvador.

Just sixteen, Manuela was young enough to be Paulo's daughter. In 2006 they flew together to Canada, using fake documents to convince border inspectors that Paulo was Manuela's loving father. Once in Toronto, Manuela realized that Paulo's promise was a lie. Confined to a residence in mid-Toronto, she was forced to have sex with dozens of men daily.

Some weeks later, she managed to escape and flagged down a taxi. In Spanish, Manuela tried desperately to explain her plight to the confused cabbie. Thankfully the driver understood that she was in serious peril and quickly took her to a drop-in shelter for exploited youth.

Because of conditions in El Salvador and her young age, Manuela was granted refugee status and allowed to remain in Canada. Today she lives in a safe place and is enrolled in a Toronto-area high school. She remains burdened with shame and guilt, however, because of all of the sex acts she was forced to perform with complete strangers.

To those who work with women like Manuela, her reaction comes as no surprise. "It happens most of the time in the cases I have seen," says Loly Rico, co-director of the FCJ Refugee Centre, an organization serving refugees and other newcomers to Canada. By addressing issues that newly arrived refugee claimants face in Canada, including lack of resources, marginalization, and discrimination, FCJ volunteers smooth the transition from refugee to citizen.

Manuela's recovery will be long, but she is safe and free to decide her own future.

## Courage to make a desperate call for freedom

Manuela is fortunate to have escaped. Less so are unknown numbers of enslaved women brought into Canada, who continue to suffer in silence. Detective Wendy Leaver of the Toronto Police Service, Special Victims Unit, fears she has encountered one such victim. The SVU has earned a reputation for helping victims of the city's sex industry, and its telephone number is a closely guarded secret among exploited women in need of immediate help.

When she answered the SVU telephone one day in April 2007, Detective Leaver heard a woman speaking broken English interspersed with Chinese. Despite the language barrier, Detective Leaver immediately knew something was terribly wrong. "My boss will kill me, my boss will kill me," the woman kept repeating. "She told me she was lodged in what she believed was a warehouse in the west end of the city, the place divided into rooms," says Detective Leaver. "She informed me she was forced to work as a sex worker. She was terrified. She had no other information about where she was.

"She was promised a certain amount of money when she arrived," continues Detective Leaver, "but when she got here she became a prisoner. They told her she would have to pay them back for her transportation for bringing her here, and also for her food and lodging, by performing sex acts for men who were brought to her. She received no payment for doing this." The victim's family back home in China was also threatened.

"Just as I was giving her my cellphone number, the line was cut," Detective Leaver recalls. Police immediately initiated a trace of the call but were unable to identify the source. Detective Leaver never heard from the woman again.

"There was nothing that we could do," the detective explains. Years later, Detective Leaver still thinks of that call. "The fact that she called was quite courageous. I still have dreams about that woman. She must have been totally desperate to call me."

## Welcome to Canada—a destination for human trafficking

It is difficult to imagine that stories such as the one related by Detective Leaver are happening in Canada. The fact is that foreign victims of human trafficking have been essentially invisible to our immigration officials for years. Analysts at Citizenship and Immigration Canada (CIC) were unable to provide any statistics or information on the number of suspected trafficking cases in Canada before May 2006, when Monte Solberg, then minister of CIC, approved a range of measures to assist foreign trafficked persons; as well, a special field was added to immigration databases to flag individual cases. Even with the field, however, senior officers at CIC readily admit that in known cases, "some potential victims … were not identified."

Between May 2006 and November 2008, CIC databases flagged fifty suspected foreign victims of human trafficking in Canada, involving both sexual exploitation and forced labour. These statistics do not include unreported cases, which can be expected to make up a significant number of total human trafficking cases. Nor do they include victims who were transported through Canada to be exploited elsewhere; victims who voluntarily returned to their home countries without seeking to remain in Canada; Canadian victims involved in domestic trafficking cases; or unidentified victims like the Chinese woman who called Detective Leaver. While the CIC data offer only a glimpse into foreign trafficking in Canada, they provide an important snapshot of the crime's victims and its geographic reach.

Women represent 74 percent of all reported instances of suspected foreign trafficking victims, although an increasing number—one in four—are men, likely victims of forced labour trafficking. Only three cases, or 6 percent, involved individuals who were minors at the time.

The spread of foreign trafficking victims in Canada is virtually national. CIC officials identified cases in British Columbia, Prairie/Northwest Territories Region (which includes Alberta, Saskatchewan, and Manitoba), Ontario, and Quebec.

The home countries of the victims proved just as diverse. Individuals from Brazil, China, the Democratic Republic of the Congo (DRC), Estonia, Kyrgyzstan, Malaysia, Mexico, Moldova, Peru, the Philippines, Romania, Russia, South Korea, Vietnam, and Ukraine were all among the victims recorded by CIC. By continent, a majority of 59 percent originated in Asia and a substantial 33 percent in Central and Eastern Europe. The Americas and Africa accounted for roughly 4 percent each. Almost three-quarters of all suspected cases of foreign trafficking to Canada stem from just four countries—the Philippines, Moldova, China, and Romania—which rank among the worst in the world for their inability or unwillingness to combat this crime.

While poverty is considered an "enabling factor" in many source countries for human trafficking, Professor Sheldon X. Zhang, chair of Sociology at San Diego State University, identifies the attitude and operations of each country's government as a significant contributor to the problem. In Professor Zhang's opinion, government corruption, ineptitude, collusion, and complicity remain core elements that make a country attractive for traffickers to recruit victims.

Officials can barely keep up with the constantly changing tactics used by traffickers to bring victims into Canada. "Some enter with genuine passports, entry documents, or work visas; instances of abuse of valid work visas have been reported," says a senior policy analyst at CIC's headquarters in Ottawa. "Others use falsified or altered entry documents, such as photo substitutions, or gain entry as impostors. Fraudulent offers of employment are also being used to support applications to obtain visas and convince border and consular officials that the victim intends to return to his/her country of origin. Traffickers may also bring victims into Canada utilizing established smuggling routes and methods."

Informants who know about the modus operandi of traffickers have made it clear to police that the criminals are always a few steps ahead: "They say there are brokers that are working in legitimate businesses bringing in the workers that are supposed to be coming in to assemble furniture or package something, and as soon as they're in, they're sold," said Sergeant Mark Schwartz of the Calgary Police Service, Vice Unit.

In December 2008, the RCMP Criminal Intelligence Unit captured national headlines when it released an unclassified report called *Project Spawn: A Strategic Assessment of Criminal Activity and Organized Crime Infiltration at Canada's Class 1 Airports.* The report found that organized crime was active at the country's major airports, with criminals bribing airport employees, as well as getting their own associates hired as airport staff. Vancouver International Airport and Pearson International Airport in Toronto were singled out as entry points for organized crime groups bringing foreign nationals into Canada illegally.

In one case in November 2007, a foreign woman arrived at Vancouver International Airport after travelling through several other countries. She was detained by the Canada Border Services Agency as a potential victim of human trafficking. She stated that an individual who'd arranged for her to enter the country had taken her passport and given her another one to use. More alarmingly, she claimed that her traffickers had infiltrated the airline company that brought her to Canada. Officials have refused to divulge the name of this company and have provided no further information about the investigation into these serious allegations.

## A nation of opportunity ... for traffickers

Foreign trafficking victims in Canada encompass a diverse group of vulnerable individuals. Some are long-term victims of the international sex slave market, transported to Canada to earn greater profits for their traffickers. Others have been lured here by false promises of wealth-generating careers and even romance. Still others are seeking to escape poverty or merely hoping to find less egregious conditions within the sex industry than they experienced in their home countries.

My research team analyzed data on sex trafficking victims brought to Canada from abroad to identify common characteristics. These factors are unlikely to be observed in any one individual simultaneously. Yet by observing several of these factors, you may be able to identify a potential victim of foreign sex trafficking in Canada:

1. in Canada primarily to engage in paid sex acts
2. providing sex acts as a means of repaying a debt of an imposed or changing amount (debt bondage)
3. encountering conditions in Canada that do not resemble those promised
4. forced, threatened, or pressured to continue providing paid sex acts
5. not in possession of immigration documents or passport

6 not free to travel where and when they want, or to leave their current situation
7 unfamiliar with the community they reside in
8 has limited knowledge of English or French
9 constantly accompanied by someone who speaks for them or monitors them
10 shows signs of trauma, including bruising, withdrawn behaviour, depression, or fear

## Exporting the casualties of war

Among the most accessible sources for sex traffickers are victims already under the control of traffickers in other countries or recent survivors of similar trauma. Both groups are easily directed to Canada. Various victims of international sex trafficking have been brought to Canada after being exploited for years as modern-day slaves in countries around the world. Thérèse, whom we met in Chapter 1, affords a dramatic example, having been brought to Canada from the DRC after over a decade of exploitation as a sex slave in her home country.

Armed conflicts such as the ongoing war in the DRC significantly and disproportionately harm women and children. Victims of sexual violence and sex trafficking during the conflict, they are extremely vulnerable to serious human rights violations in post-conflict environments. In addition to the DRC, Chechnya, Colombia, El Salvador, and Sierra Leone represent global hot spots that tend to create an excess "inventory" of sex trafficking victims who are brought to other countries, including Canada, for further exploitation.

Like Manuela, whom we met earlier in this chapter, Luisa grew up in the shadow of one of the bloodiest conflicts in our hemisphere, this time in Colombia. The world's undisputed cocaine superpower, Colombia cultivated enough hectares of coca bushes in 2008 to manufacture 430 metric tons of cocaine, over half the global supply. Drug trafficking fuels the conflict between left-wing guerrilla groups and right-wing paramilitaries, having contributed for decades to bouts of civil war and instability.

Luisa, a mother of two, lived in Colombia's countryside. When her common-law husband was killed in the high-stakes game of narco-trafficking, Enrico, his associate, entered the picture. Enrico may have announced that Luisa's husband owed him money, which he decided to "collect on" by selling Luisa for sex, or she may have represented an easy target because she was a widow. In any case, Enrico supplied Luisa with drugs, which generated dependency through addiction, while he profited by selling her for sex.

Luisa's father discovered what was happening and courageously stepped in, caring for Luisa's children and taking her away from Enrico. Luisa and her father agreed it would be best for the children to stay with their grandfather and for Luisa to leave the country for a few months to get her life back on track. They chose Canada for her fresh start.

After her student visa application to Canada was approved, Luisa travelled to Toronto to learn English. As a recent survivor of human trafficking, alone in Canada's largest metropolitan city, she was very vulnerable.

They say that sharks can detect an injured animal from up to one kilometre away in open water. Traffickers operating in Canada have developed similar sensory skills for detecting their quarry. When Carlos met Luisa at their English-language class in Toronto, he smelled the figurative blood in the water.

Carlos must have recognized from aspects of her demeanour that he would be able to exploit Luisa. With stealth and patience, he built trust by showing concern for her children back in Colombia.

With time, Luisa and Carlos became intimate, and after six months Carlos began applying all of his skills to turn her back into a commodity that could be sold. He began by reintroducing hard drugs, building Luisa's dependency on them once again. Next, he made Luisa an offer that she couldn't refuse. "I'll help bring your children here," he promised, "but you need to work for me."

Carlos took Luisa to a brothel in a pleasant middle-class

neighbourhood in North Toronto, a residence that from the outside looked like any other home. Inside, Latin American women, primarily from Brazil, were for sale. Carlos controlled Luisa's movements, taking her to and from the brothel and his house each day.

At this point, Luisa no longer had her immigration papers and her student visa had expired, raising the likelihood of immigration detention if authorities found her. Moreover, as a Spanish speaker from Colombia, Luisa had difficulty communicating effectively with the Portuguese-speaking women from Brazil. The false hope that her children would be brought to Canada, along with the influence of the drugs, Carlos's control of her movement, and the threat of immigration detention, kept Luisa firmly under his domination. In 2006, a police raid of the brothel ended Luisa's exploitation, and she was able to find support from local NGOs.

## Smuggling debt and young children

Migrant smuggling occurs when foreign nationals illegally enter a country for a fee paid to criminals who facilitate their entry. Such smugglers generally make a one-time profit from fees paid by smuggled individuals to cross an international border, whereas traffickers make ongoing profits from the sexual exploitation or forced labour of their victims. However, this distinction can become blurred, especially when young children are involved.

Traffickers have used migrant smuggling schemes as a powerful tool to recruit foreign nationals seeking a better life who will agree to be transported to a foreign destination but on arrival find themselves forced to repay massive smuggling debts as debt bonds. Such individuals may be willingly smuggled into Canada, only to find on arrival that they are sent to a sweatshop or brothel. This recruiting method, which makes possible a continuous stream of potential victims, is less risky than other means such as abduction, force, and threats of force.

The most alarming cases involve children who are smuggled into Canada and become victims of human trafficking. Trains, planes, and boats are used to this end. While few such reported cases have been uncovered here, these vulnerable foreign children are often unaccompanied by parents or relatives, owe thousands of dollars to smugglers who have transported them illegally, and have no source of income to repay the debts. Because of these factors, authorities have raised concerns that foreign children may be destined for brothels, sweatshops, or domestic servitude.

Although under-investigated in Canada, the problem has commanded major police resources in the United Kingdom, where law enforcement authorities launched "Operation Paladin" in 2007 over concerns about the number of "unaccompanied minors" arriving at major airports from abroad. Found alone in the airports, the children were placed in the child protection system but often vanished. They were previously instructed to leave their child protection shelters soon after arriving and to make contact with individuals they had never met. Unbeknownst to the children, they were destined for exploitation.

Between 2008 and 2009, Operation Paladin resulted in the arrest of twelve individuals for child trafficking. Were these children isolated cases of human trafficking or part of a more systemic problem? And is Canada witnessing the same phenomenon? At this point, we have little evidence of the latter, but Canada has yet to conduct an investigation that matches Britain's.

The British Columbia Office to Combat Trafficking in Persons (OCTIP) has expressed concern about potential trafficked children. Opened under the B.C. Ministry of Public Safety and Solicitor General in July 2007 with a mandate to develop and coordinate the province's response to human trafficking (and the first provincial body of its kind in Canada), OCTIP works with provincial ministries, federal departments, municipal governments, law enforcement agencies, and community-based and Aboriginal organizations.

OCTIP considers an individual under eighteen to be a "probable trafficked child" if one or more of the following "significant indicators of trafficking" exist:

- travelling with an unrelated person posing as a family member
- possessing neither personal identification nor travel documents
- arriving with contact information for persons unknown
- holding expectations of an unattainable job or education
- travelling in unsafe and hazardous conditions
- fearing for the safety of family and/or self
- owing significant amounts of money to a person or group who may have arranged transportation (debt bondage)

Some of the impetus to launch OCTIP as an effective response to the problem of human trafficking dates back to the summer of 1999, when four boatloads of illegal Chinese migrants arrived on the British Columbia coast. The boats were intercepted and the B.C. Ministry of Child and Family Development took 134 children into care. The children were considered to be smuggled, and only one was allowed to remain in Canada. As an official associated with the investigation points out, "In 1999, we didn't have the trafficking language." In retrospect, the OCTIP guidelines indicate that these children might have been intended for exploitation as trafficking victims in North America; they owed a smuggling debt of fifty to sixty thousand dollars, they were under tremendous pressure to keep moving to their intended destination, and their documents were missing. Recent cases continue to raise serious concerns about smuggled children being trafficked through British Columbia and elsewhere in Canada.

Each year in Toronto, for example, eighteen to twenty unaccompanied children arrive at Pearson International Airport. Often from India, China, Africa, and the Caribbean, the children in many instances are accompanied by adults pretending to be their parents. In other cases, the children board the planes accompanied by adults who abandon them upon arrival at Canadian customs. When these children are discovered alone in the customs hall, child protection workers are brought in to assess the situation.

While some children may be brought to Canada in an attempt to unite them illegally with family members or acquaintances, a representative of the Peel Children's Aid Society is concerned that some foreign teenagers carrying phone numbers of unknown people whom they are to call upon arrival in Canada may be destined for sexual exploitation.

Canada continues to appear reluctant to recognize smuggled migrants as trafficked persons where indicators of potential exploitation on arrival become evident. True, the challenge is significant. On one hand, countries such as Canada need to prevent human trafficking and protect potential victims at the earliest stage possible. On the other hand, becoming more accommodating of smuggled migrants increases the potential appeal for traffickers and other criminals to profit from illegal entry, undermining the security and integrity of Canada's borders.

Where children are involved, a cautious approach is clearly necessary, as demonstrated by the United Kingdom. The alternative is for Canada and other countries to tolerate the potential for severe abuse of children.

## Hope after decades of sexploitation

*Lawlessness* and *collapse* are the two words most appropriate, and most frequently used, to describe Ukraine through the late 1980s. As the country's economic malaise deepened and the Communist hold loosened, organized crime stepped in to fill the power vacuum.

During this volatile period Katya, a nine-year-old Ukrainian girl, was abducted to be sold for sex. For more than two decades, Katya served as a slave, devoid of comfort, rewards, or freedom. After having been sold to traffickers in Africa, Europe, and North America, she was brought to Canada by her newest "owner," who expected to reap more profit from her body. His venture did not succeed. The countless acts of rape that Katya had endured from the age of nine to her mid-thirties had made her so volatile and hard to control that her trafficker dumped her outside a hospital in Edmonton in 2005.

In addition to being diagnosed with schizophrenia, Katya was suffering from severe depression. She still walks with a noticeable limp, a persistent reminder of the brutality she suffered over much of her life. The treatment prescribed for victims like Katya is almost identical to that for victims of extended and substantial torture.

"Imagine you've been kidnapped when you're nine years old, in one of the developing countries, and then sold to a developed country," suggests Tracey Campbell, a consultant with Alberta Employment and Immigration who's assisting Katya in her recovery. "Imagine the damage it would do, how devastating it would be, and how much work a psychologist would have to do for you."

Three years after her release, Katya was continuing to improve. She completed a course in English as a Second Language (ESL) and began to dream of becoming a nurse. The first independent choice she is making in her adult life is to care for others.

"The humiliation experienced by the victims is deep and profound," says Loly Rico. "At one point they felt used, they were raped. But some begin to believe that this is their role as women. And for them to change that role is very hard."

Rico has had difficulty finding qualified counsellors to assist foreign victims of human trafficking, in particular professionals who speak languages other than English. Some victims resist counselling because they want to "forget about that life," an understandable reaction but one that delays their long-term rehabilitation.

## Mumbi—a story of resistance, courage, and survival

Like many young women in Kenya, Mumbi was eager to travel and work overseas. In 2001, she accepted an offer that proved too good to be true—help with her travel costs to Canada. On arrival, Mumbi was locked inside a Montreal-area hotel room and told that she would be sold for sex to repay the "investment."

The traffickers tried to break Mumbi's resistance. Keeping her confined, they forced her to watch pornographic movies, a "grooming process" used to eradicate sexual inhibitions and "train" victims for the services they would be expected to perform. Withholding food,

Mumbi's captors kept up the pressure for four days while she resisted their orders despite threats of severe physical abuse. Then a chance at freedom presented itself. In a moment of inattention by her captors, Mumbi escaped and made her way to a women's shelter, where she sought comfort and assistance.

Soon after Mumbi arrived at the shelter, however, staff became concerned about men lurking nearby in parked cars and telephone callers demanding to know Mumbi's whereabouts. For her safety, Mumbi was moved to another location and later granted refugee status that permitted her to remain in Canada. The situation in Kenya was too perilous for her to return.

Although cause for joy and celebration, Mumbi's escape from traffickers in sexual services is atypical. Linguistic and cultural barriers, combined with isolation, keep many foreign women trapped in operations where they are exploited "under the radar" of law enforcement agencies and society at large.

In September 2009, police in Edmonton uncovered a human trafficking operation at the "Sachi Professional Massage and Spa" where, they alleged, three women from Fiji and one from China were "forced to eat, sleep and perform sex acts for money in the same room." Many massage parlours in the Vancouver area cater only to an Asian clientele, promoting themselves exclusively in a foreign language and hanging up if a caller speaks English. These barriers make it more difficult to access potential victims.

## Dancing slaves in a strip club near you

Enslavement as a means of forcing women to perform sex acts with strangers isn't restricted to massage parlours and brothels. Whatever one may think of strip clubs and their activities, the reality often includes young women living and performing under coercion.

Federal officials in Canada express grave concerns about the exploitation of foreign women as exotic dancers, particularly women from Central and Eastern Europe. For some time these women were being brought into Canada legally and expeditiously under the federal government's "exotic dancer visa program." Concerns about exploitation and human trafficking caused the program to be largely shut down, but trepidation persists.

A March 2007 email to the Canadian Embassy in Romania from a regional intelligence officer for the Canada Revenue Agency in Niagara Falls, Ontario, identified aspects of the problem. "I have read some dancer contracts and a couple of clauses really troubled me," the officer wrote. According to her report, one clause stated, "[T]he club owners have the right to hold all ID until the terms of the contract are fulfilled," while another required "that monies will be held until terms of the contract are fulfilled, less disbursements. These two clauses themselves smack of slavery."

Frederick Matern, one of Canada's top immigration officials in Bucharest, replied in a detailed, but heavily censored, email obtained under the *Access to Information Act.* Among other things, Matern raised concerns about women from the region being brought to Canada to work as exotic dancers, including evidence of blatant deception by the contractors. "In order to conform to HRSDC [Human Resources and Social Development Canada] requir[e]ments," Matern noted, "we are getting shown very different contracts by people seeking work permits. I suspect that the contracts that conform to HRSDC are nowhere close to the truth."

Indeed, in a case documented by the Canada Border Services Agency, a woman from Romania came to Canada under a work permit as an exotic dancer. Soon after arriving, she was reportedly "forced to do things that she did not wish to do ... was unable to take sick time when required ... [and] there were elements of coercion and threats against her from the bar owners and supervisors." CIC officials subsequently found the woman to be a victim of human trafficking and offered her assistance.

## Micro-brothels—the (trafficked) girl next door

In November 2006, two investigative reporters from the *Toronto Star* uncovered a new and disturbing development in Canada's sex trade: The practice of providing sexual services through massage parlours, which were too easily identified and raided by police officers, largely had been abandoned in favour of rooms in high-rise apartment buildings. These "micro-brothels" are often right next door to apartments occupied by families, many of them with small children. While low-income neighbourhoods have been home to "trick pads" for decades, "micro-brothels" represent a recent migration of the sex industry into middle- and upper-class communities.

Micro-brothels are set up in hotel and motel rooms, as well as apartment units and luxury condominiums. Their secret locations are disclosed to men who respond to advertisements for "escorts" or more explicit advertisements on internet bulletin board websites and weekly newspapers. Embedded in our communities, they become venues for the sexual exploitation of victims of human trafficking. Because they "hide in plain sight," micro-brothels are quickly becoming common outlets for purchasing sex and keeping trafficking victims concealed, constantly on the move, and difficult to identify and assist. Once again, these victims are forced to meet the demands of the traffickers without recourse or opportunity for help.

A law enforcement officer in Peel Region, a suburb of Metropolitan Toronto, has participated in several raids on micro-brothels in his jurisdiction and constantly is appalled at what he discovers. "When you look around," he explains, "what do they have in there? A little bit of food. There are no pictures of their family. The first thing you notice is this does not look lived in. You might see a little suitcase in the closet, with just some clothing. No personal effects at all. They don't live there. They are taken somewhere every night."

The benefits of micro-brothels to human traffickers are significant. Massage parlours, as noted earlier, practically identify the true nature of their business and attract attention from law enforcement and citizens' groups. Escort services may provide the women with a measure of temporary freedom, increasing the risk that they may flee and turn against their captors. Micro-brothels involve neither disadvantage. If, as anticipated, law enforcement officers more actively investigate and prosecute human traffickers in Canada, these secretive outlets for exploitation are expected to multiply rapidly as traffickers take their victims even further underground.

# 4

# ACROSS THE UNDEFENDED BORDER

Osoyoos is a dry, dusty town of about five thousand people in the British Columbia interior, roughly four hundred kilometres east of Vancouver. The community lies close to Washington State, a crossing point along the almost nine-thousand-kilometre Canada–U.S. border. Historically, Osoyoos first served as a north–south trading route for fur and cattle and more recently as a cross-border transfer point for agricultural products. At least once in recent times, it became an entry point for the attempted trade in people.

In June 2006, local citizens in Osoyoos grew suspicious when a man in a large rental van accompanied by a group of Asian women began asking about nearby remote routes for entering the United States. In a small town, word travels fast. When local police learned of the traveller, his cadre of women, and his interest in a clandestine point of entry to the United States, they began keeping an eye on him and contacted the RCMP.

The police eventually arrested the man and the women. All of the women were South Korean and none spoke English, but the signs of intent to cross the border were clear. The women were terrified at having been apprehended, and following a series of interviews, it became apparent that they'd been duped into coming to the United States through Canada, their destiny to be sold for sex.

This revelation shocked the six women who ranged in age from twenty-two to twenty-eight, all of whom expected to be employed in restaurants. Lou Berube, the RCMP's human trafficking awareness coordinator for British Columbia and the Yukon, believed them. "I'm absolutely convinced at this point that we have human trafficking victims here," he says, suggesting the women had been recruited and transported for sexual exploitation. Although the women could have applied for temporary immigrant status to ensure they would not be mistreated or victimized if they returned home, all six chose to leave Canada.

We Canadians may be proud of many aspects of life in our country, but for the majority of people worldwide, the United States of America remains the magnet for prosperity. For some criminals, this prosperity is built upon the backs of slave labour—and for those who plan to achieve their wealth in this manner, Canada is a stepping stone to the United States, even with the heightened border restrictions since 9/11.

## An attractive transit hub

For almost a decade, the U.S. State Department has identified Canada in its annual *Trafficking in Persons Report* as a transit point for human trafficking into the United States. While not required for human trafficking, the movement of a victim is a key aspect of international trafficking.

The traffickers identify vulnerable individuals and bring them to markets where they can earn the greatest profits, a journey that often involves transporting the victims through transit countries. During this process, the victims are easier to control because they are isolated from family and friends and frequently don't understand the language of the transit or destination country.

Government reports have identified almost one hundred transit countries for human trafficking, most with common characteristics. These include the following:

- geographic proximity by land, sea, or air to significant destination countries;

- an operational criminal infrastructure to facilitate entry and exit of individuals;
- insufficient legislation and weak law enforcement to deal with migrant smuggling and human trafficking; and
- immigration policies open to abuse.

The United States is a significant destination country for forced labour and sex trafficking, with an estimated 14,500 to 17,500 victims brought in every year across land borders with Canada and Mexico, as well as by sea or air from countries worldwide. Since 9/11, airports have become "harder targets" for entry into the United States, making land crossings far more attractive to the traffickers.

Of the two countries bordering the United States, Mexico is likely the more alluring entry point for traffickers. Nevertheless, Canada's geographic proximity to the large U.S. market for human trafficking, coupled with fluid criminal networks and more liberal immigration policies, has made it an attractive option for some traffickers seeking to bring victims to the United States.

"There seems to be a good amount of information indicating at least two thousand people per year are trafficked through Canada into the U.S.," says an analyst with the U.S. Department of State. The north-to-south flow naturally attracts a good deal of media attention in the United States, but it is not a one-way street.

"Despite activity in both north- and south-bound directions, there is a significant increase in illegal north-bound migration from the US into Canada," according to the Criminal Intelligence Service Canada's *Report on Organized Crime* (2008). "Most human smuggling activity takes place at border crossings in B.C. and Quebec, and to a lesser extent, Ontario," the report continues. "A small number of organized crime groups, mostly based in B.C. and Quebec, are involved in the facilitation of international trafficking in persons."

## Plugging a leaky dike

As joint efforts to patrol the U.S.–B.C. border have intensified over the years, traffickers and smugglers have begun to move eastward, in some instances crossing over from Alberta into Montana. The phenomenon recalls efforts to repair a leaky dike, in which plugging one location merely directs the water to another where it flows more easily.

In July 2004, eleven women from South Korea (accompanied by three South Korean men) were found soaking wet, afflicted with hypothermia and insect bites, in Waterton Lakes National Park. Using sensors that identify body heat, a U.S. border patrol aircraft first detected the party near the remote Chief Mountain border crossing in southern Alberta as they were heading toward Montana. The subsequent investigation revealed that organized crime had brought the women into Vancouver under the pretence that they were students at a now-defunct school in the B.C. Lower Mainland. Once in Canada, the women were transported to Alberta, where two local men had been hired to drop them off near the border and pick them up on the other side after they had made their way through the dense woods. The two men reportedly were paid two thousand dollars for facilitating this illegal entry into the United States.

Authorities believe that the women would have become ensnared in the sex industry in the United States. Like the women in Osoyoos, they were returned to their homeland.

Criminal networks have long operated boarding houses in Vancouver, British Columbia, to harbour foreign nationals destined for illegal travel to U.S. cities such as Tacoma, Seattle, San Francisco, and Los Angeles. These networks help the individuals enter the United States, often by accompanying them on foot over uncontrolled areas until someone else meets them on the other side of the border and transports them to their ultimate destination. Many individuals entering the United States illegally are forced to pay their smuggling debts by being sold for sex in massage parlours and brothels—a common means of coercion, as we have seen.

British Columbia has been identified by the U.S. Department of State as "an attractive hub for East Asian traffickers," with several hundred South Koreans apparently having been transported through that province for exploitation in the United States. In Vancouver, one criminal network alone allegedly illegally transported at least thirty-nine South Korean nationals into the United States between August 2004 and March 2007, when South Koreans could legally enter Canada, but not the United States, without a visa.

In January 2009, South Korean nationals received permission to travel directly to the United States without a visa. Traffickers and smugglers keep abreast of changes to visa policies, routing their victims through countries that allow for more ready access to the United States. How this de facto harmonization of visa policy will affect Canada's attractiveness as a transit country remains to be seen.

In May 2007, Canadian Pacific Railway police in Windsor, Ontario, intercepted six stowaways on a freight train headed for Detroit, Michigan. Among them was Rashann, a young girl who'd been in Canada for several months and was assessed as a foreign victim of human trafficking. Sergeant Steve Richardson of the RCMP's Windsor Immigration and Passport Section investigated the incident. Rashann told immigration officials she did not know where she was going, reported Richardson. "She was extremely nervous.... She speaks no English at all and has not been in school."

In some instances, the trade in people flows in the opposite direction. Also in 2007, Canada Border Services Agency investigators found Tasha, a foreign child, among a group of illegal immigrants seeking to enter Canada from the United States. She owed four thousand dollars as a smuggling debt and had no family or friends in Canada and no obvious means of repaying the money, leading officials to consider her a potential victim of human trafficking.

In February 2001, the Vancouver Police Department identified an eleven-year-old child who'd been abducted in Portland, Oregon, and brought to Canada. The child had been forced to engage in sex acts for money, and a joint law enforcement investigation led to the prosecution and conviction of this child's traffickers, who received lengthy sentences to be served in an American prison. Under U.S. law in force today, sex trafficking of a child under fourteen years of age using force, fraud, or coercion is punishable with a mandatory minimum term of fifteen years imprisonment. In some instances, the offence even carries a sentence of life in prison without parole. Canada's legal system, which is far more lenient toward convicted child traffickers, is discussed in a later chapter.

In Hollywood films like *Taken* (2009), abduction is the method of choice used to ensnare trafficking victims. However it is high risk, being easier for authorities to detect at most stages of the trafficking chain. Nevertheless, abduction has been used to bring some victims from the United States into Canada.

Castana, a Mexican woman, had a green card and was living in the United States. In early 2006, she was kidnapped by a man from El Salvador who forced her into his car at gunpoint and drove her to Canada. Before he was able to sell her, Castana seized an opportunity to escape. After being questioned by police about the incident, she returned to the United States, believing her would-be trafficker had continued on to Toronto.

## Trafficked Canadians in the "Land of the Free"

Up to this point, all of the incidents related have involved foreign victims. However, the United States is also an alluring market for sex traffickers who transport Canadian victims to a wide range of destinations. From Central and Eastern Canada, victims are usually brought to upstate New York and down the eastern seaboard as far as Florida. From Western Canada, the usual route leads to Las Vegas.

In February 2008, police in Clearwater, Florida, asked the RCMP for help investigating an international human trafficking operation that was spiriting unsuspecting Canadian women over 2200 kilometres from Toronto to Florida's Gulf Coast. Investigations revealed that American traffickers were approaching women in Canadian shopping malls and, after earning their trust, offering to take them to Florida for a vacation. In the words of the investigating officers, on arrival the women were forced to "work in the commercial sex business under duress."

The executive director of an NGO for sexually exploited women in Toronto estimates that at least forty prostituted women assisted by his organization over the last ten years had been "flipped" into the United States for a time, destined for Las Vegas, Los Angeles, Atlantic City, and New York. The movement of women was well organized, with an individual in each U.S. city awaiting the victims' arrival and prepared to initiate and control them. There are several gangs seemingly involved, including Jamaican street gangs, as well as Asian and Russian criminal organizations.

In Western Canada, the Edmonton Police Service has publicly revealed that young women from Alberta were drugged, beaten, and gang-raped by traffickers who forced them into prostitution. Once the victims were firmly under the control of the traffickers, they were shipped to Las Vegas, where they were sold to wealthy men for up to ten thousand dollars per weekend.

Heavily censored police-incident reports released by the RCMP National Headquarters in Ottawa under the *Access to Information Act* confirm the brutality involved in some of these cases. A September 2005 "occurrence summary" by the RCMP Northwest Region stated that the victim was "lured from Edmonton to Las Vegas, raped and beaten, then flown to Fort Lauderdale, raped and beaten again then forced into prostitution." Despite all this, the victim did not want the police to lay charges.

Incidents of Canadian victims being exploited overseas have been less well documented. Nevertheless, the Criminal Intelligence Service Canada has received reports of "Canadian females being lured by false modelling opportunities overseas that result in their exploitation in the sex trade."

The Canadian parents of these suspected victims of human trafficking are going to great lengths to rescue their young daughters. Perhaps no case illustrates this in more heart-wrenching detail than that of Jessie Foster.

## What happens in Vegas ...

Glendene Grant last heard her daughter's voice on Friday, March 24, 2006, when twenty-one-year-old Jessie Edith Louise Foster (her real name) called from Las Vegas, Nevada. Jessie told her mom that she wanted to come home, that she would be leaving in the next couple of days and would arrive back in Canada in time for Easter. Tragically, she never made it.

A year earlier, Jessie, a bright-eyed slim blonde, had been working at Boston Pizza in Kamloops before moving to Calgary to live with her father. She met a man at a party who offered her an "extra ticket" to Fort Lauderdale, Florida. Despite warnings from her family, Jessie agreed to go with him. Within a few days of their arrival, the generous stranger claimed to be broke and demanded that she repay his "generosity" by being sold for sex. Over the next few months, Jessie was transferred first to New York City, then to Atlantic City, and finally to Las Vegas, where she was then introduced to a new man. A private investigator discovered that this individual, twice convicted of assault, had been offering Jessie for sale through escort ads in Las Vegas. He was the last person to see her alive.

Since the day Jessie went missing, her mother has been doing everything in her power to locate her daughter. She has launched a public website (www.jessiefoster.ca), raised fifty thousand dollars as a reward for information, hired a private investigator, written letters to countless officials, and participated in dozens of media interviews in the United States and Canada. Jessie's case has been profiled on *America's Most Wanted*, along with those of other women who have vanished in Las Vegas's seedy underworld.

Glendene wrote a letter to her missing daughter and those responsible for her disappearance and asked that it be distributed as widely as possible in the hope that someone may have information that could help locate the young woman. The letter is a loving mother's cry from the heart:

My sweet, dear, wonderful Jessie …

Hi baby, this is Mom. I just wanted to let you know how much I miss you and how hard we are working to find you and bring you home. I know how scared you must be and how worried you are about us worrying about you. With all my heart and soul I feel you are alive and out there, somewhere, needing to be found and rescued. We will do that.

Jessie, I also want you to know that we know what you have been through. We know what was happening in Vegas. Do NOT blame yourself or think that you need to be forgiven for ANYTHING. You are a VICTIM, even if you think you could have left, you were not able to—your being a victim of human trafficking is proof of that. You were trying to come home to Canada and someone stopped you.

Jessie, I have missed two of your birthdays and a lot of other special occasions and holidays, plus all the things that have happened in the 16 months since you have been missing.

Your dad is having such a hard time with all of this. He just does not know what to do or what to think. He is doing better now, but I have been worried about him. After all, he only has you and Crystal … of course he has step daughters and he knows you have your other sisters, but you guys are his and he misses you so much. Tracy is taking care of things of course. Being the mom and grandma to all the kids … she is a strong woman.

You have such a strong, huge support system, Jess. Your friends all miss you and are so worried and supportive to us.

Jessie, remember … we will find you, love Mom.

xoxoxoxoxoxoxoxoxox

I have one more thing to say, but this is not to Jessie … this is to whoever took her, or has her, or knows where she is. PLEASE, you have to understand that Jessie is loved, wanted, missed and needed back by her family and friends. We NEED her. She is part of us and without her there is a huge, huge hole. It is unbelievable how big of a hole such a tiny girl can make when she is not there. When she is missing from her family, from her place in our lives where she belongs. GIVE HER BACK TO US. Give her back to me. I am her mommy and I need my baby back, PLEASE. Jessie is a wonderful person with a huge heart and you do not need her like we do. We promise that if someone contacts us with information about Jessie's whereabouts we will keep it confidential and you will not be involved if you choose not to be. Contact us from our website: www.jessiefoster.ca or call Crime Stoppers or the North Las Vegas Police or even call your local police agency and they can get the information to us.

Sincerely,
Glendene Grant … mother of endangered missing
JESSIE FOSTER

# 5

# BUYING LOCAL—CANADIAN VICTIMS

When Canadians hear the term *slavery* in a historical context, they usually picture eighteenth- and nineteenth-century slave traders stuffing the holds of their ships with captive Africans in chains. Even the most uninformed realize that such measures are not used to recruit victims of the sex trade in Canada or, indeed, in any other Western nation. Today's methods of recruitment are far more subtle and refined but just as brutally effective.

In August 2008, the Criminal Intelligence Service Canada took the extraordinary step of publicly releasing a strategic intelligence brief. *Organized Crime and Domestic Trafficking in Persons in Canada* is akin to a 911 call from Canada's top police-intelligence organization: "Across the country, organized crime networks are actively trafficking Canadian-born women and under-age girls inter and intra-provincially, and in some instances to the United States, destined for the sex trade."

Domestic sex trafficking is a systematic national criminal enterprise whose practitioners target a large pool of vulnerable individuals, many of them homeless, sexually exploited youth, children in protective care or from dysfunctional families, all of them Canadian. These prime prospects are by no means the only ones; some victims recruited by traffickers even come from middle-class families.

## A national phenomenon

Sex traffickers use a range of tactics to make contact with vulnerable Canadian girls and young women. They patrol group homes and shelters for at-risk youth and approach girls on their way home from school, at shopping malls, bus stations, or parks. Traffickers frequently prey on vulnerable, economically disadvantaged, socially dislocated individuals, as well as those with personal problems or low self-esteem. And while Canadians may assume that sex trafficking is restricted primarily to large urban areas, it reaches rural communities and small towns as well. It is a national phenomenon—more widespread and involving more victims than the general public is aware of.

Wendy Leaver, an officer with the Toronto Police Service, Special Victims Unit, recently encountered an eighteen-year-old girl who was brought from Edmonton to Toronto to sell drugs. The girl imagined she could pay her way through university by that means, but when she arrived in Toronto she immediately was taken to a condo to be sold for sex acts to random men. "That's it. That's human trafficking," says Detective Leaver.

In Alberta, Sergeant Mark Schwartz of the Calgary Police Service, Vice Unit, describes how a teenage girl received a phone call from an ex-boyfriend who wanted to see her. She decided to bring along a friend on the drive outside of Calgary. Eventually the three arrived at a house, where a man told the ex-boyfriend that "his debt had been filled." The ex-boyfriend drove off, leaving the two girls. Turning to them, the unidentified man said, "You work for me now."

"They were sold for drug debt," says Sergeant Schwartz. "[A girl] will refuse at first, then there'll be some gun play, some assault, and she'll be locked in the basement for a few days to a point of breaking." The victim has no choice but to give in.

Elsewhere in Canada, the Vancouver Police Department, Vice Unit, recognizes the continued presence of a pimp- and trafficker-controlled sex trade at the street level. This is particularly apparent in the more expensive "high track" area where the majority of females are Caucasian and are sold for larger sums.

## Domestic sex trafficking criminal networks

Criminal intelligence reports indicate that while some domestic traffickers operate in highly organized networks, other criminal networks are rather unsophisticated and function as cells allowing individual members a degree of independence in controlling and exploiting their victims.

Traffickers operate in different regions or cities but may remain linked, relying on informal business arrangements to circulate victims for more profits and, when necessary, to avoid local police forces that may begin investigating specific (usually underage) victims. The gangs know that Canada has no national "squads" dedicated to rooting out trafficking in people, and the easiest way to avoid police scrutiny and possible charges is to keep the women hidden and on the move.

In contrast, some traffickers have been known to keep victims not only in their own cities but also in their family homes.

Detective Jim Kenney of the Vancouver Police Department recalls one such double life. Just nineteen, Ashley was living with her middle-class family in Surrey and going to school when she fell in love with a man who turned out to be a trafficker. Ashley's parents thought she was working at a restaurant. Instead, for three months she was being prostituted on the high track in Vancouver. Her trafficker controlled her by threatening to tell her parents if she ever tried to stop or go to the police.

## Music, modelling, and misery

The summer of 2006 was difficult for Genevieve. After ending a four-year relationship with her boyfriend she was injured in a motorcycle accident and, realizing she'd be unable to work for some time, moved in with her parents in Montreal.

With her self-esteem at an all-time low, Genevieve was thrilled and flattered to be offered a modelling job in October 2006. The assignment was to pose for the cover of an album produced by Urban Heat Music, an independent record label headquartered in

Montreal and specializing in hip-hop and other genres popular with young people. The glamour of the music business, the appeal of popular music, and the pride in being selected for her beauty would have been more than enough to entice Genevieve under almost any circumstances.

Twenty-two-year-old Jacques Leonard-St. Vil ("Jackie"), the Haitian-Canadian vice-president of Urban Heat Music, directed the photo shoot. After Genevieve had finished posing for the album cover, she accepted an invitation from Jackie to have drinks. In fact, they spent the night together, beginning a relationship in which affection quickly gave way to abuse.

The two discovered they had a common problem: Both were in financial difficulties. Urban Heat Music's reputation apparently was not matched by financial success. As for Genevieve, she had no income or prospects of employment beyond the modelling job she'd just completed.

Jackie had a solution for them both: There was money in hosting promotional parties, and Jackie and Genevieve could work together. With her charm and his abilities, they could keep busy and earn an impressive income, although not in Montreal—the big bucks were to be made in Toronto. Travelling in Genevieve's car, they arrived in January 2007 and moved into a condominium a block from Square One Shopping Centre in suburban Mississauga. The condo belonged to Jackie's employer.

To make some quick money to launch their "promotion" business, Jackie suggested that Genevieve become an exotic dancer. A few days after she began, he told her that she could make much more money by offering "extras," or sex acts, to men at strip clubs. Genevieve agreed to try but, within days, began to protest. Jackie threw an ashtray at her and slapped her across the face. She owed him eight hundred dollars, he informed her, and she was not to use her own car. When she resisted, he began beating her with a broom. Genevieve managed to call 911, but Jackie dialled someone on his cellphone and reported, "She's calling the police." Terrified, Genevieve hung up before she could tell the operator what had happened, and when the operator called back, Genevieve said that she'd phoned by accident. No one followed up to see if this were true.

By February, Genevieve was being sold for sex at various strip clubs six days a week. When she finally told Jackie she was going to leave, he grabbed her by the neck, threw her to the floor, and kicked her. The bruises on Genevieve's thighs prevented her from working at the strip club for several days.

With Genevieve firmly under his control, Jackie allowed her to make a short trip home to Montreal. To her parents, Genevieve explained her bruises had come from a fight at a nightclub. Soon afterwards, Jackie sent her to the United States to be sold for sex, ensuring the money was sent back to him. When Genevieve returned, Jackie again agreed to let her take a short trip to Montreal. This time she called the Montreal Police Service. Upon his return to Montreal, Jackie was arrested on multiple charges, including human trafficking. In just three months, he'd earned twenty thousand dollars from selling Genevieve for sex.

## A barrage of "love bombing" by recruiters

Poverty, the desire for love, and the desire for money, in that order, are the three key vulnerabilities that permit domestic sex traffickers to recruit and control victims, according to those familiar with the techniques. Applied with practised care, the routine proves enormously successful in coercing vulnerable underage girls and women into a life of sexual exploitation.

When traffickers encounter victims seeking love and attention, they commonly begin relationships by becoming "boyfriends" to their victims. This "falling in love" stage takes place over approximately two weeks. The girls are told they're beautiful, and they're taken to fancy restaurants and given lavish gifts. By showering a targeted girl with affection and fulfilling her material desires, the trafficker builds allegiance, eventually allowing him to manipulate her. Street gangs refer to these recruiting tactics as "love bombing." The greater the value of the targeted female on the flesh market and the more sophisticated the trafficker, the longer he can take in "grooming" her.

This particular exploitation process requires that the girls be sexually inexperienced. For this reason, most are recruited between fourteen and sixteen, with some as young as twelve. The more extreme the poverty that surrounds them, the younger the girls can be recruited. These inexperienced girls think they know more than they do, and very quickly the boyfriend will have them engaging in intercourse. He professes love while introducing other seemingly innocent acts to break down barriers, such as having a girl put on lingerie and dance for him. To create a sense of normality, the "boyfriend" will introduce sex acts that a girl may never have performed.

At the next stage, the "boyfriend" escorts the girl to parties, where she appears in very revealing clothing. The girl is usually given alcohol or drugs to facilitate the exploitation. Engaging in sex acts with other people present, or being in the same room while other people have sex, represents the next step, breaking down the girl's sexual boundaries.

The distance from participating in a voyeuristic or exhibitionistic act to performing with a second male present is short. The "boyfriend" might tell his targeted girl how much he'd like to watch her with his friend—a move that destroys the monogamous relationship based on trust. The party is over. At this point the girl will be driven to unexpected and unfamiliar settings. Strangers—associates of the "boyfriend" trafficker—begin arriving at the door. The girl is told she has to "put up with" uncomfortable touching. She knows she's about to be prostituted but has no way to escape.

Street gangs may force the victim to engage in sex acts with their members one after the other. Not surprisingly, studies have found a culture of silence about these "gang bangs." Degrading and humiliating, this type of sexual assault is designed to traumatize and desensitize the victim. It represents a yardstick against which future sex acts, with anonymous individual men for money paid to the trafficker, will seem less egregious.

The tactics practised by the "boyfriend trafficker" are not new and have been well documented across Canada and in the United States.

## Prince Charming has arrived

Naomi was skipping school. Her mom and her mom's "old man" were always arguing, leaving Naomi feeling lonely and neglected.

One night while out for a walk, Naomi met an older man who called himself "Big Daddy" and told her she was beautiful. He offered her cigarettes and didn't give her trouble like her parents did. She went home with him. The next morning he took her shopping and bought her new clothes. He made Naomi feel special. She thought she'd finally found her Prince Charming.

A few days after Naomi had met Big Daddy, he said, "We gotta talk," and then explained that he was having serious cash problems and needed help. Naomi didn't know what she could do, since she was just fifteen and no one would hire her.

Big Daddy told her not to worry; he had a friend who'd help her find a job. This "friend" sent Naomi to a strip club to dance, where she was given cocaine to "help loosen up." Big Daddy told her she was sexy and it was easy money. He told her she was in control.

After a month of dancing, Naomi couldn't understand why Big Daddy still needed money from her. She'd earned a lot of money for him and was sick of dancing for men who looked at her the way they did.

Big Daddy told her to shut her mouth; he would tell her when she was sick of something. He'd never talked to Naomi like that before. She was shocked and had no idea who to turn to for help. Since she'd started seeing Big Daddy, she'd lost touch with her friends and family—and how could she tell them she was stripping?

It was then that Big Daddy threatened her and beat her up. He started forcing her to have sex with random men and took all the money. Naomi eventually contracted an STD and became addicted to cocaine. Things got worse still when Big Daddy sent Naomi to Toronto because she could make more money there.

Naomi's story is featured in *Cinderella's Silence: A Story of Gang Prostitution*, a comic book published in 2002. Written by a teenager who "lived the gang experience," it has warned thousands of youth in Quebec against the tactics used by street gangs who target girls aged twelve to eighteen for sexual exploitation. Unfortunately, similar education about the systematic targeting of young girls is not reaching Canadians in other provinces. Without this information, young girls singled out by recruiters are like lambs before lions.

## Popular myths and tough realities

For Canadians whose contact with the world of sex traffickers is restricted to television shows or movies, the means by which young girls and women can be manipulated and controlled by pimps and traffickers is confusing and generates a catalogue of myths. Dealing in myths rather than facts makes it impossible to fully comprehend the extent and seriousness of the situation and also how to address it effectively.

The International Association of Chiefs of Police has highlighted the following common myths about human trafficking as well as its harsh realities.

Myth: Trafficking involves crossing an international border with the victim or assisting in the victim's being transported across a border.

Reality: Trafficking is about victim exploitation and need not involve a border crossing.

Myth: Canadian citizens cannot be trafficked.

Reality: Victims include Canadians as well as foreign nationals.

Myth: Individuals know what they are getting into, so they cannot claim to have been trafficked.

Reality: Victims may have low self-esteem and be forced or deceived into compliance. Even when they have foreknowledge of the situation, they may lack the power or ability to leave and end their exploitation.

Myth: The individuals committed unlawful acts, so they are not trafficking victims.

Reality: Traffickers often force their victims to commit unlawful acts such as prostitution or immigration offences. Trafficked persons are victims of crime and should be treated with compassion, dignity, and respect.

Myth: The individual was paid for services.

Reality: Many trafficking victims never keep any of the money paid for their exploitation; traffickers may provide others with small amounts of money to keep them compliant but not allow them to leave.

Myth: The individual had freedom of movement and so is not a trafficking victim.

Reality: Some traffickers forcibly confine their victims; many more control them using threats, psychological coercion, and manipulation. In many cases, traffickers are also able to make credible threats against the family members of the victim. Physical violence used against victims can easily convince them that these threats are serious.

Myth: Individuals who did not seize opportunities to escape are not trafficking victims.

Reality: Victims are often under threats that make escape impossible or are under control similar to that experienced by victims of domestic abuse.

Myth: The trafficker's actions were culturally appropriate. Who are we to question such practices?

Reality: Individual liberty is a right inherent to all people; countries across the globe consider human trafficking to be a serious problem that cannot be excused or justified.

Myth: Traffickers and recruiters are always men.

Reality: Women also recruit victims, enforce discipline for traffickers, and in some instances are traffickers themselves.

Myth: It can't be trafficking if the trafficker and victim are related or married.

Reality: This is like the old fable that it is legally impossible for a husband to rape his wife. Being married or related does not give someone the right to victimize another. Some victims have agreed to marry their exploiters in the false hope of lessening or ending their abuse.

## Five steps used by traffickers to recruit and control victims

Many recruiters are younger male members of trafficking-involved street gangs, seeking out and delivering young women just as "headhunters" locate potential executives to fill job vacancies in corporations. They may be joined in the quest for new "talent" by young women who are criminal associates of the trafficker or are victims already under their control. The process used by these recruiters is tried-and-true.

Anick Gagnon of Projet intervention prostitution de Québec has identified five steps in the life cycle of domestic sex trafficking. First, the recruiter looks for any vulnerability he or she can exploit and offers something to meet the needs or desires of the target. For example, a teenage girl hanging out at the mall alone may be offered a cigarette. If she accepts, the recruiter engages her in conversation, and if the conversation includes comments about a recent breakup with the potential victim's boyfriend or troubles at home, the recruiter senses an opening and quickly exploits it.

The second step involves moving toward an "engagement," as recruiters sometimes refer to it. Following up on news of the potential victim's concerns and difficulties, the trafficker begins building an intimate relationship with the victim. After the trafficker has identified the most effective way to "groom" the victim, he uses coercion, manipulation, and, if necessary, direct physical force to compel the victim to be sold for sex for the first time.

Gagnon suggests that step two often includes an appeal for sympathy from the victim, who will respond to her "lover's" needs if he's succeeded in establishing a relationship. "'I owe five hundred dollars, I'll get my legs broken if it's not repaid,'" says Gagnon, citing a common lie. "This leads to 'I need help. I don't know if you can help me, if you love me enough.'"

Step three is commonly referred to as the "honeymoon," when the victim holds out hope that her nightmare will end but continues to be exploited. Inevitably this leads to step four—a crisis. The victim is arrested; a social worker calls the victim's family; the victim contracts a serious STD; or she is brutally assaulted by a purchaser of sex acts.

Then comes the fifth and final step. The victim faces a dilemma: Either she must attempt escape and seek help with greater determination (and risk) than she might have demonstrated earlier, or she must resign herself to continued exploitation with no end in sight.

## The trafficker's playbook and cultural glamorizing of pimps

Domestic sex traffickers across North America consult playbooks on how to control and manipulate victims. These published manuals are read and reread by aspiring traffickers. Some are even available for purchase on popular websites like www.amazon.com.

Below is an excerpt from a 1998 "instructional manual" describing proven tactics employed by traffickers to control their victims. The manual reads like a recipe for exploitation. Even the author of this perverse guidebook speaks of the girls and women as victims and refers to them as pieces of property:

> You'll start to dress her, think for her, own her. If you and your victim are sexually active, slow it down. After sex, take her shopping for one item. Hair and/or nails is fine. She'll develop a feeling of accomplishment. The shopping after a month will be replaced with cash. The love making turns into raw sex. She'll start to crave the intimacy and be willing to get back into your good graces. After you have broken her spirit, she has no sense of self value. Now pimp, put a price tag on the item you have manufactured.

In addition to these reprehensible manuals, domestic sex traffickers in North America take full advantage of the glamorized portrayal of pimps in pop culture. Since 1974, the annual Players' Ball in Chicago has brought together self-proclaimed pimps to award the distinction of "Pimp of the Year." The pimp costume has become a Halloween staple. Canadian high schools have held "Pimp and Ho" parties, where students dress in stereotypical costumes as Kramer famously did in an episode of *Seinfeld*. Television shows are called *Pimp My Ride* and other variations. There is even a Pimp Juice energy drink owned by hip-hop star Nelly, who released a song by the same title. More recently, in May 2010, the rapper Necro released a song called "Human Trafficking King" on his album *Die!* The lyrics are sadistic and cruel. Is it all just harmless fun?

As public awareness of human trafficking grows ever so slowly, so does understanding of the evolving methods used by traffickers who are operating just under the radar. It's unfortunate—but hardly surprising—that these criminal elements are also taking full advantage of developments in technology to improve their efficiency. The criminals are outpacing the law enforcers, who are employing the same technology in their efforts to catch them.

# 6

# THE NEW TECHNOLOGY OF TRAFFICKING

In late 2007, among old sofa beds, unwanted pets, and obsolete computer equipment, a fourteen-year-old girl was advertised for sale on Craigslist, the popular internet bulletin board. Typically the rate was two hundred dollars for thirty minutes or three hundred dollars for a full hour. On slow days, the price would be lowered until a buyer was found. Men travelled across Ontario to motels in the Toronto suburbs of Brampton and Mississauga to hand over their cash and claim their "purchase."

"You can buy a used lawnmower right beside a fourteen-year-old girl," says one officer of the Peel Regional Police, Vice Unit, who investigated the situation. His partner adds, "I cannot believe these guys did not know how young she was."

We'll call the girl Samantha. In October 2007, she was a ward of the Children's Aid Society who suffered from fetal alcohol syndrome and had been in and out of group homes for most of her life. One day, Imani Nakpangi approached Samantha while she was out for a walk. He offered her a ride—and an opportunity to escape the group home.

When Samantha stepped into Nakpangi's car, she entered an even darker chapter of her life. Although twice her age, Nakpangi flattered Samantha, made her feel special, and soon persuaded her that he was her boyfriend—her knight in shining armour. He convinced her that if she earned enough money, they would move into a big house together. It would be her first real home.

Over the next two months, Nakpangi transported Samantha to various locations, selling her for sex through Craigslist and earning about sixty-five thousand dollars. His textbook recruiting tactics likely had succeeded beyond his wildest dreams—Samantha remained convinced that Nakpangi was her lover.

The police might never have found Samantha if not for a phone call from an eighteen-year-old called Eve. Like many sophisticated traffickers, Nakpangi adapted his tactics to suit the vulnerabilities and resilience of each individual victim: violence if necessary, but not necessarily violence. Whereas he manipulated Samantha psychologically, he controlled Eve with physical violence and threats against her family.

Like Samantha, Eve was a young Canadian who'd been exploited since she was a vulnerable teenager. Just fourteen and homeless, Eve had been easy prey for a man who sold her for sex acts and forced her to earn money for him over a year. He then transferred her to Nakpangi, who gave Eve false identification claiming she was twenty years old.

For the next two and a half years, Nakpangi netted an estimated $360,000 by selling Eve for sex acts almost every day, frequently by advertising her on Craigslist. She, too, was often moved to avoid detection and sold out of various hotel/motel rooms in the Greater Toronto Area. Some traffickers follow the "ten-day rule," moving the victim every ten days or so to prevent her from being identified by police, arousing the suspicions of community members, or developing friendships with people who could render assistance. Although isolated, she is always digitally present on websites like Craigslist, so that men can access her easily and anonymously. It's the perfect system for exploiters: victims are at once hidden and in plain sight.

Whenever Nakpangi suspected Eve was beginning to waver in her obedience to him, his threats were immediate, direct, and credible. "I'll fuck you up, and break your nose," he'd tell her, and Eve didn't doubt his seriousness. On other occasions, he'd threatened to kidnap Eve's two-year-old brother if she ever "got out of line." Once when Eve attempted to leave Nakpangi, he caught and severely assaulted her, demanding she pay him a one-hundred-thousand-dollar "exit fee" to secure her freedom.

In November 2007, a man posing as a client robbed Eve at gunpoint of all the cash she'd earned that night. Such acts of violence are common in the criminal underworld, since robberies of illegal operations are rarely, if ever, reported to the police. When Nakpangi blamed Eve for the robbery and his threats escalated, she finally decided to call the police. She described her situation and revealed that Samantha was being sold in the same motel that day, leading to the eventual rescue of both victims and the pressing of criminal charges against Nakpangi.

## The internet: The new recruiting ground for human traffickers

If Facebook were a country, its more than 350 million active users would constitute one of the largest populations in the world, behind only China and India. In Canada in 2010, more than three-quarters of teenagers had social networking profiles. It should come as no surprise, then, that sex traffickers have turned to social networking websites as ideal forums in which to prey on vulnerable youth and recruit them for sexual exploitation across this country, as Sarah found out.

In October 2008, Sarah made up her mind: She would run away from home to be with Tyrel, whom she had "met" online through their respective Facebook pages. Sarah, who was just fourteen, accepted Tyrel's invitation to make the trek from her family home in the interior of British Columbia to Victoria on Vancouver Island.

Whatever twenty-two-year-old Tyrel Henwood might have told Sarah during their online exchanges, he hadn't revealed that he was out on bail after having been charged with robbery and aggravated assault with a weapon. The charges alleged he'd beaten a prostituted woman with a field-hockey stick. Among the conditions of his bail, Henwood was to "keep the peace and be of good behaviour." Instead, he lured Sarah to Victoria with the goal of forcing her to be sold for sex for his benefit.

When Sarah arrived in Victoria, Henwood took away her wallet and identification before assaulting and threatening her when she tried to leave. Three weeks later, after Sarah's family had reported her missing, officers with the Victoria Police Service discovered her on the street. She was being sold for sex and giving her earnings to Henwood. Either because Henwood was an amateur exploiter or didn't have enough capital to cover the initial costs of hotel/motel rooms to keep Sarah hidden, she'd been seen by the police. Obviously underage, she'd provided the officers with two false names before breaking down and asking for help. Henwood was then located and charged with a long list of offences, including human trafficking.

## Someone has requested to be your Facebook friend ...

Sarah was not alone in befriending a stranger on Facebook. A survey by Microsoft Canada and Youthography revealed that one out of every three young people has accepted a friend request on Facebook from someone whom they didn't know, usually a "friend of a friend." Another motive in accepting a request is to meet new people. Concerns have been raised about the presence of convicted sex offenders online, many of whom are prohibited from having physical contact with children but are active in the virtual world where an introduction to a child is just a click away.

In 2007, MySpace revealed that more than twenty-nine thousand registered sex offenders in the United States alone had profiles on their website. This revelation prompted the State of New York to pass the *Electronic Security and Targeting of Online Predators Act* (e-STOP) the following year, requiring all registered sex offenders in the state to disclose their internet accounts and identifiers. If an offender is convicted of a child sexual offence or used the internet to commit a sex crime, he is prohibited from joining social networking sites as a mandatory condition of probation or parole.

In December 2009, over three thousand five hundred convicted sex offenders in the State of New York were kicked off Facebook and

MySpace, drawing praise from the New York–based Crime Victims Center. Unfortunately, Canada has yet to enact similar laws to confront the problem.

Parry Aftab, founder and director of WiredSafety, which advises children on internet risks, explains that children who are already vulnerable to sexual exploitation face increased danger on the web. "They may post sexual images," explains Aftab. "They may indicate that they're up for anything. They may indicate that they're more mature, and know a lot more things than anybody around them appreciates. And like a weak fish broadcasting to a shark, they broadcast their vulnerability to sexual predators, pimps, and sexual traffickers."

## Craigslist: A clearing house for victims

According to Katherine Chon, former executive director and co-founder of the Washington, D.C.–based Polaris Project, human traffickers have found Craigslist to be "one of the most efficient, effective, and free ways to post children and women for sale."

After falling under the influence of a sex trafficking ring, girls as young as thirteen are advertised explicitly, offering to perform erotic services, overt sex acts, or unprotected sex. The ads claim the girls are eighteen or older but use barely coded language to get their message across to prospective customers. Racy pictures accompanying the notices may or may not be of the girls in question. An email address or phone number is posted for interested men to call, and a place and time is arranged for sex acts at agreed prices. This is e-commerce at its most efficient—in this context, horrific, disgusting, and growing rapidly in size and impact.

In June 2009, the North Vancouver RCMP released the following public warning as the school year ended: "Many of these at-risk youths have been recruited by a North Vancouver ring of pimps and drug traffickers. These girls are being exploited through the use of Craigslist to advertise their sexual services that are then arranged for hotels. The pimps are using violence or the threat of violence to control the girls."

Police were alerted to the situation when staff at a North Vancouver school heard of students being sold for sex by former students, now gang members in their early twenties and allegedly involved in trafficking girls and drugs. Officers from the RCMP Youth Intervention Unit (YIU) and Sex Crime Investigations Units are working together to address the problem, along with ONYX, an organization that supports sexually exploited youth. It was the YIU that went public with the information in an effort to alert parents.

"Parents have to be really aware and educate themselves around the Internet and computers," Officer Shannon Kitchen of the YIU explained. "That's a big one." She's been involved in eleven files to date and has identified four suspected pimps, although she believes there are more. "I think that they're constantly working to increase their numbers."

One teenage girl who represents herself as eighteen online, but whom Kitchen knows to be sixteen, was sold for "car dates" with a range of sexual services up to one hundred and twenty dollars. Some services are described as "uncovered," or without a condom, exposing her to serious STDs, including HIV/AIDS.

## Cyber cops: Policing sex trafficking online

From Vancouver to Calgary to the Greater Toronto Area, police officers are beginning to investigate numerous cases in which Craigslist has been used to facilitate sex acts with minors, as well as to sell domestic and foreign adult victims of human trafficking. Despite some successes, police are under-resourced and cannot make more than a dent in the problem.

In August 2007, the parents of a missing underage girl in British Columbia contacted police after somehow discovering she was being sold for sex hundreds of kilometres away on Craigslist's Calgary website. Fortunately, the Calgary Police Service, Vice Unit, was able to rescue her.

Also in 2007, the Calgary police launched an undercover investigation called "Operation Carmel" to determine whether Craigslist was being used systematically for the illegal sale of minors and trafficking victims for sex. Over two years, the Vice Unit made more than thirty arrests related to criminal activity facilitated through Craigslist and rescued three underage girls being sold for sex on the website. In December 2008, undercover officers in the same city located two females in their late teens who'd been brought from Winnipeg to work as escorts. Their trafficker was posting their pictures and information on Craigslist to generate business. Fortunately, police were able to help these victims return to their homes in Manitoba.

A month later, Calgary police located another victim being sold for sex on Craigslist. The sex trafficker who controlled her was a known gang associate. This victim was rescued from a hotel room paid for by the criminal and returned to her home in Vancouver.

## The "medium of choice" for human traffickers

"Operation Street Fighter," a second major police investigation launched in Calgary in 2007, revealed "strong indications" of human trafficking and another Craigslist connection. Time and again, confidential informants directed police operatives to Craigslist as a conduit for Asian Organized Crime to advertise young girls who were providing sexual services for money and attracting customers to residential bawdy houses. The investigation found Craigslist to be "the medium of choice for the advertising of sexual services in exchange for money."

Sergeant Mark Schwartz of the Calgary Police Service, Vice Unit, has since been qualified as an expert in court on the use of Craigslist for advertising sex acts. He describes how men wanting to buy sex are "cruising through the listings on Craigslist ... similar to driving around in circles on a know[n] prostitution stroll, checking to see who is working, and then picking your favourite."

The problem reached such epic proportions in the United States that in November 2008 Craigslist was forced to curb this illegal use of its website. It agreed to take a number of measures, including co-operating with law enforcement to investigate sex trafficking and requiring phone and credit card verification for ads posted; the latter substantially reduced the ads in the "erotic services" section, along with the more explicit language.

Craigslist took further action in May 2009, but again only in the United States, to eliminate its "erotic services" section. In its place a new "adult services" section was created, with a requirement that a Craigslist employee manually review every ad to verify its compliance with the website's terms of use. In a 2009 interview about his company's role in sex trafficking, Craigslist CEO Jim Buckmaster said the extensive measures to crack down on criminal misuse of the Craigslist website do not fully apply to the nearly fifty Canadian sites owned by his company. He acknowledged, though, that the website "is just as popular in Canada."

## Cellphones: More technology to monitor and control victims

In recent years, the cellphone has emerged as the only new technology to rival the impact of the internet on our lives. Unfortunately, cellphones also provide human traffickers with a means to exert more control over their victims than might otherwise be possible.

Consider the system devised by twenty-one-year-old Vytautas Vilutis, a convicted human trafficker who posted his cellphone number on Craigslist so that men could arrange appointments for sex acts with his twenty-year-old Canadian victim. In this way, he kept track of who was coming and going and used this information to calculate how much the victim owed him. Vilutis would even text his victim when a man's time was up.

The irony of the situation is palpable. The phone Vilutis gave to his victim—a tool to monitor, manage, and control her—was simultaneously a means for her to call for help if only she could marshal the courage. The control exercised by traffickers over their victims is that powerful.

Some traffickers have recognized, too, the power of global positioning satellite (GPS) capabilities, which are becoming common on smart phones. The free GPS applications that allow law-abiding users to track down their friends at a coffee shop or restaurant become for traffickers a means of monitoring the precise location of their victims in real time. This Orwellian method of control is only the latest perversion of technology that makes trafficking easier for serial exploiters.

# 7

# BREAKING THE BONDS THAT ENSLAVE VICTIMS

How traffickers exert such tight control over their victims is difficult to understand. Many victims, for example, spend a good deal of time out of physical reach of their traffickers. Yet their traffickers are able to control them very effectively even when they're in cars or hotel rooms with strangers who've paid to abuse them.

The Criminal Intelligence Service Canada has identified an arsenal of tactics used by sex traffickers to control their victims. Some—such as abduction, rape, forcible confinement, and assault—are direct. Even when the victim is temporarily away from the trafficker, the prospect of suffering a severe beating and the threat of future harm or even death is powerfully inhibiting. This is especially true if the victim already has endured a beating or injury in the past or knows someone else who has at the hands of the trafficker. In many cases, traffickers portray law enforcement officers as enemies to be avoided, further discouraging the victim from approaching them. The victim is also told that she herself is a criminal and should expect to be treated as such, or worse.

Indirect forms of coercion include controlling all aspects of the victim's life and threatening her family members should she turn on her abuser. Some traffickers have reportedly impregnated their victims to create a sense of "familial loyalty."

"Nobody can get into the mindset of these girls," says a police officer familiar with the techniques of traffickers. "How does an average person relate to it? They can't. When I first came to this unit, I thought the same thing—what's wrong with these girls? Very quickly you learn they are forced to do this. They are victims."

Listen to the words of Michelle, an underage Canadian girl who was recruited by traffickers and forced for weeks to provide sexual services to men:

> I ran away once or twice at first, but he always caught me and forced me to go back. He would punch me, pull my hair.... I wound up in this cheap motel room with dirty, smelly, disgusting clients coming in all day long. Then there were the sadistic ones who took pleasure in degrading and humiliating you.... I threw up sometimes, it was so unbearable. When I did that I got punished. The guys [in the gang] wouldn't give me anything to eat: they would say, "That way, you won't throw up." It got to the point where I was begging—not for food but for drugs, pills, anything. The best thing that could happen was for me to forget where I was, who I was.... But clients don't like it when the girls are stoned. Some of them complained about me. I won't tell you how badly I got beat up after that.

## Common tactics of traffickers and torturers

Government health policy analysts and international NGOs have compared the tactics used by traffickers—the direct force and indirect coercion to which they subject their victims—to methods of torture. Consider the abuse of Michelle and other victims described earlier in light of these definitions of torture prepared by Shared Hope International and the Polaris Project:

| | |
|---|---|
| Perception: | Movement restricted; information available only from a single source. |
| Isolation: | Separation from family and loved ones; periods of time kept in closets, closed rooms, trunks of cars, etc. |

| | |
|---|---|
| Trivial Demands: | Enforcement of minute rules to demonstrate complete power over the victim. |
| Degradation: | Application of demeaning punishments, public insults, and constant emotional abuse. |
| Dominance: | Enforcing complete power over the victim's physical and emotional state. |
| Indulgences: | Occasional affectionate behaviour to build emotional dependency. |
| Threats: | Consistent and repeated threats against the victim and his/her loved ones. |
| Exhaustion: | Starvation, sleep deprivation; in the case of sexual slaves, being forced to provide sex for forty-eight hours straight. |

In some instances, the psychological power of the trafficker is rooted not in the victim's seeking to protect herself from physical harm but rather in her attempt to fulfill an emotional need.

"Part of the psychology that keeps her trapped is this codependence which says: 'I'm going to win him back, I'm going to do this,'" notes a youth intervention worker, who suggests that the mentality of human trafficking victims resembles that of many victims of domestic abuse. "[They think,] 'If I do this, he'll love me more. You know what, if I do this prostituting for just a little bit of time then he'll love me more. I can get out of it. This won't happen again.' There's the honeymoon, there's the threats, there's the violence, there's the plea for forgiveness."

Another individual working with trafficking victims, this time with the Salvation Army, also has witnessed the psychological control exerted over victims: "It's unreal the hold these guys have over these girls, you know, it's really hard to break that … especially if they've been in it for some time. Usually their self-esteem is so bad, they don't think they're worth anything else."

Most people dedicated to assisting the victims of human trafficking agree that many of them don't even identify themselves as victims.

When they define their life experiences, they minimize the abuse and don't consider that they've been exploited. Even when they've been "actively pimped," an expression used by social workers, they still refuse to define their experience in those terms.

In other instances the methods of control are much more explicit. Law enforcement officers who are battling human trafficking in Peel Region outside of Toronto have uncovered a number of rules shared by various sex traffickers. Simply called "The Rules," they provide a means of controlling victims to extract maximum profits from them:

1 Phone the trafficker every few hours to check in.
2 You cannot use your own vehicle; all travel is arranged by the trafficker.
3 You must earn a minimum amount of money (a quota) each evening for the trafficker before being permitted to return.
4 Surrender all money earned to the trafficker without exception; if money is needed for food, clothing and hygienic products, it must be obtained from the trafficker.
5 When working on the street, the rule "ten toes to the curb" must be followed to quickly attract potential clients—no hiding in the shadows.
6 When in a strip club, you are not permitted to spend more than five minutes with a potential client without receiving money for a sexual service.
7 You are forbidden to speak with other women or black men in strip clubs, due to concerns about being recruited away by competing traffickers who in Peel Region are predominantly gang members associated with North Preston's Finest (NPF) or Haitian-Canadian gang members who are black [Yes, you can add racism to the list of wrongs committed by these traffickers].

"The bottom line is that the trafficker does not want you to have any relationship besides their relationship," explains one Peel Region officer who describes sex traffickers in similar terms to cult leaders. "That's why you don't talk to girls, you don't talk to anyone in the club unless they're paying you. When you go home, you get in that car and go straight back. When you get to the hotel, you call again—they want to know that you're there with nobody. The girls are isolated."

This description recalls the strategies of convicted trafficker Vytautas Vilutis. He controlled his victim by forbidding her to buy food without his approval, as well as requiring her to keep her motel room clean at all times and depriving her of a key—a clever tool to keep her from leaving even for a moment because she would be locked out. When Vilutis visited his victim, he demanded that she be freshly showered and have hot coffee ready for him.

Research conducted by University of Ottawa criminology professor Patrice Corriveau and Laval University social work professor Michel Dorais confirmed what earlier studies have found: The majority of underage girls sold for sex "were under the control of a pimp at one time or another" and the relationship was "generally typified by emotional dependency, intimidation, exploitation, violence, and restricted movement."

## Fourteen ways to spot a domestic sex trafficking victim

Since the victims of domestic sex trafficking are frequently unable to take the necessary steps to escape their plight, others must take responsibility for alerting authorities to any suspicions. Any combination of these observed activities and behaviours should trigger further investigation, particularly where the individual is a minor:

1. lack of control over schedule or identification documents
2. unexplained absences from school or work, or failure to attend either on a regular basis
3. chronic running away from home
4. reference to frequent travel to other cities, along with excessive amounts of cash or multiple hotel room keys

5 signs of trauma: bruising, withdrawn behaviour, depression, or fear
6 signs of branding (i.e., tattoos)
7 lying about age and carrying false identification
8 inconsistencies in stories or explanations, along with restricted or obviously scripted communication
9 irregular physical appearance: hungry or malnourished, inappropriately dressed
10 troubled demeanour: anxiety, depression, submissive behaviour, tension, nervousness, inability to make eye contact
11 being watched or monitored by someone, or appearing to have an overly controlling and abusive "boyfriend"
12 spending significant periods of time with a new friend or boyfriend
13 displaying expensive gifts, such as an item of clothing, jewellery, or a cellphone, with no apparent source of income to justify them
14 substance abuse and addiction

## The powerful hold of "trauma bonds"

The abuse to which many sex traffickers subject their victims isn't always about controlling them. Often the motive is to save face with their peers. Traffickers who can't control their victims, or who allow them to keep any of the money they earn, risk being ridiculed by their associates and lose standing in the criminal underworld. Yet traffickers who go "overboard" in the amount and degree of abuse hurled at their victims may be designated "gorilla pimps."

Traffickers aspire to an almost omnipresent psychological control over their victims. Chantal Fredette, who specializes in street gangs and the girls they force to be sold for sex, describes a meeting with a teenage girl who was convinced that her trafficker had bugged Fredette's Montreal office so that he could listen in on their conversation. The girl, clearly deeply disturbed, explained to Fredette: "He does it because he loves me, to protect me."

As a defence mechanism against the ongoing harm they suffer, sex trafficking victims may develop a sense of loyalty to their exploiters because they represent the only constant people in their lives. This psychological connection has been referred to as *trauma bonds* and is similar to indoctrination, brainwashing, or Stockholm Syndrome. Dr. Patrick Carnes describes trauma bonds as "a certain dysfunctional attachment that occurs in the presence of danger, shame or exploitation. There is often seduction, deception, or betrayal. There is always some form of danger of risk."

These trauma bonds help explain why many victims are initially uncooperative or evasive during interviews with police and intervention workers, making it exceedingly difficult in many instances to identify and assist them. Police officers, social workers, and other front-line workers who come into contact with sex trafficking victims need to appreciate that the initial reactions of these victims may be counterintuitive because of defence mechanisms they've built up to protect themselves from relentless trauma.

In some instances, traffickers have even managed to control their victims while they were in foster care, group homes, or women's shelters. One teenage girl was regularly sleeping overnight at a youth centre in Quebec and participating in programs during the day while continuing to be sold for sex in the evenings.

Workers at the Ma Mawi Chi Itata Centre, which assists Aboriginal youth in Winnipeg, have witnessed a similar trend. In six separate instances, men dropped off Aboriginal girls at short-term treatment sites when they became too malnourished, unhealthy, or contracted a serious STD. Once these girls were "cleaned up," however, their exploiters retrieved them and continued to sell them for sex.

An employee at the Salvation Army's Florence Booth House in Toronto was shocked to find traffickers continuing to control women on the street while saving money by using shelters for free accommodation. "Limos would pull up across the street," she says, amazed at the audacity of the traffickers, "and everybody would hop in the limo and later be dropped off and come in here."

In virtually all of these methods of control, the chains that enslave victims of domestic sex trafficking are myriad and largely invisible. Most victims are not kept physically confined—a costly, time-consuming, and risky practice. It is far more profitable, efficient, and safe for traffickers to control their victims through the less direct means we have seen.

## Breaking the bonds between trafficker and victim

In sex trafficking cases, victims are often uncooperative and unwilling to turn on their trafficker, even when assaulted. Members of the Vancouver Police Department, Vice Unit, recall a case in which a female victim was assaulted by her trafficker in front of four witnesses but continued to tell police that her injuries were caused by a fall.

Melissa Snow, project director at U.S.-based Shared Hope International, suggests that police officers start by asking suspected victims of domestic sex trafficking questions such as "Do you have a boyfriend? How old is he? Does he take your money?" Snow's organization has also identified intervention responses to overcoming the trauma bonds between victims and their traffickers, particularly in domestic minor sex trafficking cases:

| | |
|---|---|
| Trafficker Role: | Filling emotional voids and needed roles. |
| Response: | Find out what needs are being met or are trying to be met, such as love and self-esteem. |
| Trafficker Role: | Providing hope, which they later exploit. |
| Response: | Give hope through a variety of ways, such as skill-building, education, and advocacy. |
| Trafficker Role: | Filling physical needs. |
| Response: | Provide holistic programs and services. |
| Trafficker Role: | Generating both fear and intimacy, creating instability. |
| Response: | Create a safe place for victims to stabilize and receive long-term care. |

| | |
|---|---|
| Trafficker Role: | Manipulate, lie, betray, and let the victim down, but always be there. |
| Response: | Set realistic and honest expectations, and be consistent. |

One example of a structured, conversational approach to interviewing sexually exploited youth is the Adolescent Forensic Interview Model, which seeks to minimize the trauma and the number of interviews victims must undergo. Interviewers gather facts in a non-threatening manner geared to the emotional and developmental level of the victim. This requires officers to recognize that victims, especially minors, have developed a tough shell in order to survive.

## Blackmail, extortion, and threats

As a relatively wealthy developed country with a reputation as a human rights champion, Canada attracts foreigners in search of a better life. Many foreign sex trafficking victims thus enter the country willingly, but on arrival find themselves unable to escape the control of their traffickers. Yelena, a girl from a small village in Russia whose sole contact with the outside world was via the internet, represents one such case.

Having encountered an internet ad offering passage to Canada and large sums of money in exchange for work as an escort, Yelena responded and soon received travel documents. Once in Toronto, she was met by traffickers who gave her a cellphone that she had to answer day and night and then took her to a condominium where she was to be sold for sex until she'd repaid her travel costs. While she was repaying her debt, she would receive thirty dollars per day.

"She wanted out of it and didn't know how to get out of it," says the detective who investigated Yelena's case. "What concerned her most was that they threatened to tell her parents. She was from a small Russian town, and they knew where she lived and knew the name of her parents. And they said, 'We will tell your parents that you're a sex worker.'" In a remote Russian village, the stigma of being sold for sex would have brought enormous shame to Yelena's entire family.

Fortunately, Yelena met a health care worker who helped her contact the police and arranged for her to leave her exploiters. Her domination by the traffickers ended but provokes skepticism among some who hear her story. Many people unfamiliar with the tactics of traffickers suppose that individuals like Yelena "knew what they were getting into"—an observation that is both unfair and incorrect.

That people have some degree of suspicion or even knowledge of the possibility of engaging in paid sex acts does not prevent them from being recognized as victims. As one member of the U.S. Department of Justice put it, "They may have come here because they have a better opportunity, but that does not mean they have the option to leave."

In other instances, newcomers to Canada who do not have strong social networks and are unfamiliar with laws that protect them from abuse make easy prey for urbane traffickers. Joyeuse, a twenty-one-year-old Haitian woman, immigrated to Montreal in August 2008. Soon after, she met Tyrone Dillon, a smooth-talking young man in the "record business" who drove a silver Cadillac CTS and a black BMW. The two began dating and eventually he persuaded her to move to Toronto with him. One night Dillon suggested that he and Joyeuse enjoy a romantic dinner together at a local restaurant, having arranged for a babysitter for her three-year-old daughter. After dinner, Dillon told Joyeuse she must prostitute herself for him and hand over every dollar she earned or she'd never be reunited with her daughter.

Joyeuse could see no way out. For the next seven weeks, Dillon reportedly earned up to one thousand dollars per day from selling Joyeuse to men who engaged in sex acts with this young woman who'd come to Canada looking for a brighter future. When Joyeuse demanded to be reunited with her daughter, Dillon allegedly beat her. At some point she managed to call 911, prompting a police investigation that led to her release, followed by the rescue of her daughter and the laying of multiple criminal charges against Dillon.

## A wolf in sheep's clothing: Female traffickers

Most Canadians assume that trafficking in women and exploiting them through the sex trade is exclusively a male activity—and they are usually correct. But the ensuing profits are sometimes enough to provoke similar abuse by other women.

Women's shelters are supposed to be refuges from abuse, violence, and exploitation. Unfortunately, like group homes, they are also places where traffickers know they will find vulnerable and at-risk women and girls. Female recruiters and traffickers blend in readily among these residents, quickly gaining the trust of potential victims. A common tactic in other parts of the world, the planting of female recruiters and traffickers in shelters was certain to appear in Canada. And it did, in the form of twenty-eight-year-old Laura Emerson, who went by the innocuous nickname of "Kitty."

Outside women's shelters in the Ottawa area, Kitty trolled for teenage girls and young women who could be forced into prostitution to benefit her and her thirty-three-year-old partner, Gordon John Kingsbury. She managed to persuade three girls, all under eighteen, that they'd be "well taken care of," along with a fourth victim whom she "bought" from another trafficker. Once she became the property of Emerson, the fourth victim was told she had to earn between one and two thousand dollars daily—approximately half a million dollars in annual revenue.

The teenage girls were kept in a condominium in Gatineau, Quebec, just opposite the Parliament Buildings on the other side of the Ottawa River. Emerson controlled the girls with a range of tactics, including threats, assaults, and forcible confinement. Regular doses of crack cocaine and alcohol ensured that two of the victims remained dependent on her. Sometimes men would pay for sex acts with Emerson's victims in an apartment room furnished with only a mattress; on other occasions, they'd be sent out to hotel rooms or men's homes.

On various occasions, each of the victims tried to escape Emerson's control and paid dearly for it. One was so desperate for freedom that she ran into the frigid Gatineau River until Emerson caught her, dragged her back to the condominium, and beat her severely. The other victim slipped away after a meeting with her probation officer. Days later Emerson spotted her and dragged her into her Cadillac Escalade. She ordered two of the victims to beat the young woman while she was trapped in the trunk, a tactic used by some traffickers who seek to have their victims "enforce" the traffickers' commands to harm each other. The tactic also prevents victims from trusting each other or helping each other escape. They punched her, struck her with a bottle, tore off her false nails, and ripped out pieces of her hair. Back at the condominium, they cut off what was left of her hair and tied her to a table, leaving her there for two days. It was during that assault that they forced her to smoke crack cocaine to try to get her addicted. Each victim feared not only Emerson and her associates, but also the other victims. They could trust no one.

Remarkably, Emerson's audacity in victimizing these teenage girls and young women didn't end when she was arrested. While Emerson was being held in police custody awaiting her trial on human trafficking charges, one of her victims was unwittingly placed in the same cell after an arrest on unrelated charges. "Don't testify," Emerson allegedly threatened the victim. "You won't be safe forever. I'll find you."

Emerson and Kingsbury don't appear to be independent criminals. Police believe they are affiliated with the Ledbury Banff Crips, a violent street gang that formed in the late 1990s in and around a housing project in old Ottawa South, less than fifteen minutes by car from Parliament Hill. In recent years, LBC members and associates have been publicly implicated in serious criminal activity, including attempted murder and other violent crimes, as well as trafficking in cocaine and prohibited firearms. They have spread not only across Ottawa and the provincial border into Gatineau, but also into Western Canadian cities such as Calgary.

"Members of the LBC are known to exploit and control young females for the purposes of sexual relations and … for the purposes of financial gain through the sex trade," warned Ottawa Chief of Police Vince Bevan in a May 2004 report to the Ottawa Police Services Board. Chief Bevan classified the LBC as a "hard core" street gang with an estimated twenty-eight members averaging twenty years of age and with "a significant number of female associates." In other words, they are relatively unknown to the public and small but deadly.

The LBC is such a serious threat to the community that children of five and older have become the focus of an early intervention program in Ottawa's Ledbury/Banff area—a preventative measure to discourage them from becoming involved in gang life. To complement the program, cash has been invested to improve community housing.

On April 9, 2009, Emerson pleaded guilty in a Gatineau courtroom to charges of living off the avails of prostitution, assault, forcible confinement, and human trafficking. The woman wore a dark-grey turtleneck over her white prison jumpsuit and sat slumped in her chair, rising only to confirm her pleas. Her hands were cuffed in front of her and her long black hair hung loose around her shoulders as Judge Lapointe sentenced her to serve seven years imprisonment in addition to the eight months and ten days spent in pretrial custody, for which she received two-for-one credit.

Emerson also was ordered to have no contact with the victims during her sentence, required to provide a DNA sample, and, on release, prohibited from owning a firearm for ten years. She forfeited $28,150 in cash and her 2007 Cadillac Escalade, which the Quebec General Prosecutor seized upon her arrest. Judge Lapointe's sentence is the strongest handed down by a Canadian court in a human trafficking case to date. Unfortunately, other sentences for human trafficking in Canada have been far more lenient, as discussed in a later chapter.

In December 2009, Kingsbury, Emerson's male partner, pleaded guilty to living off the avails of prostitution and sexually assaulting one of the victims. Sentenced to three years and ten months' imprisonment, he was given credit for pretrial custody to reduce the amount and, as a result, will serve fourteen months in jail followed by three years of probation.

Kingsbury's final words as he was taken away to serve his time were chilling. According to Gatineau's French-language newspaper *Le Droit*, he threatened to kill when released from prison. "I have three of them on my list," he said.

# 8

# FIRST NATIONS, LAST CHANCE

Honouring the Spirit of Our Little Sisters is a safe house in Winnipeg for Aboriginal youth between thirteen and seventeen who are at risk of sexual exploitation. The facility is managed by the Ma Mawi Wi Chi Itata Centre, which was founded twenty-five years ago to provide help for Aboriginal children and their families in Manitoba's child welfare system.

Comprehensive holistic programming at Little Sisters fosters a safe, welcoming, and respectful environment that includes support for family decision-making, cultural development, education, employment, training, mentoring, and life skills. The facility provides a unique opportunity for First Nations girls to escape the brutality of sexual exploitation and enables them to grow up free of threats from the men who pay to abuse them. But as the experience of Crystal and Sabrina reveals, even Little Sisters is vulnerable to sophisticated human traffickers.

In early 2004, the girls, both wards of the province, were living at Little Sisters when two young South Asian men befriended them. For three months, the men treated Crystal and Sabrina generously, picking them up from school and taking them for dinner or to a movie. One Friday afternoon, the men invited the girls to a party in Regina, over five hundred kilometres away. Little Sisters staff advised the girls not to accept, and Crystal and Sabrina agreed. When the girls suddenly left Little Sisters without warning, the staff grew alarmed and ran after them.

"As we got outside we saw the vehicle just turning from the back lane," recalls Jackie Anderson, a children-in-care coordinator at Little Sisters. "We did get the licence plate and the colour of the vehicle so we immediately phoned the police. We were told that, because [the girls] just left and it was a rumour at this point that they were going out of the city, that we didn't have proof of it, they couldn't respond to it."

About two hours later, the girls called Anderson from a gas station outside Brandon, Manitoba, to say that they were doing fine and were heading to Saskatchewan. The safe-house staff immediately notified the RCMP, who said the police could do nothing.

For some unknown reason, highway patrol officers pulled over the car with Crystal and Sabrina in the back seat. Up to this point, the young men had been plying Crystal with cocaine and alcohol and tried the same tactic on Sabrina, who refused. Not only were the highway patrol officers oblivious to the drugs and alcohol in the car, but also they hadn't been told about the missing girls. Police found no reason to detain or search the vehicle, which continued westward to Saskatchewan.

In Regina, a Caucasian man with long grey hair joined the young men and the girls. The newcomer appeared to be about forty years old, was carrying a briefcase, and claimed to be from Vancouver. The five transferred to a new vehicle and headed north to Saskatoon, a further two hundred and fifty kilometres away. Once they'd arrived, the older man purchased some "kinky underwear" for the girls, and on the way to a hotel, the men picked up an older woman from off the street—likely a prostituted woman.

Inside the hotel room, Crystal passed out from all the drugs and alcohol she'd consumed on the trip. The two young men, the man from Vancouver, and the woman from off the street began engaging in sexual activities. Knowing the door to the hotel room was locked, Sabrina was terrified of being sexually assaulted. She seized a cellphone, locked herself in the bathroom, and called Jackie Anderson in Winnipeg, desperate for the social worker's assistance.

Anderson, relieved to hear from the young girl, asked where she was being held.

Sabrina had never been to Saskatoon before. In fact, so limited was her knowledge of Canada that she'd never even heard of the city. All she could repeat over the phone to Anderson was "Kakatoon! Kakatoon!"

"I asked her to look around the bathroom to see, because in hotels you have soap bars," says Anderson. Letter by letter, Sabrina, who could not read, spelled out the name of the hotel: Howard Johnson.

While Anderson kept Sabrina on the phone, another staff member called the Saskatoon Police to report the situation. Police officers immediately asked hotel security to begin dealing with the matter until they arrived. Then, without warning, Sabrina's call went dead.

"She thought the men in the room were going to try to come in, so she opened the bathroom door and ran out of the room," Anderson says. "By the time she reached the end of the hall, Security was there."

They were soon joined by Saskatoon Police officers, who arrested the entire group on charges of drug possession. According to Anderson, the police said that they could hold the girls for only a maximum of six hours before releasing them with directions to a local shelter. Anderson pleaded with the police to keep Sabrina and Crystal until she could arrive, but the police could make no promises. When Anderson finally reached Saskatoon, she was relieved to find the girls still at the station. The girls' "friends," however, had been released.

"All of the factors were there," Anderson says, still incredulous that the men were gone. "These guys were recruiters. They were bringing the girls there to trade them, to sell them to this guy who was going to take them to Vancouver. Who knows what would have happened from there? We may never have seen them again."

"At the end of the day the police system, the child welfare system—everybody just pointed fingers at each other," suggests Diane Redsky, acting executive director of the Ma Mawi Wi Chi Itata Centre. "The systems could not react fast enough when our girls were taken from Winnipeg into another province." Indeed, traffickers know that the easiest way to avoid detection is to move a victim from her hometown, both to isolate her and to capitalize on the lack of national coordination to address the problem.

## The vulnerability of First Nations women and girls

According to Dianna Bussey, director of the Salvation Army's Anti–Human Trafficking Network, Aboriginal girls are known to have been transported from reserves in rural Manitoba and sold for sex in Winnipeg. Another scenario involved rural Aboriginal girls from a particular reserve being hired as "nature guides" in their community, only to be sold to men for sex.

A 2001 study found that between 14 and 60 percent of Aboriginal youth in British Columbia have been sexually abused. Providing another view, an earlier study revealed that 75 percent of Aboriginal girls under eighteen had experienced sexual abuse of one kind or another, 50 percent under fourteen had encountered the same treatment, and almost 25 percent under seven had been sexually abused. Some First Nations advocates have described the extremely high prevalence of sexual abuse suffered by Aboriginal youth as a factor in "conditioning" them for more egregious long-term exploitation in the sex industry.

Sexual exploitation of Aboriginal girls and women is more common than anyone has been willing to admit, according to NGOs and governmental officials, whose members have expressed particular concern over the growing use of trucking routes to exploit the girls.

Vancouver Rape Relief's Lee Lakeman describes the vulnerability of Aboriginal girls at truck stops: "[Often they are] very young girls who were forced into hitchhiking for lack of transportation and once they're on those hitchhiking routes, they are lured by men with small amounts of cash, small amounts of drugs, small amounts of gifts." Or by other more violent means, as in the case involving Judge David Ramsay, detailed in Chapter 13.

At least five hundred First Nations girls and women have gone missing in Canada over the last thirty years. No one knows at this point how many of these disappearances are linked to the flesh market and, perhaps, domestic sex trafficking, but some believe that the two likely are related.

"Aboriginal girls are being hunted down and prostituted, and the perpetrators go uncharged with child sexual assault and child rape," reports the Vancouver-based Aboriginal Women's Action Network. "These predators, pervasive in our society, roam with impunity in our streets and take advantage of those Aboriginal children with the least protection."

"Men see Aboriginal women not as women but as things to use and dispose of," adds Redsky. She believes the problem is largely being ignored because of racism and sexism.

The Little Sisters safe house run by Ma Mawi is, for some, a last stop. One fourteen-year-old girl had been in sixty-seven placements in foster care and a succession of group homes before arriving there.

Yet Little Sisters, whose work is important and in many cases life-saving, has just six beds. Due to a lack of funding and facilities, they've had to turn away more than one hundred teenage girls in the last six years. In need of help and protection, the girls were failed by the system and left to take their chances on the street.

What's behind the high incidence of sexual exploitation of Aboriginal girls in this country? Are the causes economic? Social? Geographic? Historical?

A landmark study in 2007 found that they are all of these and more. The root causes named in the study are myriad and complex, and are linked to other persistent social challenges facing Aboriginal communities; these include the legacy of colonization and residential schools, domestic violence and crime, poverty, substance abuse, lack of awareness and acknowledgement of the problem, isolation of Aboriginal youth, racism, and inadequate services and laws to combat the problem.

## Drugs and death

While drugs often play a role in attracting and controlling young women within the commercial sex industry, their use is not universal. In some instances, traffickers may even forbid their victims to use hard drugs such as cocaine and heroin because once addicted, the girls may become too volatile and hard to control.

Staff at the Ma Mawi Wi Chi Itata Centre have found that many victims controlled by their addiction are especially vulnerable to their drug dealer's becoming their de facto trafficker. Once addicted to methamphetamine ("meth"), crack cocaine, or heroin, victims may sell their bodies for sex acts to pay their drug dealer for the next hit, used both to satisfy their intense addiction and numb their physical and mental suffering. While under the effects of these narcotics, victims experience severely impaired judgment and a relaxing of inhibitions.

The stories of Aboriginal young women falling prey to drug dealers and sexual exploitation are almost too numerous to tell, and far too many of them end in tragedy. Such was the short life of Fonessa Bruyere (her real name), an Aboriginal girl in Manitoba who first was sexually exploited when she was only eleven years old. As well, Fonessa and her older sister soon became addicted to crack cocaine and meth. When Fonessa was just twelve, she sought help at a residential youth shelter in Winnipeg, but because all the beds were full, she was turned away. Her substance abuse and the lack of support contributed to her being sold for sex acts.

Fonessa returned to life on the street with her sister, managing to survive for five years. She was last seen alive getting into a car on a Winnipeg street corner near Selkirk Avenue on August 9, 2007. A few days later, she was found dead, her body dumped on a roadside at the city's outskirts. She was seventeen years old, and her murder has never been solved.

"Police were notified but we were greeted with indignance and disrespect to the extent that her grandmother was refused an incident number after reporting her missing," says Carla Bruyere, Fonessa's aunt. "We also made attempts to contact the press to get her picture out there as a missing child, but there was no interest at the time."

Tragically, two of Fonessa's friends, also young Aboriginal girls, were last seen alive in the same area, went missing, and were later found dead. A group of men reportedly were using them for sex acts, plying them with crack cocaine, and giving them food and clothing. Fonessa's friends were Hilary Wilson, eighteen, and Cherisse Houle, seventeen.

9

# FALLING THROUGH THE CRACKS

Often when the justice system fails victims of crime, it is said that they have been victimized twice—first by the perpetrators who harmed them and later by a system that failed to redress that harm. Even if human trafficking victims are finally freed from their exploiters, they face formidable obstacles in trying to rebuild their lives.

Unfortunately, Canada cannot claim an enviable record in its treatment of trafficking victims. In too many cases, they receive treatment of the kind that should be meted out to their traffickers. While some important progress has been made, the majority of provinces in Canada do not have a system in place to coordinate services required for trafficking victims, and vulnerable women and children pay the price. Canada also lacks a national plan to ensure that victims of human trafficking are given the protection and assistance they need to recover and rehabilitate. Combine this with a bureaucratic attitude to dealing with circumstances that are not clearly delineated in policy books and injustice is sure to follow, as it did in the case of eleven-year-old Natalie.

## Free from traffickers but confined by the state

Natalie arrived in Montreal from overseas in the summer of 2008. Border guards with the Canada Border Services Agency (CBSA) believed that the little girl was a victim of human trafficking because of the mysterious circumstances of her arrival. Authorities placed Natalie in the immigration detention centre just outside of Montreal, a prison-like complex surrounded by barbed wire. Her confinement was allegedly for her own safety.

During a routine weekly visit to the detention centre, representatives of Action Réfugiés Montréal noticed Natalie and were alarmed that such a young child was in the facility. The following week they found out that the terrified eleven-year-old was still there, now segregated from the adult population. The isolation may have enhanced Natalie's physical safety but contributed to her feeling frightened and alone. And although she'd met with a psychologist and had a social worker designated as her representative, she remained in detention.

"We were concerned among other things about the impact of her isolation from contact with others, the presence of uniformed guards, and her lengthy stay in a secure facility," said the Action Réfugiés Montréal report. In an effort to get this child trafficking victim into a safe and appropriate shelter, Action Réfugiés Montréal told the English-language child protection agency in Quebec about Natalie's case. A reputed agreement between the CBSA and the French-language child protection agency, however, prevented the English-language agency from intervening. And for its part, the French-language child protection agency refused to help Natalie because they claimed that no facility in the province could effectively protect her from associates of her trafficker. Quebec's language politics and an ice-cold bureaucratic response stood in the way of quick action. After an entire month in detention, the young girl was finally released into the care of a local community organization.

Action Réfugiés Montréal called the incident "a breakdown of the child protection system, which failed to respond to the needs of a child at risk, as well as a breakdown of the immigration system, in which, by law, children should only be detained as a last resort."

Natalie's is not an isolated case. In November 2007, a child called Tasha was found among a group of adults (whom she did not know) as they were trying to enter Canada illegally from the United States.

Officials were able to determine that Tasha had neither friends nor family in this country and suspected her to be a trafficked child. She was detained, again allegedly for her safety, and moved from Ottawa to the CBSA's immigration detention centre in Montreal, where she was held in prison-like detention for at least two weeks. Due to federal privacy laws, officials will not provide any information as to Tasha's whereabouts. We can only hope that she was placed among people whose care will help her overcome whatever trauma she suffered in custody.

## The cost of provincial inaction paid by victims

The Province of Quebec isn't alone in its inadequate response to the needs of victims of human trafficking. Ontario is home to the majority of foreign trafficking victims recognized by Citizenship and Immigration Canada (CIC). It's also the province where the most human trafficking prosecutions in Canada have occurred, yet for years Ontario has failed to develop a comprehensive system to assist victims.

Is it a problem of perception, of priorities, or of political will perhaps? No one knows. Or at least no one in a position to know will talk about it. When I interviewed Joan Andrew, the deputy minister of immigration for the Province of Ontario, not only did she have nothing to say about how her department was addressing the issue, she also demonstrated alarmingly little understanding of human trafficking in Ontario.

"I don't think anything has been done," says Detective Sergeant Mike Hamel of the Toronto Police Service, commenting on the treatment of victims of human trafficking in the province. While the "gangs and guns" issue has received funding in Ontario, Hamel is concerned about an apparent lack of attention to sex trafficking, a crime connected to several gangs operating in the province.

Another member of the Toronto Police Service shares Sergeant Hamel's concern. "We have very little infrastructure in place that would make it easy or give that victim the confidence to call the police," she points out. "We just don't seem to have the resources."

Constable Kristine Arnold of the Peel Regional Police, Vice Unit, confirms that this harsh reality affects Canadian victims as well as those from abroad. "We need money for clothes," she points out, "and they need money for food. We had one girl from Alberta that our unit paid for out of petty cash, because our battered women's shelters were full."

So bad is the situation that Timea Nagy, a survivor of human trafficking, had to start her own organization to educate police and pull together resources to help victims. The result, Walk with Me, inspires hope, as do other NGOs that are beginning to make limited progress. However, for years both CIC and the CBSA have declined to meet with NGOs in Ontario to improve the response to human trafficking in the province.

In November 2009, the issue of human trafficking finally made its way to Queen's Park when an Opposition member asked the government to explain why, unlike several other provinces, Ontario lacked a program tailored to the needs of trafficking victims. Rick Bartolucci, Ontario's minister of community safety and correctional services, dodged the question, bizarrely accusing the Opposition of failing to support provincial and municipal police. Later the minister reportedly told the media that human trafficking raises a lot of complex "federal issues," adding, "They're immigration."

This is an aloof bureaucratic response to a very human situation—one that grows more serious and daunting year by year. That Ontario is home to the largest number of foreign human trafficking victims identified by government records, as well as to the most prosecutions of domestic sex traffickers, should inspire a less cavalier response. Bartolucci's attitude also ignores the responsibility of the province to ensure that victims obtain the assistance and protection required to recover. At a meeting with Premier Dalton McGuinty in February 2010, after having set out this serious problem, I called on him to do the right thing and implement a system in Ontario to help victims of human trafficking. As this book goes to print, the provincial government has made no announcement.

The NGO representatives in Ontario who were interviewed for this book had no idea whom to contact within the provincial bureaucracy to assist victims in accessing services essential to recovery. Tragically, those who pay the price for this inaction are the victims in greatest need. It's a mark of shame for Canada that many know us only as a place of misery, suffering, and exploitation. This is indeed the memory of Canada for two Eastern European women who managed to escape traffickers in Toronto who were selling them for sex acts through escort agencies and strip clubs.

In the spring of 2008, Svetlana and Dina managed to overcome their fears of their trafficker and made their way to Toronto's Pearson International Airport with the intention of going home. Officials believed that the women were victims of human trafficking. However, Svetlana and Dina were locked up in the CBSA's secure immigration detention centre because "they had nowhere else to go" while they waited for their trip home to be organized.

Canada should have provided appropriate emergency shelter for these victims and worked with their home countries to facilitate their voluntary repatriation. Other countries have passed laws to ensure that if, as a last resort, victims need to be detained for their own safety, the facilities must be appropriate to their status as victims. Immigration detention and remand centres are not suitable and amount to imprisonment for these victims.

Another concern is the failure to properly and promptly identify victims when they come into contact with authorities. Even when traffickers use overt methods of control, some front-line officials remain unable to accurately identify the victim as a trafficked person. For example, local police may respond to complaints of domestic assault and fail to identify the incident as one of human trafficking. Here's an example:

On the evening of January 20, 2007, the Vancouver Police Department responded to a call about a domestic disturbance. Arriving at the address, officers found Shu-fei, a foreign woman, and discovered she was in Canada illegally. The CBSA immediately began processing her deportation even though officials were aware that the man Shu-fei was living with had, in the words of a CIC report, "been charged with a serious sexual assault and criminal harassment of another female. He appears to use violence and cruelty as a means to control these women." The report added, "[H]e is a dangerous man who will try to intimidate/manipulate anyone he comes into contact with."

At the eleventh hour, after the RCMP's human trafficking awareness coordinator had determined that Shu-fei was a victim, the deportation order against her and her son was cancelled at the airport. By this time, having endured negative treatment by officials, Shu-fei simply wished to return home and therefore left Canada.

## "New Beginnings"—Canadians step up to help

Fortunately, some police officers and average Canadians are stepping up to protect victims when they are identified. In Ontario, the Peel Regional Police, Vice Unit, realized that the sex trafficking victims they were encountering had specialized needs that were not being met by the typical services offered through provincial government offices and various NGOs.

In response, police officers in that region bordering Toronto launched New Beginnings, an excellent example of a local police force taking the initiative to help sex trafficking victims escape their exploiters for good, build trust with police investigators, and move on with their lives. The program relies on the goodwill of regular Canadians, who volunteer their time and skills to help sex trafficking victims become survivors. Individual citizens have supported the initiative in a number of ways:

- Pro bono tattoo artists have helped conceal the names, street names, or symbols that traffickers have branded into their victims' skin.
- A local dentists' clinic has provided free care to address chronic dental health issues.
- Various individuals have helped victims regain their freedom and

self-esteem through access to housing, counselling services, and criminal injuries compensation funds. They have also assisted victims in navigating the paperwork needed to re-enrol and finish high school.

The contributions of tattoo artists may appear surprising and shocking to many unfamiliar with the tactics of domestic sex traffickers. The branding technique is similar to that used by cattle ranchers who apply red-hot irons to their animals as a means of identifying them. In the same way, tattoos identify victims as being the property of their traffickers, thereby dehumanizing them and typically marking them for life.

The New Beginnings program already has helped victims become survivors by concealing their traffickers' imprint and offering them a fresh start. At nineteen, Chelsea is finally beginning to enjoy the simple pleasures of life after having been brutally controlled and sexually exploited for four years, all for the financial gain of her trafficker, who's now in jail. Her trafficker's name, once tattooed on the back of her neck, has vanished. The police officer assigned to Chelsea's case found a tattoo artist who volunteered to conceal the unwanted name in a beautiful floral design.

"When it comes to the tattoo, I'm not ashamed of it anymore," says Chelsea. "I'm proud of it."

Chelsea is living proof of the positive impact that New Beginnings and similar initiatives can have on victims. With help from the program she's found work, moved into her own apartment, and gone back to school. She's finishing her high school diploma and aspires to become a social worker. But not every day is easy.

"Some days I wake up and I'm in the bathroom brushing my teeth and I look at myself and I'm really happy," she says with a smile. "I'm blessed that I got the second chance. I'm blessed that I can go back to school. I'm blessed that I'm still alive. So yes, sometimes I'm really happy. But sometimes I'm really lonely and I'm sad and I just want someone to be there."

## Treat trafficked persons as victims, not criminals

Victims of human trafficking cannot be protected unless they are first identified to the front-line officials and caregivers responsible for assisting them. Very few victims of human trafficking escape and "self-report," not because they *choose* to be victims but because of the interlocking barriers erected by their traffickers.

Despite these challenges, foreign victims of human trafficking have been referred to CIC for assistance with their immigration status since the department began tracking these cases. Between May 2006 and November 2008, 41 percent of referrals of foreign victims to CIC came from police officers. The CBSA referred 20 percent, while other government departments referred 15 percent. Only 12 percent of foreign victims presented themselves, and lawyers referred just 7 percent. The remaining 5 percent of referrals originated with various agencies, including Children's Aid Societies and an NGO. Remarkably, only one foreign trafficking case was directly referred to CIC by an NGO—a sharp contrast with countries such as Italy, where NGOs play a large and significant role in identifying victims. This ad hoc approach to combating trafficking will not succeed with a problem so vast, so complex, and so serious.

## Putting it all together: The need for a coordinated approach

As we've seen, no comprehensive system to protect and assist victims of human trafficking exists in Canada. Instead, there is a mostly spotty patchwork of services that varies enormously by province and locality where the victim is identified. NGOs are a critical part of the solution, but so are supportive police officers, immigration officials, and other victim service providers. Indeed, recent cases have revealed major gaps in the ability of various federal and provincial agencies to coordinate their efforts with police and NGOs.

Without better coordination, the goal of helping these survivors to recover and rehabilitate remains unattainable. However, even the smallest steps to achieve this have been thwarted. In late 2008, for instance, a Federal-Provincial-Territorial (FPT) governmental working group on human trafficking was proposed to coordinate multiple levels of government. But even before it got started, its first face-to-face meeting was cancelled.

In spite of the difficulties, two provinces have already developed models that others could easily adapt or employ as templates.

## British Columbia's Office to Combat Trafficking in Persons (OCTIP)

In 2007, British Columbia became the first province in Canada to formally recognize the problem of human trafficking when it created OCTIP under the Ministry of Public Safety and Solicitor General. Based in Victoria with an office in Vancouver, OCTIP was launched "with a mandate to develop and coordinate B.C.'s response to human trafficking" with these defined objectives:

- reduce and prevent human trafficking
- identify and protect trafficked persons
- coordinate services for trafficked persons
- contribute to national and international efforts, including prosecutions, to eliminate human trafficking

Funding comes from the Ministries of Public Safety and Solicitor General, and Children and Family Development. For foreign trafficked children, OCTIP works closely with the B.C. Migrant Services Program to meet their specialized needs.

OCTIP struggled in the early days to engage willing partners in its efforts to enhance systems for identifying and assisting trafficking victims in the province. Arranging regular meetings with key agencies has also proved difficult. Nevertheless, changes are slowly taking effect as victims are identified and their need for assistance makes bureaucratic wrangling seem ridiculous.

In March 2009, the CIC in British Columbia issued the province's first temporary residence permit (TRP) for a trafficking victim. The RCMP had been investigating a foreign sex trafficking case in which Chinese women were being sold on Craigslist through a network of apartments in Burnaby, Richmond, Surrey, and Coquitlam. Police alerted OCTIP and provided information about the victims. In turn, OCTIP prepared shelter, packages of personal items, clinical counsellors, and interpreters, including a child protection worker fluent in Mandarin. At four locations, OCTIP staff and service providers waited to meet with the trafficked women immediately after the RCMP had executed its warrants to raid the micro-brothels. While the initial response ran smoothly, insufficient longer-term planning caused difficulties, not least because suspected associates of the traffickers discovered the location of the shelter. Despite this, one of the seven Chinese women stayed in touch with a clinical counsellor and received a TRP.

This marked a significant step forward for the province. A major raid of massage parlours in December 2006 had been heavily criticized for its treatment of the women, including the use of handcuffs by police, as well as allegations that information about the raid had been leaked beforehand. An internal RCMP review noted concerns about the raids and even found that men claiming to be husbands of the women were at police detachments and influenced their responses to police questioning.

The demands on OCTIP are significant, requiring a greater strategic focus on the aspects of human trafficking most prevalent in British Columbia. Of immediate concern are domestic sex trafficking affecting underage girls, including Aboriginal youth, internet-facilitated exploitation through popular online bulletin board websites, the plight of foreign women in the province's sex industry, the vulnerability of live-in caregivers and domestic servants, and the transit of trafficking victims through the province into the United States. In order to adapt to new threats OCTIP, in co-operation with local organizations and federal agencies, must also maintain its own intelligence information about emerging trends.

## The Action Coalition on Human Trafficking (ACT Alberta)

ACT Alberta is a diverse group of organizations comprising NGOs, the RCMP, community groups, and provincial government representatives. It is funded by the provincial government and coordinated by the NGO Changing Together. ACT Alberta operates mainly in Calgary and Edmonton, holding regular meetings in those cities to improve their response to human trafficking. Smaller cities and rural communities across the province are also becoming involved, including Fort McMurray, Red Deer, Lac la Biche, Grande Prairie, Brooks, Medicine Hat, and Lethbridge. Using a grassroots approach to encourage local communities to form their own ACT committees, chapters of ACT open their membership to any interested organization or individual.

ACT Alberta co-operates with the RCMP in assisting victims of human trafficking and benefits too from the willingness of the Government of Alberta to quickly implement key policy changes. However, not all partners have embraced this community-based approach; ACT Alberta has encountered some difficulty with federal agencies, most notably CIC. A senior official with ACT Alberta has accused the federal agency of acting as though "they [CIC] were the experts, they have the handout from Ottawa, they know what they're doing—don't question them."

ACT Alberta recognizes that it needs greater resources to meet the needs of victims. While the coalition has developed a basic network of services to help victims become survivors, it has not been without difficulty.

Thérèse is a young woman from the Democratic Republic of the Congo whose story appears in the opening chapter. She was a sex slave in her own country for over a decade before her trafficker brought her to Canada in April 2008. When Thérèse escaped her traffickers, ACT Alberta tried to help her overcome numerous challenges in getting the assistance she needed.

"There were huge pitfalls," says Sherilyn Trompetter, assistant executive director of Changing Together. "There was confusion about who was responsible for what in terms of the provincial level and the federal level." Trompetter's organization had a hard time helping Thérèse obtain legal immigration status in Canada, which put her at risk of detention and deportation.

"There were differing conclusions with the RCMP saying, 'Yes we think she's a victim.' CIC said, 'No, she wasn't,'" says Trompetter. "The RCMP said, 'She is, and you are issuing a TRP.' Then it became a pissing war between two federal agencies."

Trompetter is highly critical of CIC's attitude. "CIC is coming at it that everyone is lying to get into the country," she points out. "The CIC officers were very arrogant and protective of what they classified as their area of expertise. The RCMP used very different investigative techniques. They were more humane in their treatment of the victim."

Fortunately, the RCMP and Changing Together convinced immigration officials that Thérèse was a bona fide victim of human trafficking and they issued her a TRP. She has since obtained permanent status to remain in Canada because she cannot safely return to life in her own conflict-ridden homeland.

# 10

# HOMEGROWN HUMAN TRAFFICKERS

When grappling with the concept of human trafficking, many Canadians find the mindset of traffickers among the most difficult aspects to come to terms with. To some degree, we can understand the motive behind various crimes ranging from theft to murder. But what drives human beings to treat others as less than human? The predatory behaviour of human traffickers seems to extend well beyond a means of control to encompass sadism, brutality, torture, and psychological cruelty.

Although the reasons underlying the behaviour of traffickers are many and often complex, all are rooted in the most common motivator of criminal activity: money.

Sex trafficking is highly lucrative. The Criminal Intelligence Service Canada (CISC) estimates that domestic sex traffickers earn an average of $280,000 annually from *every* victim under their control.

The total number of females exploited across Canada by domestic sex traffickers is unknown, but individual traffickers may exploit between one and four victims at a time, whereas larger criminal networks may exploit dozens of victims simultaneously. The estimated financial gains shown in the table on the next page are consistent with those emerging in recent convictions of human traffickers in Canada. It seems that trafficking in people may be even more lucrative than trafficking in illegal drugs, and with revenues like these, sex trafficking will only get worse if it is not seriously confronted.

**Estimated Revenue of a Domestic Sex Trafficking Network**

| Number of Victims | Daily Revenue | Weekly Revenue | Annual Revenue |
|---|---|---|---|
| 1 | $900 | $5,400 | $280,800 |
| 5 | $4,500 | $31,500 | $1,638,000 |
| 10 | $9,000 | $63,000 | $3,276,000 |
| 15 | $13,500 | $94,500 | $4,914,000 |
| 20 | $18,000 | $126,000 | $6,552,000 |
| 25 | $22,500 | $157,500 | $8,190,000 |
| 30 | $27,000 | $189,000 | $9,828,000 |
| 35 | $31,500 | $220,500 | $11,466,000 |
| 40 | $36,000 | $252,000 | $13,104,000 |

## "Made-in-Canada" traffickers

North Preston, Nova Scotia, is a place of Shakespearean irony. In the eighteenth and nineteenth centuries, the community became a refuge for freed slaves. Today, it is the home base of a national human trafficking ring.

The community traces its roots back to the 1780s and the end of the U.S. War of Independence, when the first large influx of black Loyalists arrived in Canada. These early settlers had been promised land grants but instead received rocky, hilly terrain with soil unsuitable for growing crops.

In the 1790s, more than one thousand black residents of Nova Scotia and New Brunswick left for Sierra Leone, founding the city of Freetown. Many of these freed slaves were among the best-educated and most influential community leaders. Two centuries later, residents of North Preston have seen their community become a breeding ground for trafficking in guns, drugs, women, and girls.

The Scotians, also known as North Preston's Finest, are one of the most notorious street gangs to profit from domestic sex trafficking across the country. Traditionally, biker gangs in Quebec and southwestern Ontario have controlled the sex trade, but after major police crackdowns in those regions NPF moved in to fill the vacuum. NPF since has been implicated in multiple shootings and drug trafficking. Moreover, police officers have been warned to exercise extreme caution in approaching these African-Canadian gang members, who often bear NPF tattoos on their necks and are considered "armed and dangerous."

For more than a decade, NPF has actively recruited girls and young women from Nova Scotia, forcing them into prostitution in southwestern Ontario. In his 1996 book *Somebody's Daughter*, investigative reporter Phonse Jessome documented the problem, calling it a "Halifax-Toronto pimping ring." In the book, the case of Stacey Jackson dramatically illustrates the traffickers' tactics.

Shy and attractive, Stacey grew up in a home with an abusive father. When their mother left, Stacey and her brother chose to continue living with their father, because they didn't want to abandon their friends at school. The decision led to a volatile relationship between mother and daughter.

In 1992, seventeen-year-old Stacey gave birth to a son and settled in an apartment in Dartmouth, Nova Scotia, where a neighbour, Rachel, quickly befriended her. Stacey soon learned that a man known as "T-Bar" was forcibly selling Rachel for sex. Not long after meeting Stacey, T-Bar brought around a friend, Kenny, who began to spend time with Stacey and her baby boy.

One night Rachel convinced Stacey to dye and style her hair after Kenny had complimented her on her good looks. Upon seeing Stacey's new hair, Kenny bought her expensive clothes to complete the look. Within just a few weeks, Kenny had become her "boyfriend," and he often talked about visiting Toronto, an idea that excited Stacey.

Kenny also began promoting prostitution as "a game," a plausible alternative for any woman considering her career options. The longed-for trip to Toronto would happen sooner, Kenny suggested, if Stacey raised some of the money on her own. Through constant pressure, Kenny convinced his "girlfriend" to begin working at an escort agency—actually a front for prostitution. Over time, Kenny's control and psychological manipulation of Stacey led her into a violent underworld, but she continued to interpret Kenny's actions and behaviour as demonstrations of love. At least until she was too far in to get out on her own. In the end Stacey was rescued, but not before experiencing serious trauma, including sexual, physical, and psychological abuse.

Despite Jessome's revelations, NPF has only grown stronger since the early 1990s. "Our bars were rampant with the North Preston gang," says a police investigator in the Greater Toronto Area, "They would bring their girls back and forth from Peel to Niagara."

The Peel Regional Police began a sustained effort to identify individuals affiliated with NPF and have them banned from strip clubs. After some time, the gang got the message that it was no longer open season for trafficking in girls and women. However, once NPF felt pressure from police and began moving elsewhere, an opportunity opened up for other gangs in the business of sexual exploitation. Haitian gangs who call themselves "Bloods" and "Crips" (after notorious inner-city gangs in the United States), along with Jamaican gangs and individual opportunistic criminals who had been active in the background, moved into southwestern Ontario. "North Preston's Finest and the Haitian gangs have killed more people than the biker gangs," says Constable Mike Viozzi of the Peel Regional Police. "They are not afraid to cap off a round. They own Montreal more than here."

When southwestern Ontario became a less welcome place for them to operate, NPF members began spreading westward. Police officers have identified NPF members actively recruiting local girls and young women in major cities in Western Canada and claiming territory within this part of the country. Traffickers unaffiliated with NPF nevertheless will pay off NPF members in some cities to avoid a violent confrontation with them. "You don't put a woman out on the street without paying them," says Sergeant Mark Schwartz of the Calgary Police Service, Vice Unit.

## Majors in psychology, minors in exploitation

The tactics employed by groups like NPF are highly effective but not unusual. In the United States, prosecutors are aware that the most sophisticated domestic sex trafficking networks use physical force as a last resort. There, as elsewhere, victims are manipulated to be loyal to their traffickers.

"I've never met a juvenile involved in prostitution who didn't have a pimp," says Sharon Marcus-Kurn, assistant U.S. attorney for the District of Columbia. "I have also never met a juvenile in prostitution who hasn't said during the initial interview, 'I don't have a pimp—that guy is my boyfriend.'"

One Canadian law enforcement officer who's working to eradicate human trafficking sums up the approach: "These pimps say, 'You made one thousand dollars tonight, I'm so proud of you, that's great.' The next night, the girls want to make one thousand one hundred dollars for their pimp. They still get treated like shit. But all of a sudden, one night he will say, 'Hey, I wanna take you to dinner.' That's huge. He might carry the tray for her at McDonald's. They're still going out and eating food. It's anything other than eating in that hotel room where she has to stay. The girls almost well up in tears."

"These guys are psychology majors without ever going to school," adds another officer familiar with the tactics of traffickers. "They learn from other pimps. They know how to get into a girl's head. It is not unlike battered women's syndrome. They get beaten, they have an opportunity to leave, but they don't."

She tells the following tale about the deviousness of a recently convicted trafficker:

"One girl was on the bottom floor of a two-storey motel, and her pimp had another girl on the second floor and neither of them knew that each other was there. They each fully believed that this guy was their man, their boyfriend. He was saying the same thing to both of them."

Clearly, victims of domestic sex trafficking have a lot in common psychologically with victims of domestic abuse. In both instances, victims nourish the hope that if only they love their abuser enough, he will change.

It is, tragically, this hope for a better day that keeps them trapped in their horrible predicament.

During ten years of front-line police work in Montreal, Detective Sergeant Dominic Montchamp has come to know many victims of domestic sex trafficking. Most do not view themselves as victims or recognize the degree of abuse until they're out of the exploitative relationships. "Many girls say, 'Why are you arresting my pimp? I want to give him cash,'" Montchamp states, describing how some victims want to post bail for their exploiters. Only later, when they are out of their trafficker's clutches and able to see both his and their own actions in a new light, do they fully understand what was happening. "Three or four years later they tell us, 'You saved my life.'"

## You've just been sold

While many traffickers prefer that their victims abstain from hard drugs in case they become unstable, some provide drugs to both control their victim and increase their supposed "exit fee."

Convicted trafficker Vytautas Vilutis, whom we encountered in Chapter 6, exploited a twenty-year-old Canadian woman who'd initially become trapped in prostitution because of a serious crack cocaine addiction. Vilutis implemented a rule that the victim could not buy drugs from anyone but him, thereby cementing his position as her drug trafficker and the trafficker of her body.

Vilutis also imposed a system of "fines" to increase the amount that his victim had to pay him before she could be set free. Smoking in the bedroom carried a one hundred dollar fine, while sleeping in would add five hundred dollars to the exit fee. Over three weeks, fifteen hundred dollars in fines had accumulated. Of course, the point of these gratuitous fines is to keep upping the victim's "debt" so that she remains an indentured servant.

While traffickers treat their victims like property that can be used and eventually discarded, organized crime groups trade victims or sell them to one another. Victims are usually unaware that they've been bought, sold, or exchanged because the transactions rarely take place in front of them. For the victim, the change simply means having a new person take control.

The buying and selling of women takes place between two extremes. First, at the "addiction extreme," women are traded for drug debts, both their own and those of their traffickers. Sometimes johns buy women, or "rent" them, not just for an hour or two but for longer periods. At the other extreme, "high-end" organizations buy and sell women based on their "marketability"—their physical appearance, age, and other attributes—in the way that a new or used automobile may be traded. The value or price of a woman goes up if she has an exotic appearance and good social skills, carries herself like a model, and looks physically attractive. These women initially may believe they're in control but soon find they have no easy way to escape. For example, they might be "working" as a prostitute in Vancouver when their "boyfriend" sends them to Toronto; when they arrive, a new man tells them "Now you're my baby" and demands money from sex acts he arranges for her with random men. The woman might believe her "boyfriend" in Vancouver can still help her until one of the other girls explains that she's been bought and paid for like a piece of property. It's only then that the hard reality sinks in—she's just been sold.

"If you want to leave your pimp, if he will even allow you to leave, it's going to cost you money," explains Constable Viozzi. "Or another pimp will buy you out." One trafficker investigated by Viozzi had valuated a victim he controlled at three hundred thousand dollars a year—potentially a multi-million-dollar asset.

# 11

# JUSTICE TOO OFTEN DENIED

To those familiar with the extent of human trafficking in Canada, and the resulting brutality and damage, one fact remains both shocking and incomprehensible: the rarity of successful convictions and appropriate penalties meted out to the worst perpetrators.

Worldwide, nearly twenty thousand human traffickers were brought to justice and convicted between 2003 and 2008. In 2008 alone, more than five thousand trafficking prosecutions were recorded globally, leading to almost three thousand convictions.

Canada took until late 2005 to make "trafficking in persons" a *Criminal Code* offence and did not secure its first conviction until June 2008. For those who choose the career of trafficking in people, Canada has offered a promising venue in which to launch their "business"—and this may still be so, despite the relatively recent addition of human trafficking to *Criminal Code* violations.

## Obtaining convictions may not be easy, but it's essential

Perpetrators of modern-day slavery and their accomplices are systematic in their crimes and profit greatly from their illicit criminal lifestyle. Many are serial enslavers; once caught up in the enormous profits and exposed to only minimal potential penalties, they cannot imagine supporting themselves by any other means. Police officers say that traffickers consider the penalties handed down by Canadian courts to be a joke—well worth the benefits they gain while they're at large in the community.

The clandestine, mobile, and often violent nature of human trafficking operations, both large and small scale, makes them difficult to detect and investigate. Yet traffickers must be brought to justice. They must be held accountable with penalties that reflect the grave nature of their offence and, when released from prison, be subject to stringent conditions that recognize their modus operandi.

On November 25, 2005, "trafficking in persons" became an indictable offence in Canada's *Criminal Code.* Irwin Cotler, then minister of justice and attorney general, introduced the offence, which has two essential elements. First, the accused must have committed any *one* of the following acts: recruitment; transportation; transferring; receiving; holding; concealing or harbouring a person; or exercising control, direction, or influence over the movements of a person. Second, the accused must have committed one of those acts for the purpose of exploitation, defined as "causing the victim to provide labour or a service by engaging in conduct that could reasonably be expected to cause the victim to believe that their safety, or the safety of a person known to them, would be threatened if they failed to provide the labour or service."

Based on this definition, human trafficking in the *Criminal Code* protects both Canadians and foreign nationals. The offence is not conditional upon proving movement of the victim or the crossing of an international border. Rather, the focus is on exploitation of the victim. The maximum term of imprisonment for "trafficking in persons" is fourteen years; a term of up to life imprisonment is reserved for cases where the accused kidnaps, commits aggravated assault or aggravated sexual assault, or causes the victim's death.

Receiving a financial or material benefit while knowing it resulted from trafficking in persons is a separate criminal offence carrying a sentence of up to ten years imprisonment. It is also an offence to conceal, remove, withhold, or destroy any travel or identity documents that belong to another person for the purpose of committing or facilitating trafficking in persons—an offence punishable by up to five years imprisonment.

These definitions add to laws against international trafficking that involve entry into Canada, which has been a federal immigration offence since June 2002. This portion of the *Immigration and Refugee Protection Act* states, "No person shall knowingly organize the coming into Canada of one or more persons by means of abduction, fraud, deception or use or threat of force or coercion." The term *organize* is defined as "recruitment or transportation and, after their entry into Canada, the receipt or harbouring of those persons." The penalty is a fine of up to one million dollars and/or up to life imprisonment.

How many people have been charged and convicted of human trafficking in Canada? How stiff have their sentences been? There are no easy answers.

When the federal government was asked recently to provide this information to the U.N. Office on Drugs and Crime for its *Global Report on Trafficking in Persons*, no one in Ottawa or in any appropriate department was able to provide *any* official statistics. No central database in Canada collects this information, and most prosecutions are carried out locally. As a result, it is difficult to monitor progress in prosecuting traffickers, a serious oversight that hampers efforts to assess Canada's record. The absence of an appropriate database also makes it virtually impossible for individual jurisdictions to learn from successful and unsuccessful prosecutions with a view toward improving the judicial response to human trafficking.

To evaluate Canada's record in prosecuting human traffickers, I interviewed law enforcement officers and prosecutors in eight major Canadian cities. Consultations were also held with the RCMP's Human Trafficking National Coordination Centre and the federal Department of Justice. This research revealed early successes but also serious problems.

As of 2009, all convictions for human trafficking in Canada were guilty pleas with oral reasons given by sentencing judges—in other words, none of the convictions appear in databases of written legal decisions commonly used by researchers, lawyers, and judges. While the media reported some of these convictions, others were hidden from the broader public as forgotten audio files on computer hard drives in various Canadian courthouses. This absence of references makes it difficult for individual Crown prosecutors to find guidelines for the prosecution of human trafficking. There have yet to be any judicial decisions to help interpret and better understand the new offences.

Between April 2007 and April 2009, approximately thirty individuals in Canada were charged with human trafficking under the *Criminal Code*. The chart below tracks the outcome of these charges by province. Sometimes charges may be withdrawn due to a guilty plea by the accused on lesser or "trafficking-related" offences, or because the Crown prosecutor decides the evidence is insufficient to support a conviction, or the prosecution is not in the "public interest."

The majority of accused human traffickers are alleged to have engaged in domestic sex trafficking (71 percent), while the rest were

**Human Trafficking Prosecutions in Canada (April 2007–April 2009)**

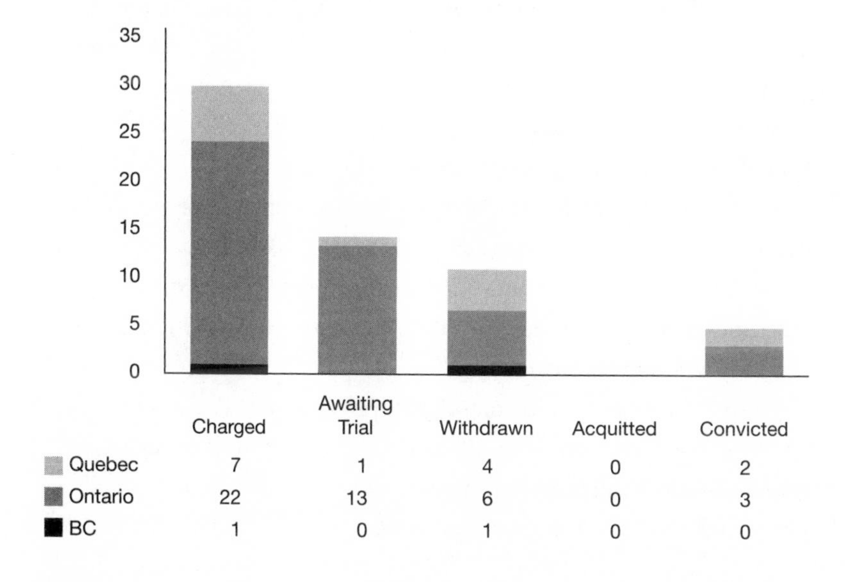

involved in cases of international sex trafficking (23 percent) and international forced labour trafficking (6 percent). One other accused was charged and acquitted of international sex trafficking under the immigration offence, mentioned above, before the *Criminal Code* offence came into force.

Although multiple investigations involving these forms of exploitation took place in the Prairie provinces over this period, no charges were laid. Edmonton's first human trafficking charges, involving international sex trafficking, came in September 2009, whereas Calgary's first charges, involving both international and domestic sex trafficking, were laid in December of the same year. Just months before, in July 2009, Terry Comfort Downey from North Preston, Nova Scotia, became the first person to be charged with human trafficking in Atlantic Canada. The Halifax Regional Police and RCMP, with help from officers from five other provinces wearing body armour, arrested thirteen people on charges of trafficking in guns, drugs, and women.

Of the five traffickers convicted in Canada to date, four were men and one was a woman. All the convictions were based on guilty pleas, took place in Ontario and Quebec between June 2008 and April 2009, and involved domestic sex trafficking of Canadian women and teenage girls. None were associated with international human trafficking, despite the ongoing discovery of such victims in Canada.

The Peel Regional Police, Vice Unit, has been leading the way in Canada in investigating and charging domestic sex traffickers. The police force is the third largest in the country and is responsible for much of the Greater Toronto Area, including Mississauga, Brampton, Streetsville, and Pearson International Airport. All in all it serves 1.2 million local residents and almost 31 million travellers passing annually through the airport.

Despite the size of its mandated jurisdiction, Peel's Vice Unit employs just four front-line officers who are responsible for investigating liquor and gambling violations, drug offences, as well as street-level prostitution and sex trafficking. Over two years, the

Peel Regional Police laid human trafficking charges in thirteen cases involving twenty-one female Canadian victims, six of whom were under eighteen. Some traffickers were also charged with obtaining a material benefit from the crime and withholding documents to facilitate human trafficking. The majority of the victims of human trafficking identified by Peel Regional Police are Caucasian-Canadians, as well as several African-Canadian females from North Preston, Nova Scotia. The victims range in age from thirteen to thirty, but most were initially "recruited" while younger than eighteen.

## Canada's first convicted human trafficker: Imani Nakpangi

In December 2007, an undercover police officer posing as a "client" made an appointment through Craigslist for sex with a fourteen-year-old girl in a Mississauga hotel room. There he found Samantha, wearing only a towel. (This teenager with fetal alcohol syndrome was introduced in Chapter 6.)

It was clear to officers that Samantha's troubled past, along with the recent sexual exploitation, had taken its toll. Yet when the police informed Samantha they would be arresting her pimp, Imani Nakpangi, she grew enraged, claiming that he was her boyfriend and she was pregnant with his child. And when Nakpangi told her he'd be going to jail to await a court date, the girl resolved to find money to cover his bail.

"I asked her what she got out of this, other than having to sleep with random men," the officer reported. "She said, 'I get respect.' That's the mind-game. He respected her. She never got that from her parents."

In fact, as we learned in Chapter 6, Nakpangi had earned as much as four hundred thousand dollars from Samantha and a second victim, Eve, whom he controlled through violence and threats against her family.

In a Brampton courtroom eighteen months after his arrest, Nakpangi pleaded guilty to charges of human trafficking, among other activities. To the court he described his behaviour as careless.

"Careless, indeed, is, I would think, applicable only to being caught," said Justice Hugh K. Atwood. "How careless can provide any insight into any degree of remorse is simply beyond me."

With respect to eighteen-year-old Eve, who had endured two and a half years of sexual slavery, Nakpangi was convicted of human trafficking under the *Criminal Code* for exercising control or direction over her movements for the purpose of exploiting her, including assaulting and threatening her and her younger brother. Justice Atwood recognized that Nakpangi's victimization of Eve was "egregious in the extreme," noting that Nakpangi used the proceeds from his crimes to finance "a life style which is lavish by any yard stick."

Nakpangi was sentenced to three years imprisonment for human trafficking associated with Eve. With the "two-for-one" pretrial credit policy, Nakpangi will serve less time in prison for exploiting Eve than he'd spent victimizing her.

When it came to Samantha, Nakpangi escaped the charge of trafficking. In Canada's *Criminal Code*, the definition of "exploitation" requires victims to have provided "labour or services" as a result of reasonably fearing for their safety or the safety of someone known to them. Although Nakpangi had psychologically manipulated fourteen-year-old Samantha into prostitution and kept her earnings for himself, he hadn't "exploited" her within the meaning of the law because she hadn't feared for her safety. His actions would have qualified as human trafficking under the *Palermo Protocol* (which, when the victim is a minor, requires only that one of the listed acts be committed for the purpose of exploitation), but he was able to evade a conviction for human trafficking thanks to Canada's unduly narrow legal definition.

## A precedent for lax punishment

The *Nakpangi* case reveals that Parliament has inadequately defined human trafficking and deviated from the internationally agreed definition after having committed to criminalizing the practice. Nakpangi is not the only accused to benefit from this oversight. His case is notable because it demonstrates how a single trafficker may choose vastly different strategies to retain control over his victims: deception and psychological manipulation versus direct threats and physical assaults.

In the end, Nakpangi was convicted of "living off the avails of prostitution" of Samantha while she was under the age of eighteen years, contrary to section 212(2) of the *Criminal Code*. While this criminal offence carries a maximum penalty of fourteen years imprisonment, Justice Atwood sentenced Nakpangi to serve only the two-year mandatory minimum.

Nakpangi was ordered to serve his sentences consecutively, resulting in a total of five years. In the absence of a guilty plea, the judge stated that he would have found a six-and-a-half-year global sentence appropriate in this case. With 202 days served in pretrial custody, however, Nakpangi received a two-for-one credit for a total of 404 days deducted from his sentence on these charges. As a result, Nakpangi was sentenced overall to spend three years and eleven months in jail. As well, he was awarded the dubious distinction of becoming Canada's first convicted human trafficker.

## A poet, a proselytizer, and a frequenter of strip clubs

In November 2008, Jacques "Jackie" Leonard-St. Vil, vice-president of Urban Heat Music, was in custody awaiting trial on human trafficking charges. Jackie, you'll recall, had lured his victim, Genevieve, with promises of modelling for album covers and CD releases, only to groom her for commercial sexual exploitation. When she attempted to leave, he beat her on multiple occasions.

The day his trial was scheduled to begin, Jackie decided to plead guilty, admitting that he'd controlled Genevieve and directed her movements for the purpose of exploiting her. Jackie also pleaded guilty to one count of "procuring" for living wholly or in part on the avails of prostitution of Genevieve. The Crown prosecutor submitted a copy of Jackie's youth criminal record to the court.

In his statement to the court, Jackie claimed to have turned his life around during his pretrial custody. His lawyer provided the court with documents indicating that Jackie had been writing poetry in jail and had participated in various educational and religious programs. However, the defence counsel also admitted that Jackie planned on returning to Urban Heat and would continue to frequent strip clubs for "business purposes."

Briefed by the Crown prosecutor on the *Nakpangi* case, Justice Durno of the Superior Court of Justice handed down a sentence that reflected the *Nakpangi* precedent and outraged many advocates for a stronger response to the crime of human trafficking. Taking into account *Nakpangi* and the typical two-for-one credit awarded for pretrial custody, the judge agreed with the Crown prosecutor and defence counsel that the eighteen months and seventeen days Jackie had already spent in jail was within "the range of appropriate sentencing for cases of this nature." As a result, Justice Durno sentenced Jackie to serve just *one day* in jail upon conviction.

The day after his conviction for exploiting this young girl, Jackie walked out of jail and returned to his "business."

Before leaving, Jackie was required to submit to a pinprick on his finger—a blood sample for the national DNA databank. Under the terms of his three-year probation order, he is not to contact Genevieve. He is also not, however, under any obligation to report regularly to a probation officer.

The Crown prosecutor had asked Justice Durno to prohibit Jackie from attending any "adult entertainment establishments" as part of his probation order, reminding the judge that Jackie originally had exploited Genevieve in strip clubs. Jackie's lawyer challenged the prosecutor's request. "As Your Honour has heard," he argued, "my client works in the music business, and, frankly, this would significantly impact with his ability to meet with other individuals apparently. It sounds odd when you say it, Your Honour, but that seems to be the practice."

Upon consideration, Justice Durno ordered Jackie not to enter any adult entertainment facility only for the first eighteen months of his probation. Jackie returned to his job as a "promoter" and, since May 10, 2010, has been free to resume his activities in adult entertainment facilities.

Genevieve had been offered the opportunity to make a victim statement in court prior to Jackie's sentencing. Not surprisingly, when she found that her abuser would be on the street the following day, she declined. The extent of the abuse she suffered and the way it violated her sense of self-worth remain off the record.

When a newspaper reporter asked Genevieve about her reaction to the case, she replied, "You feel like it's your fault. You feel like you're dumb." Then she added, "That's why a lot of girls don't go see the police."

## A slap on the wrist

The weak sentencing practices for human trafficking in Peel Region's courts have spread to other provinces, even where the victims are minors. In a Montreal courtroom in November 2008, Michael Lennox Mark pleaded guilty to human trafficking. Mark had sold Christine, a seventeen-year-old from Quebec, in street-level prostitution because her underage ID prevented him from selling her in strip clubs. He also pleaded guilty to three counts of procuring Christine and two other Canadian women. The Montreal Police Service's investigation into Mark's activities, code-named "Project Onyx," resulted in a sentence of two years imprisonment and two years probation. However, with a two-for-one credit for his year of pretrial custody, Mark served only *a single week* in prison after being convicted.

In April 2009, Vytautas Vilutis, whom we encountered in Chapter 6, also pleaded guilty to human trafficking and assault. The first person to be convicted in Canada for knowingly receiving a financial or material benefit from human trafficking, Vilutis was given a total sentence of two years (less a day) but in all served only fourteen months in jail.

The fundamental aim of sentencing in criminal law as set out in the *Criminal Code* is to ensure "respect for the law and the maintenance of a just, peaceful and safe society." On that basis, sentences should denounce unlawful conduct, deter the offender and others, keep offenders apart from society when needed, provide rehabilitation for offenders and reparations to their victims, and promote responsibility of the offender to victims and the community. None of these sentencing principles are being upheld when trafficking convictions amount to little more than time served in pretrial custody.

Sentences imposed on traffickers of children and teenagers are among the most inadequate. Canada signed the *Optional Protocol to the Convention on the Rights of the Child on the Sale of Children, Child Prostitution and Child Pornography* in November 2001 and ratified it in September 2005. According to this international treaty, "Each State Party shall make such offences punishable by appropriate penalties that take into account their grave nature." Yet the human trafficking offence enacted in the *Criminal Code* in November 2005 does not establish more serious penalties for child trafficking. In fact, the age of the victim is irrelevant.

Joy Smith, member of Parliament for Kildonan-St. Paul in Manitoba, has been a tireless advocate for trafficking victims. After I shared several cases documented in this book with her, she introduced Bill C-268 in January 2009. This private member's bill requires that convicted child traffickers face a mandatory minimum sentence of five years imprisonment and up to fourteen years. A six-year minimum and up to life imprisonment applies if the victim is kidnapped, subject to an aggravated sexual assault, or killed. Constitutional standards prevented higher minimum sentences from being set. This amendment to the *Criminal Code* was seconded by numerous members of Parliament and applauded by an array of individuals and organizations. More than fourteen thousand Canadians signed a petition calling on Ottawa to pass the proposal for reform. On September 30, 2009, the House of Commons overwhelmingly adopted Bill C-268, with a vote of 239 in favour and 46 opposed; the opposition consisted of the Bloc Québécois along with three rogue MPs from the New Democtratic Party: Libby Davies, Bill Siksay, and Leslie Megan.

British Columbia senator Yonah Martin sponsored Bill C-268 in the Senate, making an impassioned plea for it to be adopted. After months of delays, it finally moved forward. On June 3, 2010, I testified in support of Bill C-268 at the Senate Committee on Social Affairs, Science and Technology, giving evidence about several of the child trafficking cases documented in this book. That same day, the committee approved the Bill to go to the Senate for a final debate and vote, which was successful just before the summer recess—a victory for victim advocates. Bill C-268 is the only private member's bill to become law since the 2008 federal election. In the meantime, another piece of legislation recently has been adopted that also will make convicted criminals, including human traffickers, more accountable for their actions.

The *Truth in Sentencing Act* was introduced in March 2009 by the minister of justice and attorney general, Rob Nicholson, and by October 2009 had received royal assent. These amendments to the sentencing provisions of the *Criminal Code* establish a general guideline of "one-for-one" credit for pre-sentence custody when an accused is found guilty. The Act thereby limits the incentive for criminals, including human traffickers, to drag out their pretrial custody in order to obtain two-for-one or even three-for-one credit. Such games should have no place in our criminal justice system.

## Trafficking lite: Convictions for less serious offences

In Chapter 6, we saw how Tyrel Henwood used the internet to lure fourteen-year-old Sarah to Victoria, where he forced her to be sold for sex. As a result, Henwood wasn't charged merely with human trafficking but also with assault, unlawful confinement, uttering threats to cause death or bodily harm, procuring a minor, making or distributing child pornography, living on the avails of prostitution of a person under the age of eighteen, compelling a minor to engage in prostitution, and threatening violence, intimidating, and coercion—a list of offences ranking among the most serious in the *Criminal Code*, as well as in the minds of most Canadians.

In April 2009, Henwood pleaded guilty to assault, living off the avails of prostitution, and making or publishing child pornography. All of the other charges were dropped, including that of human trafficking. Henwood's lawyer tried to argue that Sarah was Henwood's "girlfriend" and that she was "complicit in the prostitution." Given Henwood's unwillingness to accept responsibility for his alleged conduct, the Crown prosecutor's decision to withdraw the human trafficking charge is puzzling.

Unfortunately, Henwood's is not the only case where Crown prosecutors have questionably withdrawn human trafficking charges. The prose-cutors are either unfamiliar with the offence, skittish about losing a case and setting a bad precedent, or do not understand that the crime is being committed in Canada.

The apparent reluctance to tackle this heinous crime, where charges have been laid based upon credible evidence, seems to permeate all regions of the country. In 2008, Crown prosecutors in Montreal withdrew human trafficking charges in two separate cases, choosing instead to proceed with the more common charge of "procuring" under the *Criminal Code*. Similarly, in the summer of 2008, Ontario Crown prosecutors were unwilling to proceed with charges of human trafficking against a domestic sex trafficking ring operating between Calgary and Toronto. "They didn't want this to be the case taken to the Supreme Court," says Detective Wendy Leaver of the Toronto Police Service, Special Victims Unit.

Depending on the facts of a given case, human traffickers in Canada may also be charged with so-called trafficking-related offences. Such charges may include the aggravated offence of living off the avails of prostitution of a person under eighteen, abduction, kidnapping, forcible confinement, extortion, conspiracy, assault, sexual assault, or various prostitution-related offences. The federal Department of Justice, Criminal Law Policy Section, has identified thirty-nine "trafficking-related" cases from 2004 through 2007, of which twenty-three were unreported and sixteen reported, including convictions and pending cases before the courts.

In 2003, the U.S. *Trafficking in Persons Report* downgraded Canada to a Tier 2 ranking for "not fully comply[ing] with the minimum [international] standards for the elimination of trafficking.... [T]here have been few convictions of traffickers, due in part to deportation of witnesses." Since then, despite the federal government having reported fewer "trafficking-related" convictions between 2003 and 2007, the ranking has returned to Tier 1. Apparently Canada was let off the hook for its lack of progress in prosecuting traffickers. Since 2008, however, the first set of actual human trafficking charges has progressed to convictions.

Canada needs more than a human trafficking offence on paper. It needs Crown prosecutors who willingly pursue these charges with vigour where evidence exists, judges who fully appreciate the enormous damage that offenders exert on their victims, and a public that recognizes the pervasiveness of the crime, coupled with an insistence that offenders receive appropriate punishment.

In many cases, charging a perpetrator with lesser offences where human trafficking appears fully justified is analogous to charging a murderer with assault, aggravated assault, or weapons offences instead of murder. Evidence of lesser charges should be used to obtain search warrants and execute wiretaps, and to initiate undercover operations and secure arrest warrants against suspected traffickers in order to fully investigate their activities and penetrate their networks. After a full investigation, the most serious charges that are supported by the evidence should be laid, along with the charges for less serious offences, to ensure that traffickers are held accountable and victims are protected.

## Unsuccessful foreign trafficking prosecutions

Admittedly, barriers to successful human trafficking prosecutions arise as they do in many other applications of the law. Police and prosecutors don't always succeed in prosecuting alleged traffickers because victims and witnesses may become unwilling or unable to testify—in some instances traffickers or their associates threaten or otherwise intimidate them—or because the cases themselves prove to be unsubstantiated or insufficiently supported by evidence to proceed to trial. The prosecution must prove its case to the high criminal law standard of "proof beyond a reasonable doubt." While these challenges are common to many criminal offences, they are exacerbated in the context of offences like human trafficking due to the vulnerability of victims, as well as the lack of authoritative court decisions that interpret the meaning and scope of these new crimes.

Although increasing numbers of international sex and forced labour trafficking victims have been identified and granted assistance and protection, Canada has not successfully convicted *any* of their traffickers.

The prosecution of Wai Chi (Michael) Ng is the highest-profile example in Canada of an acquittal for human trafficking charges due to a failure to prove the essential elements of the crime beyond a reasonable doubt. Ng was the first person to be prosecuted for human trafficking under the *Immigration and Refugee Protection Act* (IRPA), because the *Criminal Code* provision was not yet in place when he committed his alleged crimes between 2002 and 2004.

Ng ran King City Massage Acupressure Therapy Ltd. on Kingsway Street in Vancouver, next door to the Fantasy Factory, a twenty-four-hour adult store advertising twenty-five-cent peep shows. On separate occasions, Ng allegedly arranged for two Chinese women, identified in court records only as "Ms. W" and "Ms. T," to come to Canada using fraudulent travel documents. They believed that they'd be employed as waitresses in his restaurant. When Ms. W arrived, however, she claimed she was told to sleep in Ng's basement. Because the restaurant had closed, the women wouldn't be employed as waitresses but rather would be sold to perform sex acts in Ng's massage parlour. They thought they had no alternative.

Prosecutors later would argue that Ng committed human trafficking because he used deception to transport the women to

Canada, "exert[ed] psychological and financial control over [them] and ... kept Ms. W. socially isolated."

After an altercation over money that Ng claimed Ms. T owed him, Ng allegedly became violent with both Ms. T and Ms. W. According to them, Ng shouted, "You people want to die today so I'll beat you to death." Ms. T fled the massage parlour and called the Vancouver Police Department. Ng was charged with twenty-two offences under the *Criminal Code* and IRPA, including human trafficking under IRPA.

On June 21, 2007, Judge MacLean of the British Columbia Provincial Court found Ng guilty of procuring Ms. T and Ms. W and keeping a common bawdy house, contrary to the *Criminal Code*, plus several immigration offences. However, Ng was acquitted of both counts of human trafficking due to inconsistencies in the testimony of his alleged victims, along with a reasonable doubt as to whether they had been deceived in being brought into Canada.

Rather than applying the elements of human trafficking under IRPA, Judge MacLean chose instead to determine whether Ms. W and Ms. T were "trafficked persons," based on his understanding of the term and generalizations from an expert witness. The case summary for the decision states, "Not convicted of human trafficking and other offences where prostitutes did not convince court they were victims."

This appears to be an astonishing reversal of the expected process since the victims weren't on trial—Ng was.

The reaction to Judge MacLean's ruling was instantaneous, and it devastated efforts to recognize human trafficking as a high-profile and serious crime. The media lambasted police and prosecutors following Ng's acquittal for human trafficking, and the fallout likely set British Columbia back several years in its attempt to investigate and prosecute sex trafficking cases. Both Ng and the Crown prosecutor appealed the sentence handed down against him to the B.C. Court of Appeal. While the Crown prosecutor had asked for Ng's sentence to be increased to five years imprisonment, Ng's defence counsel asked for his release based on five and a half months of time served.

"All the offences committed by Mr. Ng involved significant moral turpitude, and the two complainants and other women were victims of his greed and opportunism," wrote Mr. Justice Low for the B.C. Court of Appeal. "The sentences imposed for the prostitution offences do not adequately speak to these factors and are unfit. The global sentence is inadequate."

Ng's sentence was increased by one year to twenty-seven months imprisonment. This relatively rare decision of an appeals court to increase a sentence handed down at trial suggests that the sexual exploitation of foreign nationals should be taken more seriously by sentencing judges, even if convictions do not include human trafficking.

More recent international sex trafficking charges laid under the *Criminal Code* have also failed to produce convictions. In January 2008, an Eastern European woman in her twenties shared her story with the Toronto Police Service: She'd answered a webpage advertisement for employment in Canada. Upon arrival, she was given a cellphone that she had to answer twenty-four hours a day and was expected to be prostituted in order to cover the expenses of the individuals who'd arranged for her travel. Several other women came forward with similar stories, resulting in charges being laid against several people for a range of offences that included human trafficking.

Despite the victims having come forward, the case eventually fell apart because the investigating officers weren't able to pursue the details fully. A senior officer with the Toronto Police Service's Sex Crimes Unit says, "Credibility, sometimes, can be an issue if you don't have resources to get the evidence to back them up. That's why you need a unit that's mandated to look into that [human trafficking]."

Prosecutions in Canada related to international trafficking through Canada into the United States have also proven elusive. Take, for example, the June 2006 case in Osoyoos, British Columbia, discussed in Chapter 4. Police were unable to lay human trafficking charges against the man who was transporting the women because, according to the RCMP human trafficking awareness coordinator for British

Columbia and Yukon, the driver of the rental truck knew only that he was to drive people to the border. Demonstrating their ability to work the system, the trafficking network had hired him on a need-to-know basis. As a result, the evidence to support a human trafficking charge was insufficient.

If Canada's system of dealing with human traffickers can be so easily thwarted, how truly effective is it? The human traffickers that have operated in Canada with impunity *vastly* outnumber the handful of offenders that have been convicted to date. And most of those convicted have faced sentences that pale compared with the long-term devastation experienced by their victims. A new criminal offence and a few good police officers have not been enough to end the rise of human trafficking in Canada. What more is needed?

# 12

# ENDING IMPUNITY, OFFERING HOPE

Canada's weak record in prosecuting human trafficking has captured international attention. In 2008, the U.S. State Department *Trafficking in Persons Report* criticized Canada, among other things, for its "limited progress on law enforcement efforts against trafficking offenders"—diplomatic language for sure. The effective prosecution of human traffickers requires, at a minimum, the following:

- clear and well-conceived criminal offences
- well-trained police officers with sufficient resources to investigate cases of human trafficking
- prosecutors willing to proceed with human trafficking charges
- a judicial system that is able to efficiently process criminal charges, with due regard to the rights of the accused
- protection of the safety and privacy of witnesses and victims
- judges who recognize the gravity of human trafficking in the sentencing of convicted traffickers
- continued protection and assistance for trafficking victims before, during, and after the completion of the prosecution of their traffickers

Let's see how Canada measures up to these standards.

## Fixing gaps in the law

Although Canada has ratified the *Palermo Protocol* and taken positive steps toward adopting new "trafficking in persons" offences in the *Criminal Code*, these offences are too narrowly defined. They also depart from the agreed definition of human trafficking in the Protocol in some very unfortunate ways.

The *Criminal Code*'s definition of human trafficking centres on the victim's fear for safety or the safety of someone known to the victim. This is unfortunately too narrow because it fails to criminalize other means by which trafficking is routinely committed. It could be argued that "safety" should not be restricted simply to physical harm but also should encompass psychological and emotional harm (i.e., blackmailing the victim). Yet the definition may fail to address insidious methods used by traffickers—deception, fraud, abuse of power/position of vulnerability, or payment of someone to control the victim—that should be included, as required by the *Palermo Protocol*. These methods are not clearly captured in Canada's *Criminal Code* definition unless they can be linked to the concept of "safety." As a result of this loophole, traffickers in Canada have been able to escape human trafficking charges.

Undercover RCMP officers have posed successfully as members of the criminal underworld and purchased women on the understanding that the victims would be under their full control, yet they knew they couldn't charge the vendors with human trafficking. The reason? Because the officers couldn't prove the women feared for their safety. Unfortunately, as we've seen, the most sophisticated traffickers don't resort to physical threats or abuse, but rely instead on more subtle methods. Canada's definition of human trafficking remains an oddity when compared with those of other countries that have enacted criminal offences against the practice. Furthermore, since fear for safety is an element of the crime, victims bear the burden of convincing the court they had such a fear. As a result, only the most extreme cases of human trafficking, which often involve severe physical violence or threats, are likely to be prosecuted.

Second, the *Criminal Code* definition of exploitation in the human trafficking offences does not distinguish between victims who are under eighteen years of age and those who are over that age. The *Palermo Protocol* requires no proof of the "means" by which exploitation took place for minors—if they are recruited, transported, or controlled for the purpose of sexual exploitation or forced labour, they are victims of human trafficking. Once again, however, Canada insists on the added element of there being proof of the victim's fear for safety. The prosecution of Imani Nakpangi, detailed in Chapter 11, revealed this pitfall in the case of fourteen-year-old Samantha.

Finally, as described in Chapter 11, vastly inadequate sentences in four of the five trafficking convictions to date have exposed the need for more serious penalties, especially for charges of child trafficking. While the maximum sentences provided for in the *Criminal Code* are sufficient, the sentences handed down so far are nowhere near that maximum. The "trafficking in persons" offence was adopted without any mandatory minimum penalty, something other serious criminal offences carry. Bill C-268 thankfully changes that, at least with respect to child victims.

## Improving the law enforcement response

While only five convictions for trafficking in persons were obtained nationally between June 2008 and April 2009, the number of investigations and charges are slowly increasing. Progress is uneven across Canada, however, with no convictions outside of Ontario and Quebec as of early 2010. Yet human trafficking cases have been documented across the country.

The RCMP Human Trafficking National Coordination Centre, based in Ottawa, is headed by a national coordinator and comprises five police officers and two civilian analysts. As part of the RCMP's Immigration and Passport Branch, the HTNCC is responsible for helping to coordinate human trafficking investigations in Canada, to develop policy, and to identify and share best practices with law enforcement nationally and internationally. Created in 2005, the

HTNCC is *not*, despite its name, a national investigative unit for human trafficking. Instead, it has focused on providing basic training to thousands of front-line police officers—a valuable starting point, but no substitute for dedicated teams that are needed to investigate the most active human trafficking operations in Canada.

The RCMP's training efforts are beginning to yield dividends as dozens of new investigations have opened up across the country, the result of front-line police officers identifying the warning signs. However, the RCMP needs to deliberately and proactively target interprovincial and international trafficking networks and groups in order to shut them down. Hopefully, a "threat assessment" completed late in 2009 will spur the RCMP to do just that.

Cracking down in one jurisdiction, without a coordinated response, may simply cause traffickers to relocate to areas where enforcement is less stringent. The Criminal Intelligence Service Canada warns that human traffickers take advantage of the lack of a coordinated response to escape justice, moving to cities or provinces that are less active in combatting human trafficking. Despite efforts to train police in Canada, knowledge of human trafficking as a criminal offence remains alarmingly low, even though the legislation has been in force for several years now.

In April 2009, a Toronto Police Service spokesperson was asked why charges of human trafficking hadn't been laid against Tyrone Dillon for allegedly forcing Joyeuse, a Haitian woman, to be sold for sex after he'd abducted her child (see Chapter 7 for details). "Human trafficking?" responded the police spokesperson. "Is there such a *Criminal Code* charge for human trafficking?" And yet here was a textbook case of human trafficking.

Several police officers interviewed for this book indicated that they have not received any training whatsoever on the human trafficking offences in the *Criminal Code*. How effectively can the Crown make a case for Joyeuse and others like her when law enforcement officers have little knowledge of when and how to identify the crime, gather evidence, and proceed with charges?

A lack of sufficient investigative resources compounds the challenges of gathering evidence about the exploitation of individuals in sex trafficking in major Canadian cities. The vice units of major police forces across Canada have been gutted in recent years and are often responsible for combatting gangs and drugs, as well as prostitution and sex trafficking. The smaller number of officers undermines not only the scope of direct investigations but also sharply reduces the opportunity for investigators to access informants "on the street."

In Montreal, as Detective Sergeant Dominic Montchamp puts it, "[w]hen we investigated massage parlours and escort agencies ... we built up a bank of informers. If there was a change in the sexual industry we had a phone call within an hour. Since we're not doing this, the phone doesn't ring anymore."

The Calgary Police Service, Vice Unit, which investigates human trafficking cases, has been reduced from approximately a dozen officers in 2004 to just several today. And while the Toronto Police Service has a Special Victims Unit mandated to investigate violence against prostituted persons, it has not been mandated to proactively investigate human trafficking cases. "The Special Victims Unit has one detective and four constables and they are overworked," says one member of the Toronto Police Service familiar with the situation. "If a case was discovered today involving human trafficking, say more than one victim, they would have a hard time focusing on that particular case."

Human trafficking investigations are resource intensive and, especially with international cases, can prove costly. For example, the investigation and prosecution of the case involving Wai Chi (Michael) Ng cost the Vancouver Police Department, Vice Unit, approximately $250,000 and entailed one sergeant and eight detective constables working almost full-time over six months. Since the Ng case was a human trafficking prosecution under IRPA, it involved collecting evidence in another country. Police officers in multiple jurisdictions have stated that requests to initiate wiretaps in recent human trafficking investigations have been refused due to a lack of funding, resulting in perpetrators escaping charges.

Chiefs of police who allocate resources and seek greater funding for more officers need to take note and invest more in equipment, training, and officers to eradicate human trafficking. The lack of specialized police officers to gather criminal intelligence and proactively investigate human trafficking offences represents one of the largest gaps in Canada's prosecution of traffickers.

One tool that could help to dismantle human trafficking enterprises is existing legislation that authorizes the seizure and forfeiture of the proceeds of crime and unlawful activity. If pursued by prosecutors, convicted human traffickers would not only have to hand over profits earned from exploiting their victims, but also vehicles, residences, and other property used to commit the crime or purchased with money from the crime. Only in two of Canada's five human trafficking convictions to date was the seizure of proceeds and assets of the crime ordered. Such measures are critical in dismantling the infrastructure and financial incentive of traffickers, and could provide needed funds for victim support services.

Even if the police recommend human trafficking charges be laid, Canada does not have any Crown prosecutors dedicated to human trafficking cases, nor have prosecutors or judges received systematic training in the new area of human trafficking offences. The federal Department of Justice has distributed a two-page information circular for prosecutors and police that briefly summarizes the new offences. Much more is needed. Training and, in some instances, expert evidence may be required for those involved to fully understand the control exerted by traffickers and the behaviour of victims.

There appears to be little awareness in legal quarters of the horrendous nature of human trafficking and of the difficulties inherent in investigating and prosecuting the offence to secure convictions.

## Treating victims with respect, not intimidation

Traffickers of foreign victims frequently employ the fear of prosecution and imprisonment as a means of controlling them.

Unfortunately, some procedures confirm the threats of the traffickers, making the victims feel as though they've been victimized twice—first by the traffickers and next by the Canadian legal system.

NGO representatives like Loly Rico, co-director of the FCJ Refugee Centre, argue that most law enforcement officers lack the understanding and sensitivity to encourage victims to feel comfortable telling their stories. In many cases, the victims themselves are criminalized for being found in a bawdy house, making the situation even worse. Rico says that potential trafficking victims should be entitled to have a lawyer or NGO representative accompany them whenever they meet with police and in all subsequent interviews with public officials.

Dr. Scharie Tavcer, a professor in the Justice Studies Department at Mount Royal University and the chair of the Calgary Network on Prostitution, agrees that police interviewing tactics with suspected trafficked or prostituted persons are often inadequate. "If you were a betting individual, you could say nine out of ten times that context will not permit compliance from these victims," says Dr. Tavcer. "You need to have different sorts of agencies and individuals there to attempt relationship-building, and it's not going to happen the night of the bust, and it's certainly not going to happen when they're staying in a detention cell at some type of a correctional facility."

The co-operation of victims with police is often critical in holding their exploiters accountable. However, it can be incredibly traumatic for victims to talk about the extent of their suffering—and terrifying when their traffickers have made threats against them or their loved ones. Victims may take some time before they are willing and able to share information about their exploitation with police, and they will do so only after their needs have been met and trust has been firmly established.

The Toronto Police Service, Special Victims Unit, takes a unique approach to policing by viewing prostituted women as victims of crime, not as criminals. The word on the street is that the SVU will not lay charges against prostituted persons who report experiences

of violence. This has resulted in several suspected foreign trafficked women having made contact.

Foreign victims may expect they will be deported, usually after having spent extensive time in an immigration detention facility or holding cell. However, there is now a better alternative. For victims, the preferred response from Citizenship and Immigration Canada is a Temporary Residence Permit (TRP) that allows them to legally remain in Canada for a fixed period.

A CIC officer can issue a short-term TRP allowing a victim to remain in Canada for up to one hundred and eighty days, with extensions possible. The TRP helps victims "escape the influence of traffickers so that they can make an informed decision" about whether to return home, seek to remain in Canada to recover from physical and/or mental trauma, or, if they are willing and able, assist in the investigation and prosecution of their trafficker. The TRP can also be issued "for any other purpose ... to facilitate the protection of vulnerable foreign nationals who are victims of human trafficking."

CIC policy guidelines direct officials to consider "an assessment of credibility and whether the individual may have been trafficked," including whether

- the recruitment of the individual was fraudulent or coerced and for the purposes (actual or intended) of exploitation;
- the individual was coerced into employment or other activity;
- the conditions of employment or any other activity were exploitative; *or*
- the individual's freedom was restricted.

Trafficking victims are not required to pay the usual fee for a TRP, are eligible to receive coverage under the Interim Federal Health Program (IFHP) and emergency counselling services, and may apply for a fee-exempt work permit.

Once a TRP has been issued, the victim may seek to renew or extend it beyond the initial period. In reviewing applications, immigration officials have been directed not to penalize trafficking victims for being illiterate, unskilled, or lacking support networks to help them integrate into Canadian society. Such liabilities often result from the victims' exploitation or facilitated their isolation.

When deciding whether to issue long-term TRPs, which have been approved for between thirty days and three years in individual cases, the immigration official will consider several additional factors:

- whether it is reasonably safe and possible for the victims to return to and to re-establish a life in the country of origin or last permanent residence;
- whether the victims are needed, and willing, to assist authorities in an investigation and/or in criminal proceedings of a trafficking offence;
- any other reason the officer may judge relevant.

From May 2006 to November 2008, TRP applications and renewal requests for suspected trafficked persons grew significantly—from four in 2006 to nineteen in 2007, almost doubling to thirty-six in 2008. The majority of applicants were successful in their bids to stay in Canada. Unfortunately, higher rejection rates in 2006 and 2007 may have put some cold water on the program. The higher acceptance rate in 2008 is promising for victim advocates. In total, 42 percent of all TRPs issued were for sexual exploitation, 46 percent for forced labour, and the remainder for unspecified (perhaps mixed) forms of exploitation. Forty-six percent were issued in the Ontario Region, 42 percent in the Prairies/Northwest Territories Region, and 12 percent in the Quebec Region.

Beneath these favourable statistics, however, lurk some serious problems. The decision to grant a TRP rests with a single immigration official at the regional office where an application is made. The same official may not consider such applications each time, resulting in inconsistent and incorrect decisions. Additional training for officers, and assigning complex cases to senior officials, would be a better approach for the immigration department to adopt.

In Alberta, NGOs have expressed concern about CIC's assessment of Thérèse, the long-term sex trafficking victim whom we encountered in an earlier chapter. Thérèse was fortunate in eventually being granted a TRP based on evidence from the RCMP, but the majority of referrals from the RCMP nationwide did not result in immigration officials issuing such permits for the victims. The statistics are similar for referrals from local police agencies and from border guards. In some cases, applicants were granted other forms of immigration status (i.e., humanitarian and compassionate grounds or refugee status) or could have been ineligible because they held another immigration status. Multiple cases, however, suggest substantive disagreements between immigration authorities and the RCMP: the RCMP believed the individuals were trafficking victims, whereas the immigration officers did not.

In British Columbia, the B.C. Office to Combat Trafficking in Persons (OCTIP) is familiar with one such case. In 2008, a seventeen-year-old arrived at the Vancouver International Airport under suspicious circumstances. The minor was referred to the child protection system and the RCMP determined that this child was a victim of human trafficking. But an immigration officer disagreed, so no TRP was issued.

"The dilemma for me is when you've got evidence right in front of you of a child, and you've got law enforcement saying we totally agree with you based on our own investigation, and then having it denied by CIC," says Robin Pike, executive director of OCTIP. "There's something very wrong with the system then."

Similarly, in Ontario, Clara Ho, an immigration lawyer and human trafficking activist, has heard of cases where immigration officials decided to deport individuals after the police had identified them as trafficking victims. Moreover, an internal governmental email from the CIC regional program adviser for the Quebec Region noted that "miscommunication was a problem" between federal agencies.

Fortunately, immigration officials and the RCMP do sometimes co-operate in their efforts on behalf of trafficking victims. In June 2007, the RCMP interviewed a victim in hospital and gave the interview notes to an immigration official, who later met with the victim to confirm her story and provided the TRP, health care eligibility, and information about future immigration options. It's important for immigration officials to remember that police can greatly assist in making the preliminary verification of a trafficking victim, particularly given their knowledge of other aspects of the case and their investigative capacity, which CIC lacks. Re-interviewing an individual whom the police have already identified as a trafficking victim may do more harm than good—a fact that CIC recognizes in its own TRP guidelines.

Other concerns about the implementation of the TRP guidelines for trafficked persons also need to be addressed. Records released under the *Access to Information Act* revealed that at least one immigration officer has taken the position that a foreign trafficked child seeking a TRP is required to provide his or her own interpreter, something that is well beyond a child's ability to secure. The officer ultimately relented and arranged for a translator. Article 3(b) of the *Palermo Protocol* calls for victims to receive information about legal rights in a language that they can understand. Translation services for trafficked persons applying for a TRP clearly should be available.

## Are trafficking victims refugees?

When law enforcement officials apprehend trafficked persons, the victims may attempt to claim refugee status, fearing they will be re-trafficked by the criminal groups that brought them to Canada if they return home.

In order to gain status as refugees or "protected persons" under the *Immigration and Refugee Protection Act*, claimants must establish several facts: They must demonstrate that they face persecution and violence in their home country; they must establish that this violence results from their membership in a social group that is "innate and unchangeable"; and they must convince immigration officials that effective state protection is lacking in their country of origin. As a result of these rules, very few trafficked persons gain refugee status. While refugees in Canada suffered harm or threat of harm in their home countries, trafficked persons in Canada generally suffered harm here. As a result, most foreign trafficking victims cannot benefit from the protection given to those fleeing war or persecution abroad, unless they happen to be from such countries.

In one extremely unsettling decision made before the 2006 TRP system for trafficking victims was in place, the Immigration and Refugee Board accepted a claimant's evidence that she likely would be injured or killed upon returning home but refused to find that she conformed to a particular social group. An IRB adjudicator agreed that "the claimant has been victimized by ruthless members of what seems to be an organized crime [sic] specializing in the trafficking of women from the Third World to Canada, for the sake of sexual exploitation," but denied her claim for protection because "victims of organized crimes [sic] do not constitute a particular social group."

What is the federal immigration department's view on the subject? "While some victims of trafficking may be refugees, a refugee claim may not be the best course for all trafficking victims," according to a senior policy analyst at the CIC headquarters in Ottawa. "Making a refugee claim is not a viable option for people who do not meet the definition of a Convention refugee." Instead, immigration officials point out the merits of the TRP as a vehicle for trafficked persons to obtain legal status. Unfortunately, this message from the CIC headquarters in Ottawa has not always trickled down to immigration officials in various parts of the country.

Loly Rico of the FCJ Refugee Centre has dealt with six separate cases that she considered to involve foreign victims of human trafficking. Yet when she asked the local immigration official to consider TRPs for these women, often she was told to just apply for refugee status, a process ill-suited to the situation. These cases seem to expose a disconnect between policy at CIC's headquarters and its interpretation among regional officials who implement the TRP guidelines for trafficked persons.

## Giving victims hope to become survivors

Both foreign and domestic victims of human trafficking need the protection and assistance to which Canada committed when it signed the *Palermo Protocol* in 2000. A failure to provide essential care risks re-traumatizing victims, hampering their rehabilitation, and undermining chances of holding their exploiters accountable, while raising the prospect of their being re-trafficked. Although every victim is unique, many exhibit similar needs. These include the following services that should be provided by a combination of NGOs and governmental agencies:

- Protection services: similar to those offered to victims of domestic violence;
- Shelter: emergency shelter, assisted living, or independent housing;
- Health services: short, medium, or long term, including access to public health care, mental health care, detoxification and addiction recovery services, and long-term counselling;
- Legal services: information and representation;
- Economic services: income support, access to education, training and skill development, language training, and help in finding employment.

### Protecting victims from further abuse

Physically protecting human trafficking victims from threats and reprisals by traffickers is difficult. Police officers in several Canadian cities have expressed concern at the lack of protective services for trafficked persons who serve as informants and witnesses against their traffickers.

Even if victims come forward and tell the police what happened to them, the case is far from over. Due to post-traumatic stress, fear, or direct threats from their abusers, victims may be unwilling or unable to testify in court. After providing police with a statement, victims are subject to intimidation by traffickers. One young woman controlled by North Preston's Finest faced threats from multiple gang members and thus recanted her statement, claiming the police had forced her to accuse them.

"We have to keep the pimp and their associates away from our victim," says one officer associated with these cases. "The biggest part of what we do is victim maintenance through constant contact. We have to fill a void. They're used to checking in every hour. Take that away from them, and they don't even know what to wear. Their pimps used to do that."

Offering protection to victims is more complex than it may first appear. Where should they be housed? Who will pay for protective custody? In cases involving organized crime, an array of support programs ensures that witnesses are not subject to retaliation. "The victim witness protection program protects drug dealers and murderers," says one detective engaged in investigating sex crimes. "Surely we can use the same funds to help victims of human trafficking."

## Safe houses

Not all foreign victims of human trafficking want to stay in Canada. Under Articles 6(3)(a) and 8 of the *Palermo Protocol*, Canada should provide appropriate housing for these victims and work with their home countries to facilitate their voluntary repatriation. In reality, accommodation for foreign and domestic trafficked persons in Canada is a patchwork of non-governmental and governmental options, most of them underfunded and understaffed. They also range widely in capacity, level of staff training, resources, and ability to provide long-term support versus meeting short-term needs. Some facilities accept both men and women, a practice that is not suitable for victims seeking to recover from their ordeals. Concerns arise too about cultural appropriateness, language skills and translation difficulties, as well as immigration issues, which not all organizations have the training to address.

Most women's shelters and transition houses feel their mandate is to provide safe housing for victims of domestic violence, not services for trafficked persons. Moreover, the few non-governmental agencies that are interested in offering housing for victims of trafficking receive little or no funding from most provincial governments for this specialized service. Without a safe place to stay that meets their individual needs, victims of trafficking are being set up for further exploitation. There are, however, some pioneering NGOs that are beginning to provide beds for trafficking victims—often for the first safe night's sleep the victims have had in years.

## Recovering from the trauma: Health care and counselling

Since 2006, foreign trafficking victims who are issued a TRP have access to the Interim Federal Health Program, a rudimentary medical insurance program that ensures refugees receive essential medical care: basic and emergency health services, emergency dental treatment, contraception, prenatal and obstetrical care, essential prescription medications, and covers costs related to the Immigration Medical Examination. TRP holders who can pay for their own health care or are insured by a private or public plan are not eligible for the IFHP.

When Thérèse, the long-term trafficking victim from the Democratic Republic of the Congo, received her TRP, she had difficulty getting health care to cover psychological counselling. Citizenship and Immigration Canada's TRP manual now states that in the case of trafficking victims, some psychological counselling "may be considered 'urgent and essential.'"

Unfortunately, the manual also recommends that officers grant health care coverage to TRP holders only for the initial six-month "reflection period." After that, they must rely on benevolent NGOs. This is likely inadequate for many foreign trafficking victims with significant health care and counselling needs. By appealing to the CIC headquarters in Ottawa, immigration officials in Quebec have received approval to extend health care coverage for longer-term TRP holders who don't fall under provincial health care.

Foreign trafficking victims who are covered by some other legitimate immigration status (i.e., visitor or student visas) may be ineligible for TRPs and their associated health care coverage. For example, OCTIP has had to pay for emergency dental care for a trafficked woman who didn't hold a TRP. Across Canada, many organizations are dedicated to helping vulnerable women, including victims of trafficking, but these groups are not everywhere and they usually have limited funds. Clearly, trafficked persons whose legitimate immigration status excludes a TRP need to be eligible for assistance. Furthermore, provincial governments must give allowances to victims who are Canadian citizens and permanent residents; that way, they can access services even if they're not fully registered under provincial health care at the time they're rescued or escape. After all, the victims' traffickers did not grant them the luxury of maintaining their paperwork.

## A voice for victims: Advice and representation

Navigating the immigration and legal issues that may be involved in a trafficking case, especially one involving foreign nationals, isn't a simple exercise. A person fluent in English or French easily can spend a full day researching how to apply for a TRP, what benefits are involved, how long the assistance lasts, and so on. Imagine how much longer it would take a victim of human trafficking who barely speaks either of Canada's official languages. Much of our legal system is virtually unnavigable without the help of a lawyer, and the difficulties are especially pronounced for trafficking victims.

Whether they're applying for TRPs or victim compensation, trafficked persons need access to legal information and representation. Provincial legal aid programs must ensure that trafficking victims qualify for support in the TRP application process, as witnesses in criminal proceedings, and as victims of crime seeking compensation or in lawsuits for civil damages against their traffickers. A lawyer can also ensure that the victim's rights to privacy are respected in public records. If an immigration official rejects a TRP application from an alleged foreign trafficking victim, the victim has little recourse without the assistance of a lawyer. Pro bono lawyers partnering with NGOs can play an important role in raising awareness about the various legal issues that trafficking victims are likely to encounter. For example, Covenant House in Vancouver provides a free, and confidential, daily lawyer consultation service.

Unfortunately, only a small fraction of human trafficking victims have been able to obtain free legal advice and representation—just 7 percent of foreign trafficking TRP applicants between 2006 and 2008 have arrived at CIC through a lawyer.

## A better future: Financial security for survivors

Survivors of human trafficking need immediate financial support to meet basic needs and help reclaim their independence. In the longer term, they may also need education and training to become financially secure and find gainful employment.

For Canadian victims, welfare and income support may be available, although it frequently will be inadequate. Years of being exploited have taken the place of school and job training, so it can be difficult for trafficked persons to support themselves and move on with their lives.

Income support is available for those foreign trafficking victims who've made refugee claims, but the rest generally have no access unless they live in one of the few provinces that have recognized this gap and recently changed their policies.

In 2008, officials in Alberta realized that provincial programs were ill-equipped to meet the needs of trafficking victims like Thérèse. Fortunately, however, strong advocates from NGOs and understanding public servants with Alberta Employment and Immigration secured a special policy for providing income support to victims of trafficking. The new policy recognizes that victims with TRPs are eligible to receive income support for the duration of their permits, including any extensions and renewals.

British Columbia also extended its refugee income support to TRP holders through a regulation change in 2008. This brought the province's income assistance policies for TRP holders into line with their policy for refugees, which waives the normal three-week waiting period for income assistance. Thus, trafficked persons in British Columbia with TRPs are now eligible for income assistance.

Finding stable employment is another step in the recovery process. Since 2007, foreign trafficking victims who hold TRPs can obtain work permits, and immigration officers are required to present this option to TRP applicants. Some NGOs also offer training programs and educational initiatives. The Salvation Army's Florence Booth House, for example, has a partnership with Hertzen College, which helps train women in information technology and pharmaceutical practice. Diane Redsky and Jackie Anderson, who run the Little Sisters safe house in Winnipeg, stress the need for training and education for Aboriginal girls as they "age out" of the child protection system, meaning on their eighteenth birthday they are no longer allowed to stay. For some Aboriginal girls in the system, turning eighteen is not cause for celebration but a terrifying milestone after which they fear they will be left to fend for themselves.

## A new life for Thérèse

Six months after her courageous escape from her traffickers, Thérèse began a new life in Canada. The Alberta government is providing her with income support and she has some help in the community through immigrants from her home country. She's also learning to speak English.

What's next for Thérèse? Hers is an inspiring story of renewal for others who manage to escape exploitation. The provincial government has promised Thérèse five hundred dollars this year, a small amount, to help upgrade her education and skills. Once she finds a job, her first paycheque will represent more than money to meet her basic needs—it will start to restore her dignity.

# 13

# FROM AVERAGE JOES TO AVERAGE JOHNS

Sean's request to the escort agency was simple: He asked for a woman to be sent to his Toronto hotel room. He didn't plan on cruising the streets, and wanted to avoid the tackiness of having sex in a car. This way he'd discreetly have an hour with a woman he'd never met—and who'd ever find out?

The person who arrived at his hotel room door was young. In fact, she was fifteen at most, and delivered by a couple of burly men who kept her under their control. When Sean was alone with the girl, she extended her small hand and nervously gave him a folded bit of paper. It contained just two words: *Help me.*

Sean reacted swiftly. By his own account, he "got the hell out of there," leaving the young girl to be found by her handlers. For whatever reason—the shock brought on by the girl's plea, or the shattering of the myth that paying for sex was a victimless crime—he'd lost interest.

Once out of the hotel, Sean had to tell someone what had happened, but he didn't want to make himself known to the police. Instead, he told the story of the frightened little girl to his friend Chris. The girl had begged Sean to save her. And he hadn't.

Chris could hardly believe the story and his friend's refusal to act. Well, if Sean wouldn't get involved, Chris would. He called Crime Stoppers and gave the operator the details of Sean's experience, including the name of the escort agency. Crime Stoppers relayed the information to the Toronto Police Service, which recognized the name of the individual associated with the agency's telephone number, a man already known to be running a prostitution ring.

A police officer called the escort agency, posing as a potential client looking for a young Asian girl and hoping that the girl who had been brought to Sean's hotel room would arrive in the company of her traffickers.

Detective Sergeant Mike Hamel of the Toronto Police Service, Sex Crimes Unit, picks up the story. "We had the phone number of the escort service he called, so we set it all up," Hamel recalls. "We were hoping the same thing would happen, but we got an older female. We ran into problems."

Lacking first-hand evidence of an underage girl being sold for sex, the officers had no choice but to rely on a statement from Sean. With that in hand, the police likely could obtain search warrants to investigate the escort agency and try to find the terrified girl.

However, the refusal of Sean to contact police meant that the investigation could proceed no further, and the young girl who'd appealed for help almost certainly would continue to be sexually abused.

"We never found her," says Detective Sergeant Hamel with sadness in his voice. "We go from one fire to the next. To me, that's not good enough."

## Escort agencies: Selling sex through thinly veiled language

Escort agencies represent the twenty-first-century evolution of nineteenth-century brothels. The only difference is location; instead of choosing women and rooms within the same establishment, johns now determine the environment, usually a hotel or motel room.

An obvious front for selling sex, escort agencies have played a role in several documented human trafficking cases, including those of Svetlana and Dina, detailed earlier. Fees collected from the women support the agencies' owners and managers, some of them associated with criminal gangs who frequently control many of the agencies within a single city or region.

The opportunities for the profiteers don't end there, however. Escort agencies couldn't attract the sizeable number of johns calling them, virtually 24/7, without widely accessible outlets for advertising their services, including weekly newspapers published and distributed in virtually every major Canadian city. Such papers are rife with ads incorporating thinly veiled promises of paid sex acts. These publications shouldn't be able to accept cheques for advertising from "sexually oriented businesses" without exercising some due diligence to ensure they aren't actively marketing criminal activity. Instead, the publications remain wilfully blind to the problem and little, if anything at all, is done to make them think twice.

The sheer number of advertisements for escort services confirms that the industry indeed represents big money to those who control the women being sold. "When you look at all those ads, you have to ask yourself: Are all these people, from all these countries coming to Canada to do this job?" wonders Detective Sergeant Hamel of the Toronto Police Service, Sex Crimes Unit. "It is just incredible how many escort services there are. If you spend the time to investigate some of these people, you'll find that a lot of the women are not here voluntarily."

## "Rub and tug": More than a massage

Massage parlours are places of suspended disbelief that our society has somehow come to accept. You drive past them knowing that, more often than not, they're bawdy houses where sex is for sale.

Operators of massage parlours have been profiteers who've controlled women to a degree that qualifies as enslavement in several cases. Once again, however, as with escort services and the advertising media they use, other people and organizations are collecting proceeds from the racket while pretending to be innocent of the brutality inflicted on the women employed in the "parlours."

Chief among the profiteers from massage parlours are the landlords who accept their rent. An even more egregious sector, though, may be the municipalities that collect licensing revenue from these "businesses," rarely conducting any due diligence or subsequent inspections after receiving their cut.

Police officers in cities across Canada confirm that escort services and massage parlours commonly are fronts for selling foreign victims of human trafficking, and the operators legitimize their bogus businesses by purchasing valid licences. Canada's mayors, city councillors, and by-law officers need to remove the licensing from these illegal enterprises and find less dreadful means of filling the community coffers.

Sergeant Jeff Danroth of the Vancouver Police Department believes that the Vice Unit has interacted with "hundreds" of foreign women, mainly from Asian countries, who are being sold for sex in bawdy houses in the city. Typically they've replied to advertisements for work at massage parlours, but no one knows whether the women are fully aware before arriving in Canada that they'll be required to provide sex acts, or whether they can leave the situation if they so choose.

Authorities worldwide recognize that traffickers recruit and control women who are already being sold for sex in developing and often-corrupt countries by promising better conditions in developed ones. In one of the most extensive studies of sex trafficking in the United States, Dr. Janice G. Raymond, emeritus professor at University of Massachusetts, and Dr. Donna M. Hughes, professor at the University of Rhode Island, found that "[i]nternational women, formerly in the sex trade in their countries of origin, are particularly vulnerable to recruitment in sex industries in the United States."

When sex trafficking victims in Canada appear to have been sold for sex in their home countries, some Canadians—and even some sectors of the media—tend to blame the victims. In September 1997, news reporter Rosie DiManno said of the women involved in a major trafficking operation in the Toronto area, "Indentured sex trade workers, yes. Exploited concubines, possibly. Self-conscripted whores, apparently." DiManno's point of view was telegraphed effectively in her *Toronto Star* story, titled "Sex slave 'victims' weren't captives chained to beds."

This willingness to blame victims of sexual exploitation is uninformed and misdirected. It's easier to blame the victims than to ask tough questions about who profits from their suffering and to identify the men who pay for sex acts with these women. In commenting on this attitude, one law enforcement officer says, "Our approach to these women is wrong. These people are victims from day one. They are being exploited and we label them as prostitutes. We should look at them as victims of exploitation." Sadly, the women being sold aren't the only victims of the actions of johns.

## Collateral damage: Families, wives, children

Jennifer suspected that her husband, Jeff, was cheating on her. She had no real proof yet, and with two young children to care for, she didn't want to do anything drastic that might weaken the marriage.

Everything unravelled, however, when Jennifer's doctor informed her that she'd tested positive for an STD. Jennifer hadn't been with anyone but Jeff since her marriage to him several years before. Clearly he'd been unfaithful. After the initial trauma, she set to work rummaging through her husband's dresser drawers, the desk in his small office, and his other belongings, exposing the brutal truth.

Jeff had been frequenting strip clubs, massage parlours, and escort agencies. Worse still, he had multiple credit cards in his name that were billed to his office address and showed outstanding balances totalling tens of thousands of dollars.

After an explosive confrontation with Jeff, Jennifer decided to file for divorce. As more details emerged about Jeff's wide-ranging and long-term patronizing of sex services, Jennifer realized that her husband's secret addiction would ultimately destroy her and her family. Creditors began calling every day, demanding payment for Jeff's sex bills. Eventually, Jennifer was forced to file for bankruptcy, leaving her devastated.

Jennifer, along with others who've become collateral damage of the demand for paid sex, has told her story to hundreds of men at Toronto's "John School." This education and awareness program run by Streetlight Support Services allows first-time offenders who've been arrested for communicating for the purpose of prostitution in a public place to avoid a criminal record; the only requirement is that they successfully complete the program. Jennifer hopes that the men will make a fresh start and not destroy their lives and families as her husband did.

## Human trafficking meets a demand

The simple reality is that sex trafficking would not exist in Canada or abroad without demand from men who feel entitled to engage in paid sex acts of their choosing. Yet in tackling the problem, concerned parties frequently ignore the powerful role of the purchaser.

"Why is there tolerance for buying another person?" asks Linda Smith, founder and director of Shared Hope International. "Why aren't clients going to jail? If there weren't a buyer, there wouldn't be a procurer, and there wouldn't be a victimized woman or child."

The cases of sex trafficking documented in this book reveal that traffickers have sold their victims to purchasers through various outlets, including strip clubs, massage parlours, escort agencies, internet bulletin board services, street-level prostitution, hotels and motels, house parties, and truck stops. The thousands of Canadian men who purchased these sex acts either didn't know or didn't care that they were renting victims of human trafficking, many of them minors. If we can better understand who these men are and why they behave this way, we can develop strategies to intervene.

As the executive director of Streetlight Support Services, John Fenn has met thousands of such men over the last decade. Would these men have known if they were paying for sex with someone who was in reality a victim of human trafficking? Probably not. "They go for whatever they can get," says Fenn.

A 2004 study by University of Rhode Island professor Dr. Donna M. Hughes, entitled *Best Practices to Address the Demand Side of Sex Trafficking*, found that "whether or not the woman or child is being compelled to engage in prostitution seems irrelevant to men when they purchase sex acts.... When the focus shifts to the primary level of the demand, there is no evidence that men distinguish between women and children who are victims of trafficking and those who are not." Therefore, in addressing the demand side of sex trafficking, "it is not possible to distinguish between men's demand for victims of sex trafficking from men's demand for commercial sex acts."

Purchasers of sex acts rely on multiple, often contradictory, justifications for rationalizing their behaviour. John Fenn provides some examples:

"If nobody knows about it, how can it be wrong?"

"If my wife doesn't find out, then what she doesn't know isn't going to hurt her."

"I deserve this because I've just got a new job and I feel good about myself and I deserve a little reward."

"I lost my job, my wife hasn't given me sex for three weeks, and I'm a man. I need this, I deserve it."

Compare these fanciful justifications from johns with this statement from Eve, one of the teenage girls exploited by convicted human trafficker Imani Nakpangi:

"I have low self-esteem. I feel like I'm only good for one thing, sex. I don't see why someone, a man, would be interested in me and try to get to know me because I feel unworthy, dirty, tainted, nothing."

Purchasers of sex acts attempt to convince themselves that they're helping the prostituted/trafficked person by giving her money, further rationalizing their actions on the grounds that they "are not hurting anyone." Some claim that the woman has chosen this "line of work" and enjoys it. However, studies have found that purchasers of sex acts generally do not believe that the women make a lot of money or enjoy the experience at all.

The idea that masculinity automatically implies an uncontrollable need to buy sex is a popular myth that creates false permission for purchasers of sex acts to carry on as they do. As one European study has pointed out, human beings are not born wishing to buy sexual services any more than they are born with specific desires to play the lottery or drink Coca-Cola. While having sex is a basic biological function, men have to be socialized or induced to feel that it would be pleasurable to *pay* a stranger for sex. Where commercial sex is concerned, they also have to be taught to feel that consuming such services is a sign of "having fun"—a marker of their social identity and status as "real men," "adults," or whatever. The conclusion: paying for sex is a learned behaviour, not a natural and uncontrollable urge.

By confronting the demand for paid sex, we can ensure that purchasers are held accountable for the tremendous harm that they inflict on their victims, both directly through their individual acts of abuse and, together with other purchasers, indirectly by contributing to the entire process of victimization. Seen in that light, the purchasers of sex acts are as morally responsible for the suffering of their victims as are the traffickers who meet their demand.

## Johns in high places: The scandalous case of Judge David Ramsay

Lab tests on rats have yielded information about the precise dose of ethylene glycol required to bring about death. Mixing the odourless anti-freeze with orange juice may help it go down more easily, before it viciously attacks the liver and kidneys. As a provincial court judge in British Columbia, David Ramsay was likely familiar with this means of death discussed in criminal investigation textbooks or used in murder cases. On a spring day in 2004, the former judge put this knowledge to personal use as he drank the deadly cocktail. How far he'd fallen. How much he'd given up. How great the suffering he'd caused.

The allegations against Ramsay had surfaced in the summer of 2002 in Prince George, the self-proclaimed Northern Capital of British Columbia, where many of the seventy thousand residents are Aboriginal. Ramsay enjoyed a reputation as an outstanding member of the community. Prior to going to law school at the University of British Columbia, he'd been an elementary school teacher, and after being called to the bar he opened the first legal aid office in Prince George.

Despite his busy private legal practice, Ramsay made time to volunteer on the boards of various charities, including a home for troubled youth, a shelter for abused women, and a crisis centre. Appointed to the Bench in 1991, Judge Ramsay travelled from his base in Prince George as a circuit judge to various remote communities. He appeared to be a respected judge and a doting father of four children—"a decent and caring individual." But a few knew otherwise.

Between July 1992 and December 2001, at least four girls between the ages of twelve and sixteen came to know a very different side of Judge Ramsay, a side that was callous, predatory, and violent. One of them was fifteen-year-old Cynthia.

When Cynthia entered Judge Ramsay's courtroom to face various minor charges, he made the First Nations teenager a ward of the province. Several months later, Ramsay encountered Cynthia on a Prince George street, picked her up in his vehicle, and drove her to an isolated road six kilometres outside of town, where he parked and ordered her to perform oral sex on him for sixty dollars. During the sex act, he grabbed her by the hair and demanded his money back. The girl managed to escape and Ramsay drove off, leaving her alone and naked on the abandoned forest road, but not before warning that he'd have her killed if she ever told anyone about the incident.

Sometime later, fourteen-year-old Audrey, a First Nations girl described as having a "fragile mental state, low self-esteem, limited education and [a] past with abusive adults," was taken by Ramsay to the same remote forest road and forced to perform various sex acts for him, an incident repeated a number of times over three years. Because the girl was facing criminal charges as a young offender, Judge Ramsay promised that he'd "let her off sentences" if she kept his acts secret. As the presiding judge on eight separate occasions when Audrey appeared in court, he was able to make good on his promises.

At just twelve, Hannah was Judge Ramsay's youngest victim, a girl with a troubled past who, like Audrey, appeared in the judge's courtroom facing several criminal charges. Sometime after her appearance in his court, Judge Ramsay picked up Hannah on the street and told her he wanted to "simulate aggressive sex" with her for one hundred and fifty dollars. When she became scared, Hannah pushed Judge Ramsay away and escaped from his vehicle as he yelled at her that no one would believe her if she went to the police. Remarkably, court records refer to this twelve-year-old victim as a "juvenile sex trade *worker.*" A more appropriate description would be a "sexually exploited youth" or "sex crime victim."

Judge Ramsay's most violent behaviour was directed at Sandra, a Métis girl of sixteen. Following the pattern, he picked her up off the street and drove her to a remote area, where he demanded sex acts in exchange for money. When Sandra removed her clothes and reached for a condom, Judge Ramsay became enraged, and according to court records,

> [h]e slammed her head on the dashboard, causing her forehead to bleed. After some struggle, she made it out of the truck. However, he caught up with her and pinned her to the ground. He slapped her across the face and proceeded to penetrate her with his penis as she cried. He got up, threw her clothes out of the truck and left. No money changed hands. She made her way back to the highway and hitchhiked back to town.

This was not the last that Sandra would see of Judge Ramsay. A year later, during a custody battle for her son, she was shocked to find him sitting on the bench, presiding over the hearing and deciding the fate of her child. In fact, the shock was sufficient to motivate Sandra to report Judge Ramsay's actions, launching an investigation that, over the next two years, revealed the extent of his actions and the number of victims.

Judge Ramsay's suicide attempt failed, and he was sent to hospital for twelve days before his trial could begin. Although he resigned as a judge when the allegations came to light, it was widely anticipated that he would launch a vigorous defence. Surely the allegations couldn't be true, could they?

Just before his trial, Ramsay shocked his friends, his children, and his wife by admitting that Cynthia, Audrey, Hannah, and Sandra were indeed telling the truth. Rather than endure the girls' testimony in court and cross-examination by their lawyer, Ramsay pleaded guilty to sexual assault, breach of trust, and three counts of obtaining the sexual services of a minor for money.

His statement to the court satisfied few people in understanding how he could have acted as he did. "I'm at a loss to explain to you, the complainants and my family, how I could work so hard in all other aspects of my life, yet fail by engaging in such disgraceful conduct," he said in the same courtroom where he had sat in judgment of others for years and now stood as a confessed criminal. "I cannot undo that which has been done, nor take away the pain or the indignity I've contributed to their lives."

At Ramsay's sentencing hearing, Associate Chief Justice Dohm called his colleague's conduct "utterly reprehensible," finding that Ramsay had treated the teenage victims in the same manner that

> one might discard a pair of old shoes.... He freely engaged in sexual activity, including violence, with young women who were highly vulnerable because of youth, disadvantaged backgrounds and addiction. He sat in judgment on them for the very behaviour in which he himself was instrumental in causing them to engage, when he had full knowledge of their personal circumstances.... [T]he accused used his office both to solicit satisfaction of his perverted lusts and to shield himself from their consequences. In our society judges are the trustees of the administration of justice. One can hardly imagine a more infamous breach of trust.

On June 1, 2004, Ramsay was sentenced to serve seven years in prison for his crimes. Justice Dohm, in giving his reasons for sentencing, commented on the stark contrast between Ramsay's brutal actions and his reputation in the community: "It is difficult to imagine a more astounding example of the split personality phenomenon....

He has brought shame on his former colleagues, on the judiciary generally, his family and on himself."

During the trial, it was revealed that police had probed Ramsay's actions several years earlier but had been unable to find anyone willing to testify against him. Ramsay would never have been held accountable for his actions as a purchaser of sex acts and an abuser of vulnerable girls if not for their courage in coming forward despite his threats. Encouraged by the victims' bravery, more than twenty other young women began preparing complaints against Ramsay.

Ramsay would never answer those additional allegations. He died of cancer in January 2008 while serving his sentence in a New Brunswick prison. Despite fears from several quarters that he might be released within two years of a seven-year sentence, he was denied parole on the grounds that he had made "no meaningful attempt at remorse or rehabilitation on his part since arriving at federal penitentiary."

## A demographic of Canada's johns

Purchasers of sex acts, including those who select vulnerable children, may include powerful and upstanding members of the community like Judge Ramsay. Researchers have concluded, however, "the average client is the average man." A 1988 Gallup poll estimated that 7 percent of Canadian men have paid for sex; more recent estimates are lacking.

From time to time, news reports reveal that many "ordinary johns" may not be so ordinary after all. A Quebec City investigation called "Operation Scorpion" rattled the community and captured international headlines because of the diverse array of men arrested for purchasing sex from underage girls. Their sellers were a street gang called the "Wolf Pack." The seventeen "johns" arrested included an aide to former Quebec premier Lucien Bouchard, a popular radio host, the former president of the winter Bonhomme Carnaval festival, the owner of a pharmacy chain, the owner of an upscale patisserie on Cartier Street, and a flea market proprietor. Yet the prosecutor described the number of prominent men implicated in Operation Scorpion as "the tip of the iceberg."

Patrons of these trafficked women can find themselves in unexpected situations. One social worker heard that some of the women, having escaped the pimps and traffickers, had gone to job interviews only to discover that their potential bosses were former "clients."

Older psychological studies on the patrons of purchased sex tended to characterize them as having social or physical inadequacies that drove them to seek out the women. More recent research has revealed that purchasers of sex acts generally share no special distinguishing features, instead displaying characteristics that transcend all categories of income, education, and social standing.

In Canada and the United States, studies of men arrested for attempting to purchase sex found that 60 to 72 percent of participants had some post-secondary education, and most were gainfully employed. From 1996 to 2008, over seven thousand men in Toronto who were caught attempting to purchase sex were sent to the John School at Streetlight Support Services. Officials at the school noted that the attendees represented all ages and walks of life, and most were married and employed. A 2005 study found that nearly 50 percent of sex act purchasers were fathers; whether the majority of these men were satisfied with their sexual relationships with their partners is undetermined—the research points to conflicted feelings among the respondents.

Some commonalities appear to exist among purchasers of sex acts. For example, the average age of a man who purchases sex acts for the first time is between twenty-four and twenty-seven. Additionally, in one study, the men who reported a history of purchasing sex acts averaged forty-two paid encounters.

Casual and habitual users of paid sex may differ significantly. One international study describes habitual users as "deeply troubled" men who relate to women only in a sexualized way. They "suffer from heavy sexual dependency problems and whose excessive involvement in prostitution and pornography results in a number of difficulties including financial, occupational, relationship, as well as personal.... [They] project their own psychological problems on the women by using more or less excessive violence to humiliate and degrade them."

Many studies list and explain the wide variety of motivations that prompt men to purchase sex, yet a common attribute informs them all: A *sense of power* arises when the sex act purchaser can seek out a woman or girl, enter into a "business transaction" with her that's designed exclusively to satisfy his urges and fantasies, and walk away with no strings attached. For some men, the motivation may include a lack of interest in establishing relationships with women, an inability to do so, or the craving for sex acts that they're unable to enjoy with their partners.

For the majority of purchasers, sexual behaviour becomes a transaction like any other, devoid of intimacy. The desire always to be in control and to have a variety of anonymous partners, without consequences or responsibility, has even been dubbed "McSex." "It's like going to McDonald's," one john suggested. "It's satisfying, it's greasy, and then you get the hell out of there."

To a small minority of men, sex for purchase replaces intimacy that's unavailable elsewhere. "Some of them fall in love," explains one man associated with Toronto's John School. "Some of them come back and only look for Susie, week after week, or month after month, whatever it may be, whatever their cycle is, or day after day, who knows. But they're looking for her, and they want her to leave the pimp, they want her to come and be with him, be his girlfriend. Some of them fall in love with these girls."

In contrast, some purchasers of sex acts seek a more sadistic hold over their victims. Driven by a desire for physical control, a man of this kind will incline to "forcing sex acts that were not agreed on, for longer than the allotted time, or holding the woman against her will; verbally, physically and sexually abusing the woman; and, enjoying power and control, believing that they own the woman and can do whatever they want to her while she is with them."

The sense of power extends to verbal abuse. "[H]e tells you that you are a dirty whore, a nasty skank, that fucking and sucking are really all you're good for," says Terri-Lynn, a member of the Aboriginal Women's Action Network in Vancouver. "You are nothing more than a sexualized ... collection of body parts to him. This is the so-called work of prostitution. It demeans, humiliates, and devastates women who are used in this way."

## Responding to "market demand"—why traffickers recruit younger and younger women

The demand for younger girls and women is causing traffickers to recruit them, in many cases, when they are under eighteen. Why do men insist on paying for sex acts with minors in violation of the law and society's values?

Adolescents and children are easier for men to dominate, less able to defend themselves physically, and more susceptible to manipulation by their traffickers, including enforced silence. Another factor is pop culture, advertising, and the entertainment media generally, all of which tend to project a hypersexualized vision of young girls.

The availability of child sexual abuse imagery and videos on the internet contributes significantly to men seeking to purchase sex or sexually abuse underage boys and girls. Some law enforcement officials and counsellors who assist the victims of sex trafficking believe that people who wouldn't otherwise physically act out or assault a child, or seek victims in underground markets, do so through the internet because the risk of getting caught seems lower to them. According to multiple studies, habitual purchasers of sex acts view pornography significantly more often than first-time purchasers.

## Gambling with their lives

Purchasers of sex acts often think of their crime as "victimless" and of themselves as invincible. They're wrong on both counts. In addition to harming the victims they visit, men who pay for sex acts gamble with their own careers, finances, family life, intimate relationships, reputation, health, and even their lives. These men can be subject to criminal prosecution and, in some provinces, police seize and impound vehicles used in street-level prostitution.

Serious health risks are always present. Purchasers may demand to engage in sex acts without the use of condoms, and some will pay extra for this even though STDs are on the rise. Studies in the United States have shown a rate of HIV infection of prostituted persons ranging from 2.5 percent in Los Angeles County to 28 percent in New York City. A recent study found that 26 percent of prostituted females in Vancouver were infected with HIV, a rate that has been increasing over the last decade.

As johns attending programs so often recount, the cumulative impact on their status in the community, career opportunities, family relationships, and financial security can be life altering. Here's one tale from a participant in a recent session at a Toronto John School:

> At the height of my addiction I was spending tens of thousands of dollars on sex, drugs, and gambling every year. There was a lot of shame … porn movies, strip bars, pimps, and drug dealers. The addiction cost me my business, my wife, my children and my freedom.

# 14

# DOING THE DIRTY WORK: FORCED LABOUR

Saint Vincent and the Grenadines is renowned for its historical associations with slavery and the battle to abolish it. At the height of the African slave trade, Saint Vincent functioned as a secret refuge for slaves in the Caribbean who'd either been shipwrecked during their hazardous transatlantic passage or had managed to escape from colonies in neighbouring Barbados, St. Lucia, and Grenada. In the early eighteenth century, however, even this enclave succumbed to the slave trade as French colonial settlers exploited slaves on cotton, tobacco, sugar, and coffee plantations.

All of this was abandoned more than a century ago—or so thought sixteen-year-old Chantale, who left her native Saint Vincent with her mother to visit relatives in Canada. Much of what Chantale experienced on that visit appealed to her, and she responded with excitement when she heard of an opportunity to return to Canada—this time to babysit for a Vancouver family. She didn't realize that a modern form of servitude awaited her. Yet as soon as Chantale arrived, the children's parents seized her passport and forced her to work long hours in the home, performing many chores that had little or no relationship to babysitting.

By day she was isolated in the home and toiled long hours doing every domestic chore imaginable. By night the children's father sexually assaulted her time and again. A teenager from a foreign land, she had no one to turn to for help. When the children were old

Benjamin Perrin in rural Cambodia in 2001 as part of The Future Group's prevention campaign to educate children at risk of being recruited by sex traffickers. (Courtesy of The Future Group)

Children in Northern Thailand play at a day school where girls at risk are protected from being trafficked. (Kay Chernush for the U.S. State Department)

Photographs published by Interpol on October 8, 2007, in a bid to identify Christopher Paul Neil, a Canadian pedophile in Thailand, who had disguised his face digitally in the abuse images posted on the Internet. (Interpol)

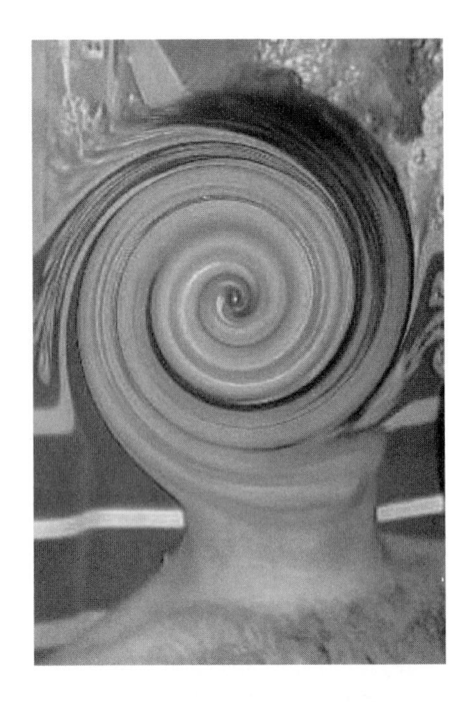

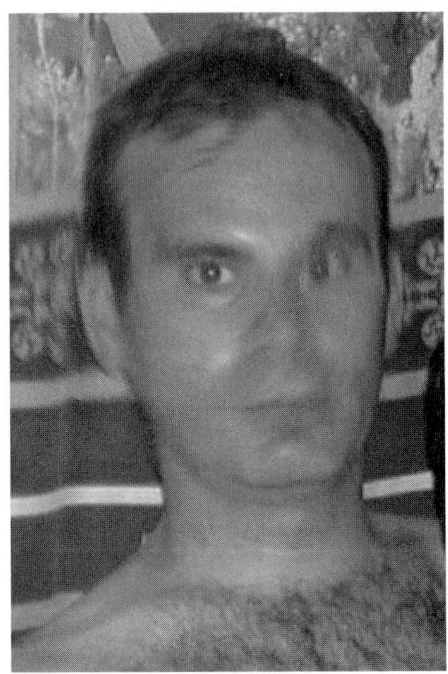

The "Elmvale 11" were forced to live in an abandoned farmhouse in Elmvale, Ontario, for two months until they were rescued by Filipino embassy officials. They came to Canada because they were promised good jobs but were instead exploited in what was called "a chain gang without the chains." (Dale Brazao/GetStock.com)

Vancouver Police Department Detective Constable Benedikte Wilkinson and Detective Ron Bieg were the key investigators in Canada's first child sex tourism conviction in the Donald Bakker case. (Martin Dee, courtesy of Vancouver Police Department)

The Hon. Monte Solberg introduced measures to protect foreign victims of human trafficking in Canada. (Courtesy of the House of Commons)

Grandmothers Protecting Our Children Council Walk in Winnipeg, Manitoba, 2008. Left to right: Velma Orvis, Mae Louise Campbell, Margaret Lavallee, Thelma Morrisseau. (Aaron Pierre)

Jessie Foster, Canadian woman missing in Las Vegas, Nevada. (Courtesy of Glendene Grant, mother of Jessie Foster)

Joy Smith, member of Parliament, has been a consistent advocate for victims of human trafficking and introduced Bill C-268 to crack down on child traffickers. (Courtesy of the House of Commons)

Manitoba's "Stop Sex With Kids" campaign targets the demand for sexual exploitation. (Courtesy of Canadian Centre for Child Protection)

Imani Nakpangi, Canada's first convicted human trafficker, 2008. (Illustration by Alex Tavshunsky)

The Hon. Irwin Cotler introduced the criminal offence of human trafficking in Canada. (Courtesy of the House of Commons)

enough to attend school full-time, Chantale was sent to Montreal to another family, where she endured the same harsh conditions as before: lack of income and free time, and once again, sexual abuse. The difference was this time Chantale became pregnant as a result of repeated rape, and when the pregnancy was confirmed, the family threw her out.

After almost a decade of exploitation and sexual abuse in Vancouver and Montreal, Chantale, just twenty-six, finally received a helping hand. She was brought to a shelter in Toronto, gave birth to a healthy baby, and found safety from her exploiters.

But the scars remain. "You can see when you talk to her," an NGO worker says of Chantale. "She acts like a child. You can see all [of] the trauma she has been suffering."

Indisputably tragic, Chantale's story isn't unique. Representatives of NGOs have described multiple forced labour cases involving victims as young as thirteen who come from the Democratic Republic of the Congo, El Salvador, Ghana, the Philippines, and Mexico, among others. Often victims were further isolated because they were illiterate or could not speak English or French. Their movements were restricted and their documents withheld; they were threatened with deportation, denied wages, overworked, and subjected to poor living conditions. Many, but not all, were physically or sexually abused, demonstrating that the line between forced labour and sex trafficking can sometimes blur. While the factors mentioned above are potential indicators of a forced labour situation, not all must be present in a given case.

## "Dirty, dangerous, and difficult"

International forced labour trafficking is a growing concern. For example, between 2005 and 2008, the RCMP's Immigration and Passport Branch (Northwest Region) received twenty-eight complaints of alleged human trafficking in Alberta, Saskatchewan, and Manitoba, many linked to forced labour practices. Foreign workers reportedly are sleeping on mattresses in factory storage rooms, are using garbage cans as wash basins, and are told to hand over their bank cards to employers, supposedly for "tax purposes."

Contrary to the expectations of many Canadians, victims of forced labour trafficking can be found across employment sectors in Western Europe and North America. These include agriculture, construction, cleaning, domestic work, and hospitality—industries that rely on "3D work," that is, dirty, dangerous, and difficult. Such jobs are low skill, offer similarly low wages, and require large numbers of flexible seasonal workers. Forced labour is defined under international law as "work or service which is exacted from any person under the menace of any penalty and for which the said person has not offered himself voluntarily." Experiencing what this legal definition meant was a harsh reality for two Filipina newcomers to Vancouver.

## Slave conditions in one of Canada's wealthiest neighbourhoods

The Vancouver neighbourhood of Shaughnessy has an average household income that's more than double the city average. In 2005, two Filipina women arrived at a home in this affluent neighbourhood as part of the federal Live-In Caregiver Program, which enables women to earn money legally by providing vital services for people who can't care for themselves. In Shaughnessy, however, the Filipinas found themselves in a situation that was not at all what they'd bargained for.

The women's employer forced them to work excessive hours, took away their immigration papers, and severely mistreated them. In addition, they lacked a proper place to sleep, feared for their safety, were constantly harassed by their employer, and are believed to have been sexually abused by him. The Live-In Caregiver Program contractually binds the worker to one employer, creating an imbalance that is conducive to exploitation and diminishes the opportunity to find alternative or better employment. With no options in Canada, the two women returned to the Philippines.

Cases of this sort are all too common, especially among members of the sizeable Filipino community who work in Canada's federal Live-In Caregiver Program. In one case, an abusive employer had allegedly mistreated at least six different caregivers over two years.

Many cases of domestic worker abuse are so outrageous, and leave the victims with so few options and protections, that they constitute a national disgrace. Records released by Citizenship and Immigration Canada (CIC) under the *Access to Information Act* revealed a case in Quebec in which a live-in caregiver was mistreated and passed back and forth among multiple families until she eventually was abandoned in an emergency room after having suffered a stroke.

Foreign nationals have also become victims of a form of abuse labelled "live-in exploitation," which exists outside formal immigration programs. This was the case with a young woman from Ghana we'll call Aba.

Sometime between 2002 and 2004, Aba was brought from Ghana to Canada on a visitor's visa and hired as a domestic servant for a Vancouver family. A woman in her thirties, she was treated at first like a nineteenth-century slave and later like a worthless object. Aba received no regular income or medical care during her years with the family—only room and board in their home. As well, she may have been physically mistreated.

Sister Deborah Isaacs of Sisters of the Good Shepherd, who eventually learned of Aba's situation, recounts the working conditions. "They'd taken her papers from her," Sister Isaacs explains. "She worked [an] enormous amount of hours.... The only thing she was allowed to do was go to church service a half a day a week. For her, some of the conditions were still better than Africa."

When the family decided to immigrate to the United States, they simply abandoned Aba as they might have done with an item of furniture or clothing they no longer wanted. "When they left, they threw her out on the street," Sister Isaacs says. "She had nothing. She had no money; she had no papers."

Aba was directed to MOSAIC, a non-governmental organization that helps newcomers to Canada. There she met Isaacs, who quickly saw that Aba's options were limited. "She was afraid to go back to her country," Isaacs notes, "and she didn't know what to do.... She was scared of the police." For their part, immigration officials could do nothing to help Aba obtain legal status and remain in Canada. Then Aba vanished, and no one knows what became of her.

## A false start on forced labour prosecutions

Despite forced labour allegations beginning to surface in Canada, there have yet to be any convictions for the crime. Senait Tafesse Manaye, a twenty-nine-year-old Ethiopian woman, was the alleged victim in the first human trafficking charges made under the *Criminal Code* to involve a foreign national. In May 2007, RCMP officials in Laval, Quebec, received anonymous tips from several people about alleged worker abuse. The tip-offs led to Nichan Manoukian and his wife, Manoudshag Saryboyadijan, being charged with trafficking in persons, receiving a financial or material benefit from human trafficking, and withholding travel or identity documents for the purpose of committing or facilitating trafficking. Manaye allegedly had worked for the couple for eight years as a live-in nanny, first in Lebanon and then in Canada.

According to the charges, Manaye was largely confined to the house where she worked long hours, was not allowed outside alone, and was denied access to her identity papers. In their defence, the accused couple claimed they had treated the alleged victim like family. Then without warning, on December 6, 2007, Crown prosecutor Isabelle Briand withdrew all charges against Manoukian and Saryboyadijan based on "new evidence." No details of this evidence were made public.

Following the withdrawal of charges, the couple demanded an apology from the RCMP and, in May 2008, filed a civil lawsuit against the federal force, Laval Police, and the Government of Quebec, seeking five million dollars in damages. Two years later, the lawsuit was still pending. Meanwhile, Manaye reportedly obtained refugee status in Canada and was not sent back to Ethiopia.

## "A chain gang, without the chains"

Any situation in which a worker can be isolated and controlled carries the risk of abuse, potentially leading to an intolerable master–slave relationship, as the Filipino men now known as the Elmvale 11 allegedly experienced in the summer of 2007.

The eleven men were attracted to Canada to help build two icebreakers for the Canadian Arctic for an advertised twenty-three dollars per hour, plus overtime, food, and lodging. The Canadian employer had obtained legal work permits, so the men had every reason to expect the terms would be honoured. Not only did they quit their jobs in the Philippines, but also many sold their belongings to cover their transportation costs and the recruiting agency fees, and some went deeply into debt.

Unbeknownst to the men, the project was cancelled before they'd even left Manila.

Upon arriving at Toronto's Pearson International Airport, the men were met by a woman who claimed to work for the Manila-based recruiting agency. She escorted them to a suburban Toronto home where they were confined in cramped quarters and slept four to a bed in the basement. The woman allegedly demanded their passports and work permits, then removed all telephones from the house and warned the now-confused Filipinos against attempting to contact their relatives. After having spent a week in these conditions, the men were informed that the shipbuilding arrangement had been cancelled. Instead of returning home, the men would work for a new "boss" at a company outside of the city.

Soon they found themselves at a filthy farmhouse in Elmvale—a hamlet near Barrie, Ontario, about one hundred kilometres north of Toronto. "Inside there was mud on the floor everywhere," recalls one of the men. "We had to spend a week cleaning it up." Their living space was cramped and food arrived only intermittently. When the workers questioned their "boss" about the situation, he retorted that he'd paid four thousand dollars for them and they should cease their complaints.

The Filipinos spent six weeks doing physical labour and menial tasks at bottling plants and on the rural estate where they were confined. The hours were horrendously long; at least two of the workers laboured on occasion for seventeen to twenty-four hours without rest. Only rarely were the workers permitted a day off, and they were never paid the wages promised. Complaints were met with threats of deportation. Finally, one worker managed to escape and contacted the local Filipino consulate, which in turn contacted the police, who launched a raid on the farm and rescued the other men.

From the perspective of the labour attaché at the Filipino consulate in Toronto, the treatment of the men entailed nothing short of slavery. "This was a chain gang without the chains," he commented.

No charges were laid in the Elmvale 11 case, even after months of investigation. The reason cited by authorities was, once again, the narrow definition of "exploitation" in the *Criminal Code*, which differs from the *Palermo Protocol* definition that Canada had agreed to adopt. "The way exploitation is phrased in the *Criminal Code*, they have to fear for their safety or their lives," says Constable Julie Meeks of the RCMP. In her opinion, "they just didn't have that fear."

As of June 2010, no one in Canada has been convicted of forced labour trafficking, despite the fact that authorities continue to discover growing numbers of such cases.

## Needed: A "source country" means of preventing forced labour trafficking

The federal government is starting to take steps to address the treatment of foreign workers based on a growing number of cases involving serious forms of labour exploitation.

At the international level, CIC says that "[i]mproving the integrity of the Temporary Foreign Workers Program, including worker protection measures, continues to be a priority." CIC officers stationed in embassies and consulates worldwide are involved in preventing human trafficking "through information-sharing and intelligence-gathering." In 2007, the federal government announced improvements to the Temporary Foreign Workers Program, which CIC says "will increase program integrity and reduce potential worker exploitation." While these efforts are laudable, concerns remain about the promise Canada holds for newcomers and the degree to which traffickers and profiteers misrepresent opportunities to vulnerable workers.

In October 2009, Jason Kenney, minister of citizenship and immigration, announced proposed changes to the Temporary Foreign Workers Program, including two important regulatory reforms to help protect foreign workers from mistreatment and abuse. First, officials will conduct "a more rigorous assessment of the genuineness of the job offer," including any past violations of labour laws by the employer. Second, employers who have "provided significantly different wages, working conditions or occupations than promised" will be banned from hiring temporary foreign workers for two years.

Monitoring and enforcement of employers will be vital to the effectiveness of these important preventative measures as will providing foreign workers with "whistle-blower" protections for reporting on offending employers (i.e., support in finding alternative employment and seeking redress for lost wages and misrepresentations).

Canada has taken action on behalf of other regions and continents as well. The Canadian International Development Agency has worked with the UN Interagency Program to address the issue of trafficking in the Great Mekong Sub-Region (which includes Cambodia, Laos, Myanmar, Thailand, Vietnam, and China). It also committed to provide three million dollars to combat trafficking in West Africa. Moreover, the government has funded prevention projects in Latin America and the Caribbean.

While these efforts are admirable, focused co-operation between Canada and its main source countries for human trafficking (i.e., the Philippines, China, Moldova, and Romania) should be enhanced to more effectively prevent the abuse. When engaging in diplomacy and development, Canada should encourage these source countries to improve their response to human trafficking. For example, the Canada Border Service Agency's Migration Integrity Officers and the RCMP's Liaison Officers should enhance co-operation to prevent human trafficking at the source country stage.

As has been emphasized throughout this book, human trafficking remains a global blight that must be eradicated on the same scale. This requires that Canada focus greater attention on the problem and co-operate more closely with affected countries.

# 15

# BATTLING TRAFFICKING ACROSS CANADA

The soft, steady beat of drums echoes through the streets of Winnipeg as more than a hundred people walk side by side from Thunderbird House to the Forks at Odena Circle. There a sacred fire is lit in the four directions. It will burn from sunrise until sunset.

This is the Grandmothers' Sacred Walk, an annual procession of Aboriginal women leaders who aspire to reclaim the streets of Winnipeg from child sexual abuse and exploitation. The grass-roots initiative began in 2007 when clan mothers, elders, and grandmothers formed Kookum Gaa Na Da Ma Waad Abinoojiig, the Grandmothers' Protecting Our Children Council. In the words of the group's founders, its purpose is to "emphasize the sacredness of children and the importance of keeping them safe.... We are here to say that despite our damaged and painful history, our hearts are not on the ground, our nations are not conquered, and we don't want to see our children hurt anymore."

Having decided that they could no longer passively witness the abuse in their midst, members of the community took it upon themselves to raise awareness and educate the public about the sexual abuse of First Nations children in Manitoba. They hoped that greater understanding would bring about change.

We can learn a great deal from the wisdom and inspiring example of the grandmothers. They understand that a broader response from our society is needed to end exploitation in its many forms. If we fail to prevent this exploitation, it will continue to threaten and destroy the hopes, dreams, and lives of many vulnerable individuals.

In the *Palermo Protocol*, Canada committed to initiating comprehensive policies, programs, and other measures to prevent human trafficking, including the following:

- establishing educational campaigns in co-operation with non-governmental organizations
- launching measures to improve the detection of trafficked persons at the border
- alleviating factors that make individuals vulnerable to trafficking
- discouraging the demand that fuels human trafficking

In pockets across the country, there are some encouraging examples of such initiatives. By profiling these programs, I hope to inspire a wave of new and expanded initiatives that could make Canada a global leader in preventing human trafficking.

## Prevention education and raising awareness

Chantal Fredette works for the provincially supported Centre jeunesse de Montréal—Institut universitaire, which developed the Cinderella's Silence program, introduced in Chapter 5. Reaching out to young girls who could be recruited by street gangs or others, the program explains the methods used to entice girls into sexual exploitation and the harsh realities that ensue.

Cinderella's Silence includes a detailed facilitator's handbook with discussion guide, relevant laws and statistics, information about victim psychology, lesson plans, activities and handouts, as well as contacts for resources. Targeted at youth between twelve and eighteen, the program is widely used. For instance, Projet intervention prostitution de Québec, which provides prevention programs in high schools, is one of the organizations that deliver Cinderella's Silence to about seven thousand students each year in and around Quebec City. Coordinator Anick Gagnon feels it is essential to reach students at an early age when they are the most vulnerable and having various first-time experiences.

In Manitoba, the "Stop Sex with Kids" campaign aims to prevent the sexual exploitation of children and youth through public awareness and education. Billboards, leaflets, and a powerful website portray tragic stories accompanied by shocking statistics from the provincial government, including the fact that an estimated four hundred children and youth are exploited each year in Winnipeg's street-based sex trade. While the majority are girls, boys are sexually exploited too. Yet whereas women's rape crisis lines and shelters are available in many communities, few, if any, similar services exist for sexually exploited boys and men.

Most sexually exploited youth in Winnipeg—as many as eight out of ten—are of Aboriginal descent, and the average age at which they were first violated is thirteen. Some were as young as eight, however. Almost three-quarters of those identified as sexually exploited children were at the time in the care of the provincial government's Child and Family Services, and more than 80 percent of child sexual exploitation is conducted in "gang houses" or "micro-brothels," small apartments or condos where the victims are isolated and to which johns are directed. Manitoba is one of the few provinces to mount a high-profile awareness campaign confronting demand.

At the national level, the Canadian Centre for Child Protection has developed excellent educational materials for children of all ages on topics such as sexual abuse and exploitation, and healthy relationships versus controlling ones, the goal being to build resistance to sexual predators. Unfortunately, however, most school boards across Canada have yet to incorporate the voluntary prevention materials into their curricula.

For its part, the federal government in recent years has launched modest awareness and educational initiatives to prevent foreign human trafficking. It produced an information booklet in fourteen languages for distribution in Canada and at embassies abroad that outlines the risks and warning signs of human trafficking. Citizenship and Immigration Canada has also distributed information about trafficking to temporary foreign workers and live-in caregivers, so that potential victims are familiar with employment, health, and safety standards.

In January 2009, Ottawa announced a partnership with the Canadian Crime Stoppers Association to raise awareness about human trafficking and to encourage tips about specific cases. Crime Stoppers is planning more public awareness efforts as part of the international "Blue Blindfold" campaign, which calls on citizens to acknowledge and report suspected human trafficking.

Public awareness about human trafficking is growing slowly, but a greater knowledge and understanding of the problem is needed, along with an appreciation of how to identify and assist victims and where to report suspected cases.

## Open to trade and tourism, closed to terrorists and traffickers

The pristine blue skies, billowing white clouds, and swaying fields of golden wheat in southern Alberta are the latest backdrop to the fight against modern-day slavery. Farmers and border-town communities are being asked to report to the Integrated Border Enforcement Team any suspicious activity along the province's expansive boundary with neighbouring Montana. IBET represents a joint Canada–U.S. multi-agency initiative to identify, investigate, and effectively eliminate illegal movement of people and goods across uncontrolled stretches of the forty-ninth parallel.

To the west, the border between British Columbia and Washington State has also been made less porous thanks to the efforts of IBET officers, including those who participated in the foiled transit trafficking case at Osoyoos, British Columbia, described earlier. Criminal networks moving women from South Korea through Canada and into the United States for sex trafficking have been further disrupted because of successful prosecutions in Washington State. Keeping up with the changing routes used by these criminal networks is a constant effort requiring extensive co-operation between Canadian and American authorities.

High-tech measures are also being used to extend the watchful eye of law enforcement and border agencies across remote stretches of the land border. Unmanned aerial "drones," or remote-controlled aircraft similar to those used in Afghanistan and Iraq, fly on the U.S. side of the shared border with Canada to beam real-time video images to analysts who may be thousands of kilometres away.

Just how effective are these cross-border programs and activities? We can only guess. Officials with the U.S. Human Smuggling and Trafficking Center, U.S. Immigration and Customs Enforcement, and the RCMP's Human Trafficking National Coordination Centre were unwilling to discuss any details of their joint efforts. In the absence of such information, independently evaluating their progress is impossible.

It is critical that Canada and the United States provide timely legal assistance to each other in confronting the problem of human trafficking. They must work together with source countries to dismantle entire criminal networks involved in human trafficking cases. It is not enough simply to prosecute the individual who moved the victims or directly exploited them in a sweatshop or brothel. A full investigation into all of the links in the trafficking chain is needed to take apart the criminal network. With anything less, the network can simply adapt and rapidly replace a convicted individual with another criminal.

Internationally, the CBSA Migration Integrity Officers network is trying to reduce illegal migration to Canada from over forty countries, including smuggling and human trafficking. The increased vigilance has led to a substantial increase in undocumented or illegal migrants with aspirations to come to Canada being intercepted in their native countries. Documents released by the CBSA under the *Access to Information Act* reveal that whereas only 30 percent of inadmissible persons attempting to enter Canada were intercepted overseas in 1990, the number had increased to more than 70 percent by 2005.

## Outreach to youth at risk

In 2009, the Assembly of Manitoba Chiefs received funding from the federal government to combat sexual exploitation and trafficking of Aboriginal women and children. That July, a conference organized by Grand Chief Ron Evans brought together front-line First Nations social workers, government officials, and police officers to develop programs to prevent these atrocities. The event received extensive media coverage and contributed to the provincial government's announcement that it would launch a task force to investigate missing and murdered First Nations women and underage girls in the province.

This general effort, having produced some early achievements, must be maintained. As Gord Mackintosh, Manitoba's family services and housing minister, puts it, "We are in a constant race to keep at-risk youths out of the clutches of sexual predators and street gangs."

As well, the Government of Manitoba continues to expand "Tracia's Trust," its Child Sexual Exploitation Strategy named after a fourteen-year-old victim. The $2.4-million strategy provides for increased resources to promote accountability of offenders who sexually abuse children and to raise awareness of the problem and develop services for victims, along with educational campaigns.

Also in Manitoba, StreetReach is a promising new initiative whereby community outreach workers help identify missing or runaway children and coordinate services to assist them, as well as track individuals suspected of sexually exploiting children. The program already has been credited with shutting down drug houses and other locations used to lure and exploit vulnerable youth.

Unfortunately, few other provincial governments have been similarly proactive—and yet prevention strategies are key to stopping human trafficking both in Canada and abroad. That's why the *Palermo Protocol* also includes an obligation for countries "to discourage the demand that fosters all forms of exploitation of persons, especially women and children, that leads to trafficking."

## Sex, car seizures, and videotape

Cars start circling the block as the sun begins to set. Like the men inside them, they're all makes, models, and years: luxury sedans, mid-sized cars, mini-vans, and vehicles whose next stop is the wrecking yard. Noticeably, some of the cars sport empty baby seats. The drivers seem like any others in the sprawling suburbs of the Greater Toronto Area, except they're not out for the evening air—they're cruising for women and girls.

On this night, the men have no idea that they're in the crosshairs of an undercover "reverse-sting" operation run by the Peel Regional Police, Vice Unit. Within a few hours, ten men will have been arrested for "communicating for the purposes of prostitution," meaning they negotiated for paid sex with an undercover police officer posing as a prostituted woman.

The female undercover (the "U.C.") has smudged her teeth, avoided washing her hair for several days, and put on worn-out clothes. The men know that prostituted women in the area are disadvantaged and can't afford proper dental care, so a woman with good teeth is a dead giveaway.

The entire operation takes place under the watchful eye of electronic surveillance equipment and fellow officers who will rush in if signalled by the U.C. To conceal her identity as a police officer, the U.C. is "arrested," along with the male perpetrator.

The prospect of arrest deters some but not all. One man arrested in this evening's operation will return again tomorrow night, intent on satisfying some desperate urge that costs him his money, his reputation, and perhaps his self-respect.

Such are the challenges of controlling street-level prostitution in the suburbs of Canada's largest city. To increase the deterrent effect of these operations, the Vice Unit resorts to other tools, including seizure of the vehicles used by the men. One officer comments, "We were seizing their cars after a sweep ... and we also brought a reporter along with us. It was all over the news: The police are stopping cars and seizing vehicles. How are they going to explain that to their wife?"

Another officer notes, "The registered owner has to go before a judge to get their car back. If a wife has to go to court to get her car back, she's gonna find out."

Similar operations are carried out sporadically in cities across the country. In November 2009, the Winnipeg Police Service announced the seizure of vehicles from thirty men attempting to purchase sex on the street, in some cases with underage girls. The men were charged with a range of offences, but their names weren't made public.

Undercover operations that include vehicle seizures are often a response to complaints by local residents about "strolls" (circuits where prostituted women are on display to men in vehicles), and they result in short-term police activity. A major limitation of these programs is that they target only street-level prostitution, just one avenue of exploitation. They don't reach behind the closed doors of brothels, strip clubs, massage parlours, or private residences, all of which are increasingly common sites where human trafficking victims are exploited and remain hidden.

## Taking false comfort in assumed anonymity

Purchasers of sex acts assume they're anonymous, especially when their activities take place indoors. They might be surprised to learn that a victim of human trafficking in a recent case in Canada kept a detailed logbook of her abuse: She recorded hundreds of telephone numbers, along with the dates and times of specific sex acts, as well as the amount paid. All the data went to the police when she was rescued. The underage victim kept this financial ledger to track how much money she'd given her trafficker, who claimed she owed him an exorbitant exit fee before she could leave. If the victim's clients were found, each would be liable under the *Criminal Code* for a minimum of six months in jail and up to five years imprisonment for paying for sex with a minor.

While it is illegal in Canada to communicate in a public place for the purposes of prostitution, the same is prohibited indoors only if the prostituted person is younger than eighteen. A public place is defined as anywhere to which the public has access by right or invitation, and includes a motor vehicle in plain view. From the perspective of trafficking victims being sold for sex, it is of course entirely irrelevant whether their trafficker advertised them in a public place or behind closed doors. Instead of defining the illegality by location, a more effective legal response would be to criminalize the purchase of sex acts regardless of where they take place. As we'll see in the next chapter, this technique has been used with some success in Sweden and is becoming an attractive international model. But what happens when johns are caught and convicted? John School furnishes one answer to this question.

## John Schools have no happy students but many informed graduates

As discussed earlier, John School attempts to discourage men from continually purchasing sex acts by confronting them with the consequences of their behaviour and the damage to the victims.

Vancouver, Edmonton, Winnipeg, Hamilton, Toronto, and Ottawa have used John Schools, or "First Time Prostitution Offender Diversion Programs," as part of their response to the demand for paid sex. The Toronto John School operates as a diversion program, which means that participation is open to "first-time, non-violent" offenders who've been charged with solicitation. In other words, the program is only available once to the accused, the first time he is apprehended for solicitation. If the accused completes the program, the prosecutor will withdraw the charges and the accused escapes with no criminal record.

According to Professor Alexis Kennedy at the University of Las Vegas, this program and others like it recognize that whereas the prosecution of offenders "may act as a deterrent, the social and community issues, along with the human consequences of prostitution, are largely ignored." John Schools typically require offenders to pay about five hundred dollars for a program—usually six to eight hours over one day. As one John School advocate puts it, "If they don't get the point in six hours, they won't get it in sixty." Many John Schools direct the fees to programs for victims. For example, Streetlight Support Services in Toronto applies the revenue from its John School to pay wages for female counsellors who are survivors of the sex trade and to fund programs that help women break the cycle of exploitation.

While each John School is unique, most cover the following key elements:

- laws and "street facts" on prostitution
- health awareness regarding risk and prevention of HIV/AIDS and other STDs
- effects on the community or neighbourhood and other victims
- survivor testimony from former prostituted women, and education on effects of prostitution on the lives of the women
- pimping / human trafficking
- child exploitation
- sex addiction

The Toronto John School uses real case studies to illustrate its points:

> Here's a guy who picked up a prostitute, went into a hotel room, got his trousers off, the door swings open, a couple of hooligans bust in, and the next thing you know not only has he lost his wallet and all of his identification, he's lost his clothes and now he's stuck at the hotel room, and he doesn't even have his car keys, and you know, so who you gonna phone?

The scenarios are "to scare the bejesus out of them," says John Fenn, who administers the Toronto John School. "We're starting to show them that they can be victims, too."

Survivor testimony and information about the effects of prostitution, as well as the reality of the sex industry and pimping, aim to dispel myths and fantasies. Fenn describes a "typical" survivor's testimony, delivered directly to the johns in the classroom: "She explains her story, how she got in, what it was like while she was there, the abuse on her, the johns, when business was bad what she needed to do to bring money in, the beatings, the whole scenario of what the world's really about. The branding, the cigarette burns, the sexual assaults by more than one man at a time, being in a room with a john and three of his buddies show up. It's hard to hear sometimes."

As well, community speakers try to connect with the johns who are also fathers, husbands, or neighbours to make them understand that this could happen in their communities, to their wives or daughters. "They tell the stories of ... the teenage daughter going to the corner and being harassed by a guy in a car thinking she may be a sex trade worker," says Fenn.

## Are John Schools an effective response or just window dressing?

Evaluations of the effectiveness of John Schools are based on participant surveys that measure changes in attitude toward prostitution and sexual exploitation throughout the program. Re-offence rates by participants have also been used to monitor the success of the programs.

The Vancouver Prostitution Offender Program recorded a significant increase in agreement with the following statements by participants who completed that city's John School classes:

- Prostitution is a serious problem in our society.
- Prostituted persons are victims of pimps.
- Most prostituted persons live in poverty.
- Prostitution exists because of the demands of the customers.

Evaluations of Toronto's John School are also encouraging. According to the program's directors, participants were more likely to accept responsibility for their actions, more likely to admit that they might have sex addictions, and less likely to report favourable attitudes toward prostitution.

The number of John School attendees who re-offend is also encouragingly low. Having completed the program at Toronto's John School, fewer than 2 percent of participants were subsequently arrested by police for solicitation.

Some critics question the validity of relying on this low rate of re-offence, however, suggesting it may be more attributable to the arrest itself than to the educational and awareness program exclusively. Being caught by police, appearing in court, and confronting the possibility that others could learn of their illegal conduct may suffice to discourage some johns from future offences. This explanation applies only to those John School programs that include arrests, charges, and court appearances, which not all do.

Alternatively, the low re-offence rates among John School participants could suggest that graduates understand more fully how police operate and are better able to avoid detection; or they may opt to purchase sex acts in non-public venues to conceal their ongoing activities.

On balance, the available evidence supports the effectiveness of John School as a preventative measure for first-time offenders. The program inspires other debates: Should attendance at John School be voluntary or should it be court-ordered? Should the police lay criminal charges against the men and only have those charges withdrawn upon completion of the John School program?

Proponents of John School as a pretrial diversion program believe it's more effective when the participants attend voluntarily because they have an incentive to complete the program. In some U.S. cities, the court also may order John School upon conviction, as a condition of the offender's sentence or probation. This also ensures that a criminal record is registered against the offender.

At the other extreme, Vancouver's Prostitution Offender Program offers John School to alleged offenders before charges are laid. Women's rights groups have expressed concern that this approach, which fails to expose and publicly condemn the behaviour, undermines the seriousness of the offence and doesn't serve as an effective deterrent.

Lee Lakeman of Vancouver Rape Relief believes that men caught for solicitation should not benefit from the privacy and secrecy of pre-court diversion. "Why are they getting diverted?" asks Lakeman. "If the police think that's such an effective sentence, charge the guy, convict him, and let's have the sentence be that. But why the secrecy? Why is he being protected? Why is his reputation being protected? Why are we all going along with that?"

Lakeman feels too that John School reduces the incentive for police to investigate further to determine whether or not more serious crimes also were committed. "So men in fact never ... get charged with any of the related crimes, including more serious charges," says Lakeman.

The criticism that Lakeman and others level at John School is not without merit. At the same time sending non-habitual, first-time offenders to John School before trial can help to change their attitudes and behaviour. So when and how should John School be used?

The police and the criminal justice system must address the role of men in driving demand for sexual exploitation and human trafficking to a greater extent than they currently do. A better approach would insist that men caught soliciting for the purposes of prostitution be arrested and charged with the offence in order to drive home the seriousness of their actions. If a man used a vehicle to commit the offence, it should be seized and released to the registered owner on a court appearance based on the relevant legal provisions. Moreover, police investigations should be complete before a Crown prosecutor decides how to proceed with a case, and a case that includes any of the following should always proceed to trial:

1 The accused previously has been arrested, charged, or convicted of any prostitution-related offences or violent crimes.
2 The accused is alleged to have solicited a minor under eighteen years of age, or a probable victim of human trafficking of any age, regardless of whether the accused knew, or suspected it.

3 The police investigation includes allegations of a more serious nature beyond solicitation.
4 The accused is unwilling to accept responsibility for his conduct.

If none of these factors are present, the Crown prosecutor should carefully review the evidence against the accused to determine whether or not John School represents an appropriate option as a diversion program, assuming the accused accepts responsibility for his conduct in open court and agrees to complete the program. In addition to attendance at John School, measures such as community service and donations to charitable organizations that assist victims of sexual exploitation should be requested by Crown prosecutors. Once the accused has completed this program, including the payment of the registration fee and any other terms, the charges against him should be withdrawn. Trial judges also should consider separate John School classes for convicted offenders as part of their sentences.

John School can be valuable in preventing first-time offenders from becoming habitual users of prostitution. However, a more complete response to prostitution and human trafficking is needed, including stronger laws against the purchasers of sex acts, wherever they take place; increased law enforcement efforts to investigate and arrest purchasers, both in public and indoors; routine use of car confiscation where available; greater media coverage of policing activities that target purchasers and of the harm caused by the commercial sex industry; and stronger sentences for convicted purchasers of sex acts, particularly repeat offenders.

Even these measures aren't enough in some circumstances. As we've seen, especially from my experiences in Cambodia, some purchasers of sex acts who target children seek to escape the scrutiny of Canadian authorities by travelling to poor and often-corrupt countries. Fortunately, many of the tools needed to bring these perpetrators to justice are already in place. They simply need to be applied more vigorously.

## Ending vacations for Canada's travelling child sex offenders

Canada's child sex tourism law is valid and enforceable, as discussed previously, but it requires more proactive implementation. A recent article of mine in the *Canadian Criminal Law Review* catalogued the existing treaties between Canada and child sex tourism destination countries—and it found that all of the necessary tools are in place to hold Canadian citizens accountable for child sex crimes abroad. What's missing are the political will and resources to implement those laws effectively.

To put it bluntly, Canada's record in prosecuting its child sex offenders abroad is an international embarrassment, especially compared with the proactive approach taken by countries like Australia and the United States. For years, federal law enforcement agents from both of these countries have been investigating, arresting, and prosecuting their nationals for sexually exploiting children abroad. The results speak for themselves.

From 1995 to 2007, the Australian Federal Police conducted 158 investigations into extraterritorial child sex offences committed by Australian nationals, resulting in 28 persons being charged and leading to 19 convictions, with several cases in process. Between 2003 and early 2008, U.S. Immigration and Customs Enforcement made 67 arrests under the child sex tourism provisions of the *PROTECT Act*, resulting in 47 convictions and others still being prosecuted. The United States has even caught Canadian citizens in its dragnet.

Canadian John Wrenshall, a sixty-three-year-old former Scout leader who had been convicted of sexually abusing young boys in Calgary, was free to travel abroad without any restrictions. He moved to Thailand in 2000 and became the mastermind of an operation that arranged trips for foreign pedophiles to sexually abuse children as young as four. Wrenshall's "customers" even photographed and videotaped their unspeakable abuse. Although Canada could have pursued Wrenshall, it was U.S. authorities that successfully prosecuted him in May 2010 because some of his "customers" were American.

"Unfortunately, we are totally dropping the ball," says Rosalind Prober, executive director of Beyond Borders, about Canada's inadequate enforcement of its travelling child sex crime legislation. "We seem to find ourselves able to prosecute cases that fall in police laps, but in terms of doing any sort of proactive work to stop this crime, Canada's doing absolutely nothing." Prober is pleased, however, that under U.S. law the sentence for Wrenshall likely will be substantial—over twenty years in jail.

Only four individuals have been convicted in Canada for child sex offences committed abroad between 1997 and 2010. In June 2008, the U.S. Department of State *Trafficking in Persons Report* specifically criticized Canada's progress in addressing child sex crimes committed by its nationals abroad and recommended that it "increase efforts to investigate and prosecute, as appropriate, Canadians suspected of committing child sex tourism crimes abroad."

The following October, the *Report of the Canada–U.S. Consultation in Preparation for World Congress III Against Sexual Exploitation of Children and Adolescents* also found "the lack of enforcement of the law against child sex tourism [to be] the most glaring law enforcement gap" in Canada's response to child sexual exploitation.

"Internationally, we've got to be set up better," concedes Staff Sergeant Rick Greenwood of the RCMP National Child Exploitation Co-ordination Centre (NCECC), who has publicly stated that police forces globally are "overwhelmed" with the number of child sex tourism cases.

Though Canada maintains RCMP liaison officers in sex tourism destination countries such as Thailand, these officers are assigned primarily to issues ranging from drugs to terrorism and money laundering. This contrasts with the mandate for liaison officers from other countries, which include child sex crimes on their priority list in global hot spots.

## "The whole system in Canada was asleep"

It took over a decade before Canadian authorities extradited Ernest Fenwick MacIntosh, a Canadian citizen, from India to Canada in 2007 to face charges of child molestation. During this period, his passport was renewed several times while he remained in India where he allegedly sexually abused two young boys. Canada's failure to take swift action confused and outraged Indian officials. "I don't understand why he was able to get a new passport, or why we weren't asked to arrest him sooner," says Inspector Awanish Dvivedi of the New Delhi Police. "It appears to me the whole system in Canada was asleep."

Canada routinely issues passports to convicted sex offenders, even since the MacIntosh incident. When these men pay hard currency abroad in exchange for sex with impoverished children, they power the local demand for human trafficking. Above all, in their quest to evade detection and prosecution, they gravitate to countries that are both poor and corrupt where they can abuse children with impunity.

International co-operation remains a key component in securing convictions for sexual exploitation and human trafficking. Interpol—with 187 member countries, the largest police organization in the world—is foundational in supporting international requests for information and assistance among countries with respect to these crimes. The Interpol International Wanted Persons notices, or "Red Notices," can be issued to facilitate the apprehension of suspects before the filing of formal extradition requests. Red Notices are supported by detailed arrest warrants issued by national judges and contain information about fugitives, including physical descriptions, photographs, and fingerprints, as well as occupations, languages spoken, specifics of identity documents, and other details. The Red Notice system played a vital role in the 2007 identification and apprehension of Canadian Christopher Paul Neil in Thailand, a case discussed earlier.

"Green Notices" are another Interpol tool. They help prevent previously convicted child sex offenders from travelling abroad and re-offending by equipping all Interpol member countries with warnings about the presence of known offenders. Since 2006, the United States has had a separate criminal offence for convicted child sex offenders who fail to notify their government of travel abroad. The notification must be made twenty-one days before travelling to a foreign country, and again on the convicted offender's return to the United States. The law also requires that appropriate authorities in the relevant foreign country be notified, leaving them to decide whether or not to admit the individual.

Canada has yet to take decisive action to restrict and punish offenders who fuel commercial sexual exploitation and human trafficking abroad. Convicted sex offenders from Canada are free to roam the globe. Their vacation must come to an end.

# 16

# DEALING WITH TRAFFICKING ON A GLOBAL BASIS

While this book focuses on Canada's failure to effectively combat human trafficking, the crime is global and demands a coordinated response. Countries around the world have addressed human trafficking in various ways and with diverse results. Some are complicit in the crime, while others punish and blame the victims. Many simply ignore it.

A growing number of countries, however, are no longer content to condone human trafficking through inaction. Their strategies to protect victims, prosecute offenders, and prevent the crime are worth reviewing, evaluating, and considering for adaptation by Canada and other nations.

Belgium, Italy, the United States, and Sweden offer innovative examples of laws, policies, and programs that have succeeded in fighting human trafficking. Each signed the *Palermo Protocol* in December 2000 and quickly moved to meet its commitments under that international treaty. While none have eliminated human trafficking completely within their borders, all have made tremendous progress. They continue to invest money and effort in ending the abuse, often through unique approaches that have saved thousands from a lifetime of suffering. These countries have created national action plans, backed up with funding and resources for victim services and specialized police and prosecutors. They have created human trafficking offences that reflect the *Palermo Protocol*, recognizing subtle means of coercion used by traffickers and highlighting the particular vulnerability of child victims. These initiatives have brought hope to survivors and accountability to their exploiters.

Although Canada signed the *Palermo Protocol* in 2000, its response has instead been slow, tentative, and poorly coordinated. Canada can learn much from the techniques and successes of other countries.

## Belgium: A small country with a big plan

With just ten million people in a country roughly the size of Vancouver Island, Belgium has been an innovator in tackling human trafficking as a priority crime issue. In 2007, the Belgian government reported 1204 active human trafficking investigations and secured 223 convictions.

Belgium's position between the United Kingdom and continental Europe makes it a key transit zone for human trafficking. The country thus was among the first to respond to the problem, setting standards in the early 1990s and adopting its first human trafficking legislation in 1995, more than a decade before Canada's human trafficking offence in the *Criminal Code* came into force.

Belgium and the United Kingdom have co-operated in maintaining tight security and detection efforts at major seaports in their respective countries. Additionally, the United Kingdom imposes high fines on shipping companies who bring illegal migrants into its jurisdiction—so far with good results. This coordinated approach involving both government agencies and private corporations is unique.

Belgium also has updated its legislation to comply with the *Palermo Protocol* and to facilitate the prosecution of offenders. Belgium's *Penal Code* states that human trafficking occurs with the "recruiting, transporting, transferring, housing, [or] receiving [of] a person, as well as passing or transferring control exercised on the person concerned" to enable sexual exploitation, labour exploitation, and exploitation of organs. In other words, human trafficking takes place when any of the actions is for exploitation.

Threats, physical violence, or the victim's age are not considered elements of the crime, but all serve as factors that could increase the sentence for a convicted trafficker. In contrast, since Canada's human trafficking offence in the *Criminal Code* requires the victim to have a fear for safety, a human trafficker convicted in Belgium could escape punishment in Canada for committing the same act.

Belgium's approach facilitates prosecutions by recognizing that traffickers may control their victims in a variety of ways. The elements of the offence that require proof are straightforward, and the length of the sentences may vary depending on the means used by the trafficker. These well-conceived laws help explain why Belgium has been effective in prosecuting traffickers, but they are by no means the only reason.

## Protecting victims and encouraging co-operation with law enforcement

Belgium has provided temporary residence status to foreign victims of human trafficking since 1994, twelve years before Canada. The law requires that front-line officials who make initial contact with suspected victims present them with available options, including the possibility of obtaining legal immigration status, and refer the individuals to a specialized "reception centre."

Of 495 adults referred to the reception centres in 2008, 202 subsequently were identified as potential trafficking victims and 169 received some form of residency status. These centres are privately operated but coordinated and funded by government. They offer shelter and guidance to victims, as well as psychological, social, legal, and medical assistance. Representatives from the reception centres are the only people authorized to apply for residence permits on behalf of trafficking victims, ensuring they operate both as specialized advocates for victims and as a preliminary screening measure for potential cases.

A permit for a forty-five-day protection period can be granted at the outset so that a trafficking victim is able to begin recovery and regain stability. This has proven most useful for individuals who initially do not identify themselves as victims, who distrust authorities, or who fear reprisals from their traffickers. It also allows victims to decide whether or not they wish to co-operate with authorities. Should victims choose to file criminal complaints during this time, they can apply to remain in Belgium; if they choose not to make statements against their alleged abusers, then they typically must return to their home countries when the period expires.

A renewable three-month special residence or renewable six-month temporary residency permit may be issued, depending on the status of the investigation, along with a work permit, if necessary.

When criminal proceedings are complete, victims may also apply for permanent residency, which is granted based on the significance of the information they contributed to the criminal procedures, whether their complaints led to convictions, the degree to which they've adapted to Belgian society, and similar concerns. In some cases, residency may be granted before an investigation is over.

On the advice of child protection officers, children may also apply for residence as foreign "unaccompanied minors" if they do not meet the requirements for trafficking victims. One study on the treatment of 889 unaccompanied minors found that although about 15 percent were required to leave the country within five days, more than 80 percent were issued identity documents and referred to child protection officers for assessment.

Belgium's approach to human trafficking has been described as "the result of a compromise between two concerns: on the one hand there is the necessity to offer to the victims a series of measures for aid and assistance; on the other hand there is the fight against persons and networks involved in trafficking in human beings."

Victims of human trafficking who return to their countries of origin may seek assistance from the International Organization for Migration (IOM). This assistance typically consists of temporary housing and care, psychological follow-up, and guidance toward education and/or vocational training. These are important protective measures to ensure victims are not as vulnerable to being re-trafficked when they return home. Canada's failure to co-operate similarly with the IOM is putting victims at risk.

### Specialized police and prosecutors

Belgium has approximately five hundred police specialists in human trafficking, federally and locally. An additional thirty officers who develop and implement action plans to combat human trafficking and migrant smuggling comprise the country's central human trafficking unit. Specially trained public prosecutors and labour auditors are appointed for each judicial district to ensure that suspected cases of human trafficking are prosecuted.

Criminal proceedings in Belgium depend primarily on written statements. As a result, victims and witnesses rarely are obligated to testify against their traffickers in court. Should the victims' presence prove essential, the law permits audiovisual statements in order to minimize the victims' fear of testifying against their abusers.

The Belgian system is not without flaws. The initial residence permit for foreign victims has been criticized for its infrequent use, and in some cases the evidence in support of trafficking charges has been inadequate, perhaps because front-line workers encouraged victims to press charges quickly and take advantage of a secure residence status. Nevertheless, Canada can learn from Belgium's holistic approach.

### Best practices from Belgium

- Create human trafficking offences based on the *Palermo Protocol* that are straightforward to prove, with stiffer penalties for offenders who employ egregious means and whose victims are minors.
- Make human trafficking a priority crime with specialized police officers and prosecutors to investigate and prosecute offenders.
- Provide victims with access to a range of services for recovery and rehabilitation, as well as "victim-friendly" procedures to ease their role in the prosecution of their traffickers.
- Co-operate with the IOM to assist with the voluntary return of trafficking victims, thereby reducing the risk of re-victimization.
- Collaborate with neighbouring countries and private companies to disrupt transit trafficking.

## Italy: Counting on non-governmental allies

A powerful strategic alliance between NGOs and the Italian government has proven effective in combatting the country's serious human trafficking problem. In contrast to Canada, NGOs in Italy have worked more directly and co-operatively with police and government officials to help identify trafficking victims and then offer them assistance and protection.

### Development of an NGO network of support services

In 1998, the Italian government enacted legislation recognizing key roles for NGOs to protect and assist victims of human trafficking. The resulting Programme of Social Protection and Assistance committed to financing projects that are directed by accredited NGOs, such as faith-based organizations and women's groups. This unique approach encourages a countrywide collaborative network. In 2008, U.S.$9.41 million in funding supported sixty-six victim assistance projects.

Through this program, survivors of human trafficking receive a variety of support services, including counselling, health care, legal assistance, shelter and protection, social support, Italian lessons, vocational guidance and training, and assisted return home at the victim's request.

The services run by the NGOs include several kinds of shelters: short-term emergency facilities, second-care shelters for stays of a few months while the victims become stabilized, "autonomy houses" for victims starting to work and waiting to find their own housing, and alternative housing where victims live with families or other support groups. Minors often are placed with families for longer-term recovery.

NGOs seek to break the cycle of exploitation that ensnares survivors. In developing vocational training programs, for example, an NGO called "On the Road" avoids economic sectors that are unstable or traditionally linked with marginalized categories, such as domestic labour. Instead, based on their individual skills and with support from psychologists or tutors, victims work as trainees or interns in reputable companies. While the program covers salary and social security costs, companies may elect to hire victims after training. The program's employment rate is an impressive 90 percent.

NGOs, supported by funding from the Italian government, provided literacy courses for 588 victims and vocational training for 313, while helping 436 find temporary jobs and 907 locate permanent work in 2007 alone. In the same year, the Ministry of the Interior issued 1009 residence permits to victims who assisted in a law enforcement investigation, and the government ensured the safe return of 62 foreign trafficking victims, funding the costs of repatriation, reintegration, and resettlement in their home countries.

## Innovative measures to identify victims

Italian law allows foreign trafficking victims who are at risk of exploitation to obtain renewable six-month special residence permits. Victims can seek to convert these to regular residence permits for work or education and eventually apply for permanent residency. Between 2003 and 2006, about 950 foreign victims annually were granted residence permits. Child victims of trafficking receive automatic residence permits until they are eighteen.

NGOs and Italian police effectively identify trafficking victims and refer them for care and assistance. One NGO, Transnational AIDS Prevention Among Migrant Prostitutes in Europe Project (TAMPEP), sends out *unita di strada* (street units) whose members are from the same ethnic background as women and girls commonly trafficked to Italy. For example, a Nigerian "cultural mediator" is in place because until 2005, more than half of the 1575 trafficking victims assisted by TAMPEP were from Nigeria.

These street outreach teams identify likely victims of violence and trafficking, establish trust, and offer them health information and testing along with general guidance. Inside health clinics, social workers inform the victims of their rights and options for assistance.

Outreach units play a further role in sensitizing local authorities to the problems of trafficked persons, and in mapping the pattern of arrivals, departures, and prolonged stays of potential victims. They also strive to create networks in given areas to reach those victims "behind closed doors" who are harder to identify—a significant initiative because the sex industry in Italy is increasingly concealed.

Police officers also receive training in identifying and assisting victims. In 2006, a report from an independent commission found that government measures were not fully effective in identifying victims on boats arriving from North Africa. In response, the government began to allow international organizations and NGOs to inspect detention facilities and interview migrants.

### Collaboration in prosecuting human traffickers

In 2007, when the Italian Ministry of the Interior created a committee to improve the process for convicting human traffickers, it invited NGOs to join the assessment and policy-making committees. In Canada, however, NGOs and federal government agencies rarely interact and often are suspicious of each other.

Italian prosecutors also have won the co-operation of victims of human trafficking in denouncing their exploiters, a development that some NGOs attribute to the recovery period and services available before testifying. In some cases, victims chose to testify after consulting with other victims who had done so. As one Italian judge noted, "[T]he trafficked women want to act as witnesses because once they are confident about their own situation, once they know that they are protected, that they can get a job, they want their traffickers to be punished."

### Best practices from Italy

- Provide funding to develop a network of support services to assist trafficking victims, and to encourage collaboration between NGOs and the police.
- Help trafficking survivors break the cycle of exploitation through short-term recovery and long-term rehabilitation, including job training and employment with private companies.

- Give special consideration to child trafficking victims in obtaining legal immigration status.
- Implement innovative measures to identify victims using ethnic and community-based outreach teams.

## The United States: Life, liberty, and the pursuit of happiness

Over the past decade, the United States has invested hundreds of millions of dollars, improved legislation, and launched innovative programs to confront what it views as modern-day slavery—both a tarnish on the legacy of President Abraham Lincoln's Emancipation Proclamation and a violation of the Thirteenth Amendment to the U.S. Constitution, which abolished slavery. President Barack Obama has recently recognized the ongoing problem: "Sadly, there are thousands who are trapped in various forms of enslavement, here in our country.... It is a debasement of our common humanity."

### Comprehensive laws to combat human trafficking

President Bill Clinton signed the *Trafficking Victims Protection Act of 2000* (TVPA) into law just six weeks before the United States committed to the *Palermo Protocol*. Moreover, the TVPA has been reviewed and updated in 2003, 2005, and 2008 in response to ongoing monitoring of results and increased understanding of the problem. Traffickers readily adapt to meet changing circumstances, but so, too, has Congress.

By comparison Canada, which signed the *Palermo Protocol* one day after the United States, has yet to enact any federal legislation remotely as comprehensive as the TVPA.

The TVPA includes educational and public awareness campaigns and assures victims of access to federally funded social services like health care, housing, education, and job training. In fact, foreign victims of human trafficking qualify for the same federal and state services as refugees.

From 2001 to 2008, the U.S. Department of Health and Human Services certified assistance for 1696 foreign trafficking victims, about 10 percent of them minors; since 2002, the number of foreign victims receiving assistance each year has increased steadily.

Case management for victims has emerged as an important step in helping them recover and achieve self-sufficiency. A case manager links the trafficking victim to the services, programs, and support required, often becoming the first and sometimes the only person whom the victim trusts.

The TVPA also created the "T-visa," which permits foreign trafficking victims to remain in the United States as temporary residents, allowing for permanent residence after three years. To obtain this assistance, foreign victims are required to co-operate with U.S. law enforcement, but this does not mean they must testify publicly against their exploiters. Between 2001 and 2008, more than 2300 T-visas were issued to foreign victims of human trafficking and members of their immediate families. In 2008 alone, 394 foreign victims of human trafficking applied for T-visas, and 80 percent were approved. Trafficking victims also can qualify for the Witness Protection Program.

The TVPA's tough criminal laws hold traffickers accountable for their crimes, especially when their victims are under eighteen. Furthermore, unlike Canada's *Criminal Code*, U.S. law recognizes "the subtle means of coercion used by traffickers to bind their victims into servitude, including psychological coercion, trickery, and the seizure of documents." The TVPA also specifies no need to prove child victims were subject to force, fraud, or coercion, but if they were, higher penalties apply. Again, Canada's criminal offence of human trafficking is much narrower, limiting its effectiveness.

In 2007, the U.S. attorney general created a special Human Trafficking Prosecution Unit. Its mandate includes providing technical expertise and training to police agencies, along with legal support during the investigation of major cases. From 2001 to 2008, the U.S. Department of Justice, Civil Rights Division and Attorneys'

Offices, prosecuted 531 alleged human traffickers. Of these, about 28 percent were charged with labour trafficking and the balance with sex trafficking, resulting in 419 convictions. Almost one thousand new human trafficking investigations have been launched. The average sentence for cases involving adult victims was nine years and four months, with the maximum being fifty years imprisonment. These prosecutions also led to traffickers having to pay millions of dollars to their victims.

## Bipartisan support for improving the response

The United States has not treated human trafficking simply as another partisan issue. While President Bill Clinton originally signed the TVPA, President George W. Bush signed into law the *Trafficking Victims Protection Reauthorization Act of 2003* (TVPRA), which expanded the TVPA. This law created stronger provisions to prosecute travelling child sex offenders and to help trafficking victims sue their traffickers. It also requires an annual report from the attorney general to Congress evaluating the progress of the United States in combatting human trafficking. The TVPRA also authorized two hundred million dollars (U.S.) for projects to combat modern-day slavery.

In 2005 and again in 2008, the TVPA was reauthorized and expanded to fund new victim rehabilitation services, support state and local efforts, and enhance the criminal offences. To ensure political attention, a Cabinet-level task force chaired by the U.S. secretary of State was created to coordinate federal counter-trafficking efforts, in addition to a senior policy group to keep bureaucrats on task.

## U.S. Human Trafficking Task Forces

Human Trafficking Task Forces (HTTFs) are financed by the U.S. Department of Justice in forty-two jurisdictions. They bring together key players from federal, state, and local agencies, as well as non-governmental victim services organizations, to investigate cases and assist victims. Locally, some police have also formed task forces and working groups to confront human trafficking more effectively.

A 2008 study by Northeastern University confirmed that task forces produce results. Jurisdictions with task forces have identified and investigated more than double the number of cases of non–task force jurisdictions, and these were twice as likely to result in federal charges than offences investigated by non-task force jurisdictions.

In spite of the many successes, the Office of the Inspector General found in July 2008 that not all HTTFs were performing acceptably. Improvements in oversight were introduced, many of them to local programs dealing with regional issues or concerns.

## Proactive initiatives on the front lines

Some of the best ideas to combat human trafficking in the United States have come from those on the front lines.

In Boston, the police department introduced a process to identify youth at risk for sex trafficking and to give priority to those most in need of immediate intervention. Through this new system, one hundred and fifty girls were identified and twenty were rescued.

In Dallas, Texas, police officers with specialized knowledge of child sexual exploitation and human trafficking are assigned to cases of potential victims. Whenever a victim comes to the attention of police officers, they contact the relevant detective, whose ongoing relationship with the victim increases the prospects that she will disclose information about her exploiters. The detective also ensures that child protection services and other providers offer assistance to the victim.

The Innocence Lost Initiative targets child commercial sexual exploitation and trafficking throughout the United States. Since its launch in 2003, the program has grown to twenty-eight dedicated task forces and working groups across the country, which bring together state and federal law enforcement, prosecutors, and victim service providers to expose child sex trafficking, prosecute the perpetrators, and rescue the victims. In the first five years, the initiative secured convictions against over 350 traffickers and associates who were exploiting children through prostitution. The ongoing success of the program comes in part from its ability to launch a national "blitz" that draws attention to human trafficking. For example, in October 2008, the Federal Bureau of Investigation coordinated an operation involving 630 police officers, which succeeded in rescuing 49 children, between thirteen and seventeen years of age, from sexual exploitation. Of the rescued children, 10 had been identified as missing. All now have the chance to rebuild their lives thanks to this highly focused and coordinated effort.

The National Human Trafficking Resource Center operates a toll-free twenty-four-hour hotline to accept tips on suspected human trafficking. If the caller may be a victim, the call centre gives them information about local services that can help. Interpreters are available to assist callers. Although the centre receives some government funding, it is operated by the Polaris Project, an NGO; this arrangement encourages callers who would not contact a law enforcement or immigration hotline. The hotline averages four hundred calls per month, plus email inquiries.

Having become aware that technology facilitates sexual exploitation, police are developing innovative ideas to identify and prosecute purchasers of sex acts in the United States. Sting operations on the internet have led to the identification and arrest of would-be purchasers of sex acts with minors.

In another initiative, front-line police officers, social workers, and health care professionals receive training through the "Rescue and Restore" campaign developed by the U.S. Department of Health and Human Services, which provides toolkits, training materials, posters, brochures, fact sheets, and pocket cards about human trafficking—all online. Other community-based efforts have shown some positive results. In Florida, for example, local organizations are performing outreach where trafficked persons likely are being exploited. Many communities are using building and restaurant inspectors, along with officers in alcohol and tobacco enforcement, as effective partners in spotting potential victims of trafficking. All of these initiatives contribute to a nationwide and comprehensive attack on human trafficking that is increasing public awareness.

### Best practices from the United States

- Create legislation that recognizes the insidious methods used by traffickers, with higher penalties for child trafficking.
- Support multi-agency Human Trafficking Task Forces, with NGO involvement, to identify cases in specific cities and regions.
- Develop proactive initiatives at the local police level to identify potential victims by building trust and offering help.
- Establish a special team of prosecutors to litigate human trafficking cases and routinely seize proceeds and assets of the crime, with compensation paid to victims.
- Ensure that foreign victims of human trafficking are eligible to receive at least the same services as refugee claimants.
- Provide case management to help individual victims navigate the maze of services they need to rehabilitate and make decisions about their future.
- Launch targeted public awareness and educational campaigns about the warning signs of trafficking and provide a 1-800 number and website for easy access to information and to report tips.
- Ensure that victims are eligible for the Witness Protection Program to protect them from their traffickers.

## Sweden: It's more than Ikea

Sweden is increasingly winning acclaim for tackling the demand for sex trafficking. In 1999, the country pioneered a creative way of addressing the link between human trafficking for sexual exploitation and prostitution: Rather than criminalize those who are sold for sex, the country held the purchasers of sex acts liable for their activities. Purchasers thus face fines or imprisonment of up to six months, and the Swedish government has implemented a comprehensive national plan of action to help those who are exploited.

The so-called Swedish model is gaining traction because it promotes the equality of women and has documented successes in confronting and dealing with sexual exploitation. As in other countries, prostituted women in Sweden suffer from poverty, substance abuse, and control by human traffickers. In response, the Swedish government recognizes prostitution as an institution of male violence against women that cannot be tolerated or condoned.

Swedish policy also recognizes that it is impossible to address human trafficking for sexual exploitation without dealing with prostitution and vice versa. We saw previously how purchasers of sex acts either do not know, or do not care, whether the women or underage girls they are purchasing have been trafficked, thereby contributing to these often interrelated problems.

Sweden also seeks to educate men and prevent them from purchasing sex acts. Those convicted of soliciting sex are assigned to KAST groups (*Köpare Av Sexuella Tjänster*, or Purchasers of Sexual Services) to encourage them to change related attitudes and behaviours.

## Comprehensive national action plans

To implement its national action plan, Sweden allocated 213 million Krona (Cdn$32.2 million) to fund numerous initiatives to comprehensively address prostitution and sex trafficking. In addition to evaluating and enhancing measures directed at purchasers of sexual services, the national action plan is helping women and children being sold for sex to escape exploitation. Initiatives include the following:

- increasing support and rehabilitation for victims of trafficking for sexual purposes
- intensifying substance abuse and addiction care services for women exposed to prostitution
- supporting programs that target adult substance abusers and young people at risk of prostitution or trafficking for sexual purposes
- mandating the Crime Victim Compensation and Support Authority to evaluate the processing of compensation for criminal injury
- promoting a safe return to their countries of origin for victims of prostitution and trafficking for sexual purposes

Having become law over a decade ago, the Swedish model has succeeded in prosecuting purchasers of sex acts, deterring human traffickers from operating in Sweden, and changing public attitudes toward women in the sex industry.

From 1998 to 1999, the number of women in street prostitution reportedly decreased from 280 to 170 in Stockholm, from 286 to 90 in Göteborg, and from 160 to 80 in Malmö. By 2008, over 500 men had been charged with purchasing sex acts in Sweden. The head of Sweden's national human trafficking unit estimates that the overall number of women being sold for sex in the country dropped by 40 percent between 1999 and 2003. By 2007, according to one Stockholm police officer assigned to the sex trade, between 105 and 130 women were estimated to be prostituted in his city, whereas in Norway's capital, Oslo, the estimate was 5000.

A 2005 study commissioned for the European Parliament on the impact of prostitution legislation on human trafficking found that traffickers were having problems finding enough sex buyers in Sweden, confirming earlier evidence of traffickers expressing frustration about the difficulty of selling women in Sweden.

Traffickers in Sweden must be very discreet. "They can only run two or three women at a time," one Swedish police officer notes with some satisfaction, "and they have to keep moving around because neighbours complain to us." The Swedish National Police also believe that Swedish law serves as a barrier to the establishment of trafficking in human beings in that country.

The symbolic effect of the Swedish model may be even more important than the pressure it has put on the sex trade. Prohibiting the purchase of sex sends a clear signal that women are not objects to be bought and sold. Indeed, the holistic approach likely is the key. Raising awareness is emphasized as much as enforcing the criminal law. A 2002 national public opinion poll found that 80 percent of the population supported the law and its principles.

Other countries will have to do more than rubber-stamp the Swedish model to achieve similar success. One international observer noted, "[W]ithout significant investment in programs designed to undercut patriarchal hierarchies and promote the equality of women, the program is destined for failure."

### Best practices from Sweden

- Recognize that purchasers of sex acts fuel sex trafficking and that the sexual exploitation of females is unacceptable in a free and equal society.
- Criminalize the purchasers of sex acts, but not those who are sold.
- Invest in programs that increase public awareness about women's equality and help prostituted and trafficked persons "exit" their exploitation.
- Provide support for prevention services for those at risk, including substance abuse and detox programs.
- Shift attitudes toward women and children to reduce demand for purchasing sex acts and make the country less attractive as a destination for human traffickers.

### Sweden's approach versus legalizing prostitution

Since purchasers of sex acts are the principal cause of human trafficking for sexual exploitation of women and children, how should the law deal with them?

Countries worldwide are fiercely debating how to address prostitution, including Canada, where legal challenges have been mounted against laws prohibiting aspects of the activity. One side argues that prostitution is a form of male violence against women—the world's oldest form of *oppression*—that must be abolished. The other side claims that prostitution is a form of commerce that should be recognized, taxed, and regulated.

Laws are important for at least two primary reasons. First, they state the values of a society. Second, they can produce positive changes within society over time. The evidence indicates that Sweden's approach is more compelling on both of these fronts.

Margareta Winberg, deputy prime minister of Sweden, describes her position and her country's:

> I argue that any society that claims to defend principles of legal, political, economic and social equality for women must reject the idea that women and children, mainly girls, are commodities that can be bought and sold. To do otherwise is to allow that a separate class of females, especially women who are economically and racially marginalized, is excluded from the universal protection of human dignity enshrined in the body of international human rights instruments developed during the last fifty years.

Dr. Melissa Farley, a clinical psychologist and researcher who has studied human trafficking and prostitution in nine counties, concurs. "Prolonged and repeated trauma precedes entry into prostitution," Dr. Farley points out, "with most women beginning prostitution as sexually abused adolescents. Homelessness is frequently a precipitating event to prostitution.... [W]omen in prostitution are frequently raped and physically assaulted." She has found, too, that 85 to 95 percent of people being sold for sex "want to escape it but have no other options." Proponents of legalized prostitution, whose positions are threatened by Dr. Farley's findings, attack her research.

Those who suggest that society accept and condone the purchase of sex acts deny a central truth: The vast majority of those sold for sex are women and children who have experienced physical and sexual abuse, substance issues, poverty, racial inequality and, in cases of human trafficking, the use of force, fraud or coercion—often in combination.

In Australia's state of Victoria, where prostitution is legal, it is a punishable offence for people being sold for sex to offer their "services" if they have an STD. No requirements exist, however, for male clients to be tested for STDs. This one-sided regime acts to protect purchasers from STDs, but not those who are being sold. Illegal brothels also inevitably exist because many prostituted women fail the health tests.

Victoria's regulatory approach has not prevented human trafficking. In June 2010, the Victorian Parliament's Drugs and Crime Prevention Committee identified "a clear and close connection between sex trafficking and the legal and unregulated sex industry." It also recognized "growing concerns" about the prevalence of sex trafficking, finding evidence that the state capital of Melbourne is second only to Sydney—the largest city in the country—as a destination for sex trafficking in Australia.

Legalization normalizes the purchase of sex acts, sanctioning the prerogative of men to treat women as commodities—and the state, in its role as tax collector, serves as pimp. "When legal barriers disappear, so too do the social and ethical barriers to treating women as sexual merchandise," says activist Dorchen Leidholdt.

Claims that legalized prostitution will exclude criminal elements are also false. Amsterdam's red light district has had vast sections shut down due to serious concerns about the infiltration of organized crime and human trafficking. At one point, the city was investigating more than eighty violent pimps. As well, more than three-quarters of the women being sold for sex in Amsterdam reportedly hail from Eastern Europe, Africa, and Asia, often from economically depressed regions or continents where full equality for women is a distant prospect.

The 2005 report commissioned by the European Parliament, mentioned earlier, found that legalized prostitution generally results in *higher* levels of violence. In the Australian state of Victoria, officials have warned that escort workers who are alone in an unfamiliar environment may encounter "unpredictable client behaviour." In New Zealand, officials say that regulation of the sex trade has not improved conditions in brothels with a history of problems and that exploitative contracts continue to be used.

In short, it is impossible to simply *regulate* the abuse, misery, and exploitation out of the commodification of women and girls as mere sexualized objects. The social experiment of regulated prostitution has failed miserably and done nothing to stop human trafficking.

In contrast, Sweden's innovative approach aims to *abolish* sexual exploitation by criminalizing sex act purchasers and offering help to those being sold. In July 2010, an independent inquiry headed by an eminent judge resoundingly endorsed the Swedish model in a much-anticipated report entitled *Prohibition of the Purchase of Sexual Services: An Evaluation, 1999–2008.* It found that the Swedish model has disrupted organized crime, deterred sex act purchasers, changed public attitudes, and cut street-level prostitution in half. Plus it found no evidence that the problem simply moved indoors as some skeptics had speculated.

Importantly, the inquiry also found nothing whatsoever to suggest that Sweden's abolitionist model had negatively affected those being exploited. It recommended sustaining support for those being sold, creating a national centre against prostitution and human trafficking, and doubling the maximum penalty for purchasing sex acts to up to a year in prison.

Sweden's approach is growing in popularity and has recently spread to neighbouring countries like Norway and Iceland, such that it is now called the "Nordic Model." In Ottawa, the House of Commons Standing Committee on the Status of Women has recommended adopting the Nordic Model, as have numerous Canadian NGOs, women's groups, and faith-based organizations. In the words of a British NGO, the model offers "a broad and progressive political vision … that actually aims to end the exploitative industry of prostitution rather than legitimise it, which essentially ends up expanding it."

# 17

# BUILDING A NEW UNDERGROUND RAILROAD

*I'm on my way to Canada*
*That cold and distant land*
*The dire effects of slavery*
*I can no longer stand—*
*Farewell old master,*
*Don't come after me.*
*I'm on my way to Canada*
*Where coloured men are free.*

—"THE FREE SLAVE," GEORGE W. CLARK (CIRCA 1850)

In the mid-nineteenth century, an extensive network of secret paths and safe houses, known as the Underground Railroad, formed the escape route to Canada for fugitive slaves from the United States. Over thirty thousand slaves travelled this path north on foot or by wagon, seeking liberty for themselves and their families. Abolitionists developed a code language to help slaves avoid detection—they called Canada "The Promised Land."

Some one hundred and fifty years later, Canada is no longer a safe haven from exploitation but rather a destination for human trafficking. Once again, we have a moral duty to protect and assist the exploited, whether they are foreign nationals or Canadian citizens. The time has come for Canada to resume its role as a defender of freedom.

## A draft national strategy gathers dust

In 2002, the federal government created the Interdepartmental Working Group on Trafficking in Persons (IWGTIP) to coordinate Canada's response to human trafficking. Its mandate was to propose a national plan of action by 2005. While multiple drafts of *A Federal Strategy on Trafficking in Persons* have been circulating in the bureaucracy for years, none have been adopted yet.

The House of Commons Standing Committee on the Status of Women has also recommended that the federal government work with the provinces to create a comprehensive strategy to tackle human trafficking—again to no effect. In 2007, the entire House of Commons unanimously passed a motion introduced by MP Joy Smith calling for the same. However, no strategy has been adopted.

When I discovered that human traffickers literally had manuals on how to recruit and control victims, and how to maximize profits from their abuse, I realized Canada was in serious trouble: Whereas traffickers in human lives have a plan, Canada does not.

As this book reveals, human trafficking has taken hold across the country and is thriving due to a lack of a coordinated response from federal, provincial, territorial, and municipal governments. Canada must take greater steps to ensure that traffickers are prosecuted, victims are protected, and this assault on fundamental liberties is stopped. But government alone cannot solve the problem. The solution lies in a community response—and the realization that we all share in the responsibility to end trafficking and restore Canada as a safe and prosperous society for all of its citizens and newcomers.

Central to the country's failure to deal with human trafficking is a lack of leadership and accountability. Although the IWGTIP comprises seventeen government departments, it is a lethargic and ineffective body with no funding and no independent authority; it does not consult regularly with NGOs, nor does it have the ability to coordinate provincial and territorial efforts. After eight years, the IWGTIP has failed to produce results, leaving Canada significantly behind other countries in confronting this problem.

Victims of human trafficking have paid the price for this inaction over the decade since Canada signed the *Palermo Protocol.* We have only to recall a few described in this book: Natalie, who at eleven was locked in segregated immigration detention in Montreal for a month due to a lack of appropriate housing; Katya, whose two-decade nightmare of sexual abuse ended only when she was dumped outside a hospital in Edmonton, her life shattered; Genevieve, who felt stupid reporting her trafficker to police—he was released within days of being convicted.

To significantly enhance Canada's response to human trafficking, I am proposing action at all levels, from the federal government down to individual citizens, including every reader of this book.

The more we pretend that human trafficking does not occur or that we bear no individual responsibility in battling it, the closer it will come to our own front doors—as it already has for parents like Glendene Grant, whose daughter Jessie Foster, a likely victim of human trafficking, is still missing in Las Vegas.

## Leadership from the federal government

The Canadian government must take the steps below, following the lead of other countries worldwide, to make combatting human trafficking a national priority:

### Step one: A national action plan

Canada must create an effective, well-funded, and proactive federal bureau to combat human trafficking as a first step toward getting serious about eradicating human trafficking within its own borders. The bureau should be staffed with top officials possessing specialized expertise and mandated by the Privy Council Office; the latter would assist the bureau in coordinating other government departments and agencies, as well as liaising with provincial governments.

With sufficient funding, the bureau should meet the following objectives:

1. *Develop a National Action Plan to Combat Human Trafficking for approval by the federal Cabinet within a year.* The bureau should organize a series of federal/provincial/territorial meetings, including consultations with NGOs, to develop an effective plan. The National Action Plan should highlight time-sensitive objectives; propose necessary legislative, regulatory, and policy reforms; establish funding requirements; and identify strategic priorities to assist in the prosecution of traffickers, the protection of victims, and the prevention of human trafficking generally.
2. *Support the implementation of the National Action Plan to Combat Human Trafficking and monitor progress* by government departments, agencies, and provincial governments.
3. *Administer the Canada Freedom Fund,* a new federal fund to support counter-trafficking programs in areas of greatest need across the country and abroad. There are examples of excellent community programs in Canada that could be expanded for greater impact; for example, Cinderella's Silence in Quebec and the StreetReach program in Manitoba, both discussed in Chapter 15.
4. *Report quarterly to the federal Cabinet and annually to Parliament* on progress and further action needed to combat trafficking in persons. The annual report to Parliament should include up-to-date data on prosecutions for trafficking in persons, the status of foreign victims granted temporary and permanent residence in Canada, progress on the National Action Plan, and identification of priority areas for the bureau to address in the forthcoming year. The bureau would gather statistics and monitor investigations with assistance from the RCMP Human Trafficking National Coordination Centre (HTNCC), Department of Justice, Citizenship and Immigration Canada, Canada Border Services Agency, Criminal Intelligence Service Canada, and Statistics Canada.
5. *Ensure respect for victims' rights* by working with the federal ombudsman for victims of crime to complete a public report

about the challenges faced by victims of human trafficking in Canada, with recommendations to ensure their proper and fair treatment. In particular, the ombudsman should investigate whether the treatment of domestic and foreign trafficking victims complies fully with the Canadian Statement of Basic Principles of Justice for Victims of Crime.

## Step two: Enact stronger and more effective laws

The definition of "exploitation" in the *Criminal Code*'s human trafficking offences should be amended to recognize the subtle means of coercion used by traffickers, including all of those identified in the *Palermo Protocol.* As discussed in Chapter 12, the current fear for "safety" requirement is too narrow. Where the victim is under eighteen, there should be no requirement to prove that any particular method was used to exploit the child for sex acts or forced labour.

Penalties for child trafficking, in particular, must reflect the particularly grave nature of this crime. The recent passage of Bill C-268 is a major step in achieving this goal. To make certain that child traffickers are held responsible, Crown prosecutors need to ensure that appropriate charges are laid and sufficient sentences sought.

Canada's current laws do not adequately punish purchasers of sex acts who fuel human trafficking and sexual exploitation. The laws on solicitation for the purposes of prostitution of adults apply only in public places and carry a summary conviction offence suited to a minor transgression. The *Criminal Code* should be amended as follows to emulate Sweden's pioneering approach to addressing demand:

- prohibit the purchase of sex acts wherever they take place;
- make the offence prosecutable either by summary conviction or a more serious indictable offence at the discretion of the prosecution;
- ensure that penalties increase with each subsequent offence;
- provide more stringent penalties for purchasing sex acts with a minor.

Preventing Canadian men from driving the demand for human trafficking through sexual exploitation of women and children abroad must also receive greater attention. Amending the *Criminal Code* so that convicted sex offenders must give notice of their intent to travel abroad and using the Interpol Green Notice system to warn the destination country would enable that country to decide whether or not to admit the offender. If an offender failed to notify the relevant authorities, the omission would be detected readily when the offender sought to re-enter Canada or renew his passport abroad—and it would rank as a serious offence. With this system in place, individuals like child sex offender John Wrenshall of Calgary would not have been allowed to travel abroad freely on a Canadian passport and to organize child sex tours in Thailand for Western pedophiles.

Convicted sex offenders should be required by law to disclose their internet accounts and social networking website profiles to the RCMP National Child Exploitation Coordination Centre. In turn, the NCECC should be authorized to share this information with social networking websites such as Facebook and MySpace, who have agreed to remove sex offenders from their listings. Offenders convicted of human trafficking, sexual offences against minors, or those who have used the internet to facilitate sex crimes should be prohibited from accessing social networking websites as a mandatory condition of probation.

## Step three: Ensure victims are protected, not criminalized

The House of Commons Standing Committee on the Status of Women studied how prostitution laws should be reformed to address sexual exploitation and human trafficking. Having heard the evidence of dozens of witnesses, as noted earlier, the committee recommended that Canada adopt the Swedish approach and abolish criminal offences that punish individuals who are sold for sex acts. As seen in Chapter 16, these individuals should instead be granted support and treated with dignity and respect, not punishment and censure. The time has come for Canada to take this step as well.

The treatment of victims of human trafficking also requires attention. In October 2003, federal, provincial, and territorial ministers of justice established principles to ensure proper treatment of victims of crime. These tenets must also be applied to human trafficking victims:

1 Victims of crime should be treated with courtesy, compassion, and respect.
2 The privacy of victims should be considered and respected to the greatest extent possible.
3 All reasonable measures should be taken to minimize inconvenience to victims.
4 The safety and security of victims should be considered at all stages of the criminal justice process and appropriate measures should be taken when necessary to protect victims from intimidation and retaliation.
5 Information should be provided to victims about the criminal justice system and the victim's role and opportunities to participate in criminal justice processes.
6 Victims should be given information, in accordance with prevailing law, policies, and procedures, about the status of the investigation; the scheduling, progress, and final outcome of the proceedings; and the status of the offender in the correctional system.
7 Information should be provided to victims about available victim assistance services, other programs and assistance available to them, and means of obtaining financial reparation.
8 The views, concerns, and representations of victims are an important consideration in criminal justice processes and should be considered in accordance with prevailing law, policies, and procedures.
9 The needs, concerns, and diversity of victims should be considered in the development and delivery of programs and services, and in related education and training.

10 Information should be provided to victims about available options to raise their concerns when they believe that these principles have not been followed.

Canada should also adopt legislation to provide foreign trafficked persons with temporary and, in appropriate cases, permanent residence. The current system relies on a ministerial policy decision that does not afford certainty or the permanence of legislation—a concern cited by numerous NGOs. A better system for providing temporary residence for trafficking victims would improve relations among NGOs, law enforcement, and CIC, which are strained in several regions of Canada; for instance, in Alberta, where the RCMP and Changing Together had to fight for Thérèse to remain in Canada after she'd been enslaved in the Democratic Republic of the Congo and then was transported here for even greater profit for her "owner."

The *Immigration and Refugee Protection Act* should be amended in the following ways:

- A "protection permit" should be issued for an initial period of up to six months when a specially trained immigration officer has reasonable grounds to suspect that an individual may be trafficked according to the *Palermo Protocol* definition. The narrower definition of human trafficking currently in the *Criminal Code* and IRPA should *not* be used as some have proposed.
- If police officials and NGOs believe that an individual is a trafficked person, their views should carry significant weight with the immigration officer.
- Immigration officers should minimize the number and duration of interviews for a trafficked person; in some cases, if a trafficked person has already given an interview or statement to police, a separate interview by immigration officials could be forgone.
- The decision to renew protection permits for trafficked persons should rely on the same criteria as those for the temporary

residence permit guidelines for trafficked persons and not require co-operation with law enforcement.

- Whenever immigration officials decide to interview an alleged or suspected trafficked person, they should provide a translator and allow the individual to be accompanied by a support person of his or her choice in addition to legal counsel, if available.
- Trafficked persons holding protection permits should have access to the Interim Federal Health Program, emergency counselling, and work permits for their duration, including any renewals. Further, the fees that usually apply to any of these applications/permits should be waived.
- If a suspected or confirmed trafficked person wishes to return home, Canada should work with the International Organization for Migration (IOM) to reduce the risk of re-trafficking associated with voluntary repatriation.
- If concerns arise over the safety of foreign trafficked persons, they should be treated similarly to those under witness protection.
- Canada's immigration regulations should be amended to state explicitly that foreign trafficked persons who cannot be at large in the community for reasons of personal safety should be accommodated in facilities that are appropriate to victims, i.e., not in correctional or immigration holding facilities. Placing victims like Svetlana and Dina in immigration detention while they await return to their home countries deepens the trauma for women who have fled their traffickers, only to find themselves confined by border officials.
- Protocols between the Canada Border Services Agency (CBSA) and provincial child welfare authorities must be reviewed, updated, and monitored to ensure that suspected trafficked children obtain immediate access to a child advocate and assistance from child protection officers.

## Step four: Enhance federal law enforcement capacity to investigate trafficking

The RCMP Human Trafficking National Coordination Centre must go beyond raising awareness and providing training to actively targeting and disrupting human trafficking operations in Canada; provincial, regional, and local police forces must co-operate in these initiatives. There are some indications that this shift is slowly taking place in pockets of the country, but resources for detecting human trafficking through undercover operations, wiretaps, and international investigations are currently insufficient.

Similar to the U.S. Human Trafficking Task Forces, integrated law enforcement teams of RCMP, provincial, and municipal police should be tasked with dismantling particular criminal organizations and networks that are engaged in human trafficking on a systematic basis. Specialized integrated child exploitation units already in place as well as the RCMP Centre for Missing and Exploited Children should also collaborate with these teams. The House of Commons Standing Committee on the Status of Women recommended that funding be given to establish such counter–human trafficking police units that operate across multiple jurisdictions. The need for this is clear: Failure to mount a coordinated police response will only shift the problem elsewhere. As we've seen, violent street gangs like North Preston's Finest have expanded throughout southwestern Ontario and into Western Canada, due in part to increased enforcement activity in Peel Region outside of Toronto.

At a higher level, Canada, the United States, and Mexico should work together to help address the movement of trafficking victims across North America's borders. Along the forty-ninth parallel, Integrated Border Enforcement and Intelligence Teams should increase activities to detect and identify illegal border crossings. Further training in identifying victims in transit is necessary, along with greater public awareness in border regions about human trafficking. Prosecutors on both sides of the Canada–U.S. border should work together to dismantle international trafficking networks, while NGOs should co-operate more closely to meet the needs of cross-border victims.

Cracking down on Canadian child sex offenders travelling abroad must be a priority for the RCMP National Child Exploitation Coordination Centre. The NCECC should be given the mandate and resources to take the lead in enforcing Canada's extraterritorial child sex crime legislation. Similar to initiatives by the Australian Federal Police and U.S. Immigrations and Customs Enforcement agency, RCMP liaison officers should be stationed abroad in established child sex tourism destinations to investigate Canadian citizens and permanent residents who are sexually abusing children there. In addition to identifying and charging Canadians committing child sex crimes abroad, the officers should develop relationships with NGOs in key destination countries and receive support from committed Crown prosecutors to ensure the prompt processing of extradition and mutual legal assistance requests.

## An action plan for provincial and territorial governments

While some provincial governments have recognized the problem of human trafficking and their responsibilities to assist and protect victims, many continue to ignore their obligations. It is particularly alarming and unacceptable that the most populous province, Ontario, has no comprehensive system in place to assist trafficking victims. To combat human trafficking, provincial and territorial governments should ensure that they take the following steps:

- Designate a single point of contact for each region within a province to coordinate services for domestic and foreign victims of human trafficking—either a government office like the B.C. Office to Combat Trafficking in Persons or an NGO like ACT Alberta. Victims cannot be expected to navigate the bureaucracy of governmental and non-governmental programs designed to assist them and risk falling through the cracks. Every known victim should be assigned a case manager who will be an independent advocate and support person throughout recovery and reintegration, assisting the victim to make decisions and access needed services from NGOs and government.

- Review provincial laws, regulations, and policies, amending them as necessary, to ensure that both foreign and domestic trafficking victims are eligible for protection services, shelter, health care, legal advice and representation, and economic assistance, all of it culturally, age, and gender appropriate. Foreign victims should receive at least the same services as refugee claimants.
- Combat the demand for human trafficking by funding police investigations that target sex act purchasers, including their arrest, prosecution, and car confiscation where a vehicle is used in the commission of the offence.
- Establish guidelines for the use of John Schools, as proposed in Chapter 15; draw on child protection legislation to investigate and prosecute suspected purchasers of sex acts with minors; and launch public awareness campaigns about the harms associated with purchasing sex acts.
- Fund and support "exit" programs that help prostituted persons leave the sex industry. This assistance should include detox support and counselling, job training, employment opportunities, and housing support.
- Train front-line professionals (nurses, child protection officers, social workers, immigration settlement agencies, and NGOs) in how to detect and assist victims of human trafficking as well as conduct outreach to affected communities, particularly First Nations and ethnic communities.
- Incorporate preventive educational information about child sexual abuse and exploitation into school curricula. The Canadian Centre for Child Protection has already developed age-appropriate material for this purpose.
- Ensure that both foreign and domestic victims of human trafficking are eligible for criminal injuries compensation

programs and other victim support services and that they are able to sue their abusers under provincial law.

- Train Crown prosecutors about new human trafficking offences and appoint specialized lawyers to prosecute the crime.
- Amend Crown prosecution manuals to include guidelines for human trafficking cases that ensure the rights of victims are respected and prosecutors recommend sentences to reflect the gravity of this crime. Prosecutors should be instructed to demand the seizure and forfeiture of all assets and proceeds of the crime, as well as to seek restitution (compensation) for victims as part of the sentence handed down against convicted traffickers and their accomplices.

## An action plan for local police

Local police officers in our cities and towns are key front-line players in the battle against human trafficking. Most municipal police forces in Canada, however, do not have sufficient resources and officers to combat human trafficking and commercial sexual exploitation in their communities, allowing traffickers to operate with impunity.

The International Association of Chiefs of Police and others have called for greater resources and action by local police forces to identify and investigate human trafficking. In Canada, local police forces should adopt the following measures:

- Conduct department-wide training on human trafficking for dispatch staff, school liaison officers, and new recruits, among others.
- Educate the community about the crime of human trafficking.
- Identify government and non-profit agencies that assist victims, and develop collaborative relationships.
- Contribute to integrated law enforcement teams that identify, assist, and protect victims, and to investigate and prosecute their traffickers.

- Increase capacity in vice units, including resources and officers for investigating human trafficking and sexual exploitation.
- Provide specialized training for vice unit officers, including victim identification, investigative tactics, analysis of psychological effects and the mindset of trafficking victims, and advanced interviewing techniques.
- Investigate suspected cases of human trafficking within their jurisdiction, including online, and liaise with neighbouring police agencies.
- Initiate sting operations to prosecute individuals attempting to purchase sex acts, using relevant legislation to seize vehicles used in the commission of the offence.
- Recommend charges of human trafficking when reasonable grounds exist to believe the offence has been committed, and assist with actions to seize the proceeds of the crime and charge associates of the trafficker.
- Reach out to at-risk individuals and potential victims through youth intervention programs, school liaison initiatives, and protocols like those used by the Boston and Dallas police forces, as discussed in Chapter 16.
- Ensure that officers who respond to prostitution-related complaints or reports of domestic disturbances document and investigate possible indicators of human trafficking.

## An action plan for businesses

Sweden's experience has proven that law enforcement agencies alone cannot eradicate exploitation. Since social, cultural, economic, and often racial factors play a part, involving a wide cross-section of society in the battle against human trafficking can reduce its incidence and impact. So what about private enterprise? Human traffickers use hotels, taxicab companies, airlines, websites, weekly magazines, and so on to facilitate their crimes—frequently without the knowledge of these companies.

Almost fifteen thousand companies worldwide have signed the *Athens Principles to End Human Trafficking Now*, a global initiative launched by Egypt's first lady, Suzanne Mubarak. The goal is to acquire millions of signatories by enlisting the companies supplying the offenders to ensure they play no part in human trafficking. The Athens Principles commit companies to the following:

1. explicitly demonstrate the position of zero tolerance toward trafficking in human beings, especially women and children, for sexual exploitation
2. contribute to prevention of trafficking in human beings, including awareness-raising campaigns and education
3. develop a corporate strategy for an anti-trafficking policy that will permeate all corporate activities
4. ensure that personnel fully comply with the anti-trafficking policy
5. encourage business partners, including suppliers, to apply ethical principles against human trafficking
6. call on governments to initiate a process of revision of laws and regulations that are directly or indirectly related to enhancing anti-trafficking policies
7. report and share information on best practices

Sex traffickers use some specific businesses, including travel and tourism, to exploit their victims, and many such businesses have begun to take action. The Code of Conduct for the Protection of Children from Sexual Exploitation in Travel and Tourism (www.thecode.org) is an example of a sector-specific initiative to combat sex trafficking of children. Tourism service companies that adopt the code agree to

1. establish an ethical policy regarding sexual exploitation of children
2. train the personnel in the country of origin and travel destinations
3. introduce a clause in contracts with suppliers, stating a common repudiation of commercial sexual exploitation of children

4 provide information to travellers by means of catalogues, brochures, in-flight films, ticket slips, homepages, etc.
5 provide information to local "key persons" at the destinations
6 report annually to the Code of Conduct Secretariat

As of November 2009, a total of 947 companies in 37 countries around the world had signed the Code of Conduct. Unfortunately, among Canadian firms, only the Association of Canadian Travel Agencies and Incursions Voyages (Quebec City) have signed on so far.

All companies should have explicit corporate policies that prohibit employees from purchasing sex acts while travelling on company business or when using corporate assets. The policy should be clear that disciplinary action, up to and including dismissal, is the consequence. Companies that are even more proactive have partnered with NGOs to offer training and jobs to survivors of human trafficking.

## An action plan for parents

Criminal networks in Canada frequently recruit underage girls for sex trafficking, in some cases making initial contact through social networking websites. "Kids in the Know," an online resource guide from the Canadian Centre for Child Protection (www.kidsinthe know.ca), offers age-appropriate information and strategies to help protect children from sexual abuse and exploitation. It provides parents with ideas on how to talk with their children about sexuality, dating, and the internet.

Understanding the difference between a loving relationship and a controlling one is among the most difficult and important challenges for young people who are starting to date—often years before their parents may know about their activities. As we've seen, domestic sex traffickers routinely seek to convince their victims that they are in boyfriend–girlfriend relationships, while the attention is merely part of the psychological manipulation or grooming process.

We learned in Chapter 15 that the Canadian Centre for Child Protection has developed an entire curriculum for school-aged children and made it available to school boards. If your child's school has not included education on preventing child sexual abuse and exploitation in the curriculum, you or your parents' advisory council could insist that it take this important step.

### Internet safety for kids

Few parents would let their children go out alone late at night in the worst part of town, yet children with unrestricted access to the internet are at comparable risk. Cybertip.ca recently listed the following top five risks to Canadian children on the internet as a result of actions by sex offenders:

1 targeting online games with chat rooms
2 hijacking instant messaging (IM) accounts and coercing children to send nude or partially clothed images of themselves, a practice that has doubled in recent years
3 using 3-D animated characters (avatars) to engage youth in online conversations
4 invading social networking sites where children and youth are encouraged to create online diaries and connect with new people
5 encouraging youth to send nude images to peers without understanding the images could be forwarded or permanently posted online

In response to these risks, the Family Online Safety Institute (www.fosi.org) has developed the "Family Online Internet Safety Contract," which sets out expectations and commitments from both parents and children to ensure a safe online experience.

Parents should discuss safety tips with their children and warn them about the risks of life online. The following tips for Canadian children and youth come from the "Kids in the Know" campaign:

- Keep your personal information to yourself and off the internet.

- Check with your parents before sending any photographs online.
- Obtain your parents' approval before meeting someone in person whom you met on the internet. Remember to meet in a public place and bring a trusted adult with you.
- Inform your parents before entering a chat room. Remember that people on the internet are not always who they say they are.
- Trust your instincts. If something does not seem right or makes you uncomfortable, speak to a trusted adult.
- Talk with your parents about what you are doing online and who you are speaking with.

## Community responses save lives

Identifying and assisting victims of human trafficking takes a community response from NGOs, faith-based organizations, and average Canadians. In January 2010, four Filipina women were rescued in Vancouver with the help of members of a Roman Catholic Church, a local NGO, the police, and the B.C. Office to Combat Trafficking in Persons (OCTIP). Their exploitation could very well have continued, however, had it not been for an average Canadian who first identified the case.

In 2009, the four women had entered Canada legally in response to a promise of work from a businessman in Calgary. Once in the city, however, they were confined to a hotel owned by their "employer," and their passports were seized. He demanded that the women work up to sixteen hours a day—and for little pay—as cleaners and in the hotel gift shop. Heavily supervised, they were unable to interact with outsiders during work hours and then were transported to a second location at night. They were directed to clean their employer's home and provide manicures, pedicures, and massages to the employer and his family. Any complaints about their treatment produced threats.

In late 2009, the four women were transported to a hotel in Vancouver, also owned by their employer, where they performed the same services under the same conditions, except that they were permitted to attend church on Sundays. Fortunately, a member of the church congregation who recognized the signs of human trafficking befriended the Filipina visitors. The Filipinas confided enough in this woman to set off warning bells, and she put them in touch with a member of the church who was part of a committee to stop human trafficking.

The church contacted Robin Pike, executive director of OCTIP, who acted promptly. Within twenty-four hours, the Filipinas were in a specialized NGO shelter and had access to a lawyer. CIC swiftly issued temporary residence permits for the women, who qualified as forced labour trafficking victims with access to the Interim Federal Health Program. Meanwhile, the hotel owner fled Canada with the women's passports.

This case, in which community members collaborated in treating the women as victims, not criminals, should serve as a model for future initiatives. The road to freedom for these Filipinas started with an average Canadian who knew enough about human trafficking to glimpse the invisible chains that bound these women, even as they knelt in church asking God to help them.

## An action plan for you

If you've read this far, you know the horror and extent of human trafficking, and the trauma and damage it inflicts on children and adults all over the globe and right here in Canada. Now you can set this book aside ... or you can do something about it.

Here are the top ten initiatives you can take to fight human trafficking:

1 *Tell someone.*
Share what you've learned in this book with a family member, friend, or colleague.

2 *Help the heroes.*
Support organizations that help survivors by volunteering your time, language abilities, or professional skills. Donate money,

clothes, or equipment to them, and perhaps plan a fundraising event to help one of the organizations listed in the Appendix.

3 *Raise awareness.*
Host an awareness event with your friends, work associates, church group, or service club to tell them about human trafficking and commit to doing something to address the problem.

4 *Call for change.*
Email, call, or write a letter to your municipal, provincial/territorial, and federal politicians asking what they're doing to address the problem of human trafficking, and ask them to implement the recommendations for government shown above—they're supposed to be working for you, after all.

5 *Take a stand.*
Become an advocate for at least one recommendation in this book that you personally want to see adopted. The will to end exploitation must be marshalled for laws, policies, and programs to be reformed as part of the solution.

6 *Let your dollar talk.*
Buy fair trade products where possible and, if you can't be sure, avoid products whose makers are notorious for using forced labour, as shown below:

*Global blacklist of forced labour trafficking products*
A 2009 report by the U.S. Department of Labor identified 122 common goods from 58 countries that ranked among the worst for forced labour or child labour. The most problematic were cocoa, cotton, and rubber. Here are ten products made by forced labour trafficking victims (for a weblink to the complete list, see the Notes at the end of this book):

Brazil nuts from Bolivia
Christmas decorations from China
Coffee from Côte d'Ivoire
Diamonds from Sierra Leone
Garments from Malaysia
Gold from Burkina Faso
Cocoa from Nigeria
Rice from India
Shrimp from Thailand
Sugarcane from the Dominican Republic

7 *Speak up.*
Raise the issue of human trafficking in letters to the editor, at political debates, in the classroom, and at town hall meetings.

8 *Be a woman against human trafficking.*
Talk to your husband, boyfriend, partner, or male friends and family members about the realities of women and girls exploited in the sex industry.

9 *Be a man against human trafficking.*
Don't pay for sex or go to places where commercial sex acts take place, either in Canada or when travelling abroad, and discourage your friends from doing so if you're invited to go along to such places. Explain your concerns.

10 *Report it.*
Be aware of the warning signs of human trafficking in your community, at work, and when travelling. Report suspicious activity to your local police or Crime Stoppers by calling 1-800-222-TIPS (8477). You can also report online child sexual abuse imagery, child sex tourism, child trafficking, and child luring to the Canadian Centre for Child Protection at www.cybertip.ca. Don't just stand idle when you suspect that someone may

be a victim of exploitation. Call the police immediately. If you wait, it may be too late. We know that traffickers move victims frequently to avoid detection—help the police get one step ahead of the offenders.

## Restoring Canada's promise

*Deep in our history of struggle for freedom Canada was the North Star.*

—DR. MARTIN LUTHER KING JR.

William Wilberforce and Dr. Martin Luther King Jr. both grasped a basic natural law: Oppression thrives where it is unseen and unheard. These courageous men knew that exposing the truth banishes oppression and nurtures freedom.

In painstaking detail, Wilberforce presented the barbarity of slavery to the Westminster Parliament, where the facts could no longer be ignored. King put his case against segregation and discrimination before the people—he recognized the need for a "collection of the facts to determine whether injustices exist" as the first step toward positive change.

Wilberforce's and King's appeals were met with noxious lies, fraudulent justifications, and phoney excuses from those who either directly or indirectly benefited from the systems of exploitation being challenged or could not picture a world without chains. The well-funded pro-slavery propagandists of Wilberforce's era claimed that each slave had a "snug little house and garden, and plenty of pigs and poultry," and that slaves benefited from labouring for their masters. For his part, King was attacked on the grounds that non-violent protests against discrimination were "extreme." As more people saw and heard of the oppression for themselves, however, the momentum to right these injustices became unstoppable.

Human trafficking is modern-day slavery that can be traced back to the earliest of recorded histories. So, too, can the calls for its abolition.

"When one is deprived of one's liberty, one is right in blaming not so much the man who puts the fetters on as the one who had the power to prevent him, but did not use it," wrote the Greek historian Thucydides in *The Peloponnesian War* in 431 BC. His wisdom prevails today.

For millennia, philosophers and world religions alike have recognized the inherent obligation we have to take a stand against injustice. They recognized that the failure to prevent or mitigate harm when it is within one's power to do so is as blameworthy as directly committing the harm itself.

Our society has too many people willing to sit on the sidelines while their communities crumble around them. The proliferation of micro-brothels in homes, apartment buildings, and condominiums, together with the widespread availability of child sexual abuse imagery online, has brought sexual exploitation into our own neighbourhoods and living rooms. Traffickers expect people to mind their own business and not get involved when they suspect something is amiss. Otherwise, they wouldn't have the audacity to sell victims for sex in residential areas and in apartments and condominiums surrounded by neighbours. Remember how in Calgary, women from Southeast Asia were serving as indentured sex slaves in a massage parlour that was just blocks from an elementary school. Even more outrageous was the network of apartments and condominium brothels revealed in 2009 throughout the B.C. Lower Mainland.

"I just normally hear a lot of banging upstairs, but I never thought nothing of it," said a neighbour in the Downsview apartment directly below Joyeuse. In this Toronto building, Tyrone Dillon allegedly forced the twenty-one-year-old Haitian mother to be sold for sex for a full seven weeks. "It wasn't like I heard screaming," the neighbour added. Only after Joyeuse was allegedly beaten and called 911 was she finally free.

There are heroes in Canada's battle to combat human trafficking—but not enough of them. These heroes are police officers who've identified the victims being sold and held their traffickers accountable. These heroes work for NGOs that give victims a shoulder to cry on, and the dignity of a bed to sleep safely in at night. But the greatest heroes of all in this struggle are the survivors of human trafficking themselves. Despite the brutality and suffering they've endured, many are optimistic about the future and are rebuilding their lives one day at a time.

We must commit to end the shameful and unjust practice of human trafficking with the same urgency and persistence we would if the victims were our sister or brother, daughter or son, mother or father, wife or husband—because victims of human trafficking are these people to someone. Human trafficking is not a partisan issue of right and left but rather a critical question of right and wrong.

Ours is a country that aspires to be a beacon of hope, a bright North Star that can be seen on even the darkest night. We aspire to be a nation where there is freedom from fear, where all enjoy the liberty to live a life of their own choosing. Canada must renew its place as the "Promised Land" for those seeking emancipation. We must build a new Underground Railroad to freedom.

Let us earn the accolade bestowed upon us by Dr. Martin Luther King Jr. that Canada is a symbol of hope. Let us reclaim the fierce resolve of William Wilberforce to end exploitation based on our belief in the inalienable rights and dignity of all people. Together we can unearth the injustice that has taken root in our country and around the world. The national conscience requires that we restore our pledge to citizens and newcomers alike: Canada is a land of the True North, strong and *free.*

*Having heard all of this you may choose to look the other way but you can never again say that you did not know.*

—WILLIAM WILBERFORCE, SPEECH TO WESTMINSTER PARLIAMENT CALLING FOR THE ABOLITION OF SLAVERY

MAY 12, 1789

# APPENDIX

## ORGANIZATIONS COMBATTING HUMAN TRAFFICKING

### International Organizations

**Not for Sale**

(United States, Thailand, Philippines, Mexico, Uganda, Peru, Ghana, Canada, and Cambodia): www.notforsalecampaign.org

Not for Sale started in San Francisco in 2006 as an abolitionist movement. It reaches out to survivors of human trafficking by mapping and documenting situations around the world and supporting projects abroad to help those in bondage.

**International Justice Mission, Canada**

(Head Office: London, ON; Field Offices: Bolivia, Cambodia, India): www.ijm.ca

IJM is a human rights agency that assists in rescuing and caring for victims of slavery, sexual exploitation, and other forms of violent oppression in developing countries. IJM staffers also work with local officials to prosecute perpetrators and to promote functioning public justice systems.

**World Vision**

(Active in nearly one hundred countries): www.worldvision.ca

World Vision is a Christian relief, development, and advocacy organization that works with children, families, and communities to overcome poverty and injustice. They try to prevent and mitigate the effects of human trafficking through awareness raising, education, victim care, and advocating for change both in Canada and abroad.

### Shared Hope International

(United States, Jamaica, India, Fiji, Nepal): www.sharedhope.org

Shared Hope International works to prevent, rescue, and restore victims of sex trafficking by raising awareness, empowering communities, and developing holistic restoration facilities. They've compiled several key reports on the international and domestic exploitation of women and children.

### The Ratanak Foundation

(Canada, United Kingdom, Cambodia): www.ratanak.org

The Ratanak Foundation has worked exclusively in Cambodia since 1990 and focuses on the secure aftercare, rehabilitation, and social reintegration of trafficked children rescued from brothels. The founding director, Brian McConaghy, was previously with the RCMP.

### Human Smuggling and Trafficking Center

(Washington, DC)

The HSTC serves as a multi-agency platform for the United States government on matters concerning illicit travel. It collects, collates, and vets information and disseminates actionable leads to U.S. law enforcement, intelligence, and diplomatic agencies, as well as U.S. foreign partners.

### Ukrainian World Congress Task Force to Stop Human Trafficking

(Head Office: Toronto, ON; contacts in over thirty countries, including Ukraine): www.ukrainianworldcongress.org

UWC coordinates Ukrainian communities in the diaspora, representing the interests of over twenty million Ukrainians. More specifically, the UWC Task Force to Stop Human Trafficking coordinates the anti-trafficking activities of UWC member organizations worldwide and provides awareness resources and educational assistance. To encourage future collaboration, UWC strives to connect member organizations with local NGOs.

### Help Us Help the Children Anti-Trafficking Initiative

(Toronto, ON, and Ukraine): www.chornobyl.ca

This project of the Children of Chornobyl Canadian Fund is committed to improving standards in orphanages throughout Ukraine. The initiative began because many young Ukrainians, some of them orphans, are being used as pawns in prostitution rings throughout Europe. The organization's objectives include exploring ways to eliminate the exploitation that many orphans experience after leaving the institutions; organizing anti-trafficking educational seminars for orphans and orphanage directors; and providing trafficking awareness and life skills for high school students and graduating orphans.

## National Organizations

### The Salvation Army

www.salvationist.ca/trafficking

The Salvation Army is an international Christian organization that began its work in Canada in 1882 and has become the largest non-governmental direct provider of social services in the country, supporting four hundred communities across Canada. In 2004, the Canada and Bermuda Territory of the organization created an anti-trafficking network that seeks to raise awareness of sex trafficking and empower people to do something about it.

### Canadian Association of Sexual Assault Centres

www.casac.ca

This is a pan-Canadian group of sexual assault centres that have come together to implement the legal, social, and attitudinal changes necessary to prevent, and ultimately eradicate, rape and sexual assault. As feminists they recognize that violence against women is one of the strongest indicators of prevailing societal attitudes toward females.

The Canadian Association aims to act as a force for social change regarding violence against women at the individual, institutional, and political levels.

### Canadian Centre for Child Protection Inc.

www.protectchildren.ca and www.cybertip.ca

A charitable organization dedicated to the personal safety of all children, the Canadian Centre aims to reduce child victimization by providing programs and services to Canadians. Initiatives include public awareness activities, a personal safety education program ("Kids in the Know"), a national tip line to report online sexual abuse of children (Cybertip.ca), and a program to help organizations prevent child sexual abuse ("Commit to Kids"). Cybertip.ca is a part of the Government of Canada's national strategy to protect children from online sexual exploitation.

### Stop the Trafficking Coalition

cuias@cuias.org

STT was formed in Toronto and consists of members from numerous organizations and motivated individuals across the country. The group coordinates anti-trafficking efforts in the Ukrainian Canadian community, as well as liaising with other anti-trafficking organizations in Canada and abroad. Activities include lobbying and supplying information to government and police organizations, organizing human trafficking awareness events, and providing a valuable internet information service about current events (pertaining to Canadians) surrounding human trafficking. Goals include raising awareness, prevention of sex trafficking, and victim support.

### Beyond Borders

www.beyondborders.org

National, bilingual, and volunteer driven, Beyond Borders is the Canadian affiliate of ECPAT International, a global network of more than eighty groups in seventy-five countries. Activities include awareness initiatives, advocacy for improved legislation, monitoring of court cases, and promotion of effective prevention and protection strategies. Beyond Borders also provides education and training and intervenes in court cases to make sure victims have a voice.

### Sex Trade 101

(Toronto, ON): www.sextrade101.com

Sex Trade 101 offers training on all aspects of the sex trade and trafficking in Canada, replacing myths and stereotypes about prostitution with facts and true stories from women who've experienced it. Likewise, the group believes in helping those trapped in the sex trade to get out alive, with their minds and their lives intact.

### The Future Group

www.thefuturegroup.org

TFG's work has centred on confronting human trafficking and child sexual exploitation in Canada and abroad. The organization co-operates with source countries to address the root causes of human trafficking, working closely with local NGOs. In Canada, TFG conducts awareness raising activities and policy research to improve the country's response.

### Walk with Me

www.walk-with-me.org

Founded in May 2009, this NGO provides education, awareness, and training programs for the public, law enforcement officers, social agencies, and others who are concerned about human trafficking in Canada. Walk with Me also offers immediate victim services and long-term case management for human trafficking victims in collaboration with other organizations across Ontario.

## Provincial and Local Organizations

### B.C. Office to Combat Trafficking in Persons

www.pssg.gov.bc.ca/octip

OCTIP is responsible for the development and overall coordination of British Columbia's strategy to address human trafficking under the Ministry of Public Safety and Solicitor General. Hotline: 1-888-712-7974.

### REED (Resist Exploitation, Embrace Dignity)

(Vancouver, BC): www.embracedignity.org

REED works to end trafficking and sexual exploitation and strengthen the anti-trafficking movement. It provides safe spaces and companionship for women, public education on trafficking, and community empowerment on how to end prostitution through systemic change.

### Servants Anonymous Society

(Surrey, BC): www.sasurrey.ca

This is a non-profit organization that provides long-term safe homes, free education and pre-employment training, hope and wholeness for women and female youth who've been sexually exploited and trafficked. Servants Anonymous Society works to sensitize and promote awareness of the special needs of survivors of human trafficking while offering women and female youth a way out of sex trade slavery. It serves local and international victims from across Canada.

### Vancouver Rape Relief and Women's Shelter

(Vancouver, BC): www.rapereliefshelter.bc.ca

A member of the Canadian Association of Sexual Assault Centres, VRRWS is a non-profit feminist group that collectively operates a twenty-four-hour rape crisis line and a transition house for battered women and their children. VRRWS sees prostitution and trafficking of women for the sex trade as part of the same continuum of male violence against women and fights for the abolition of prostitution. The group houses women escaping any form of male violence, including prostitution and trafficking, and offers advocacy and accompaniment to hospital, courts, and the police. All services are free and confidential.

### SCION Project (MOSAIC)

(Vancouver, Burnaby, and Lower Mainland, BC): www.mosaicbc.com

The project, which is part of MOSAIC's settlement services, assists separated minors, including trafficked children, who are outside their countries of origin without parents or legal guardians. Support can include settlement and integration services, help with immigration, and employment and translation assistance. Designated as representatives at the IRB, MOSAIC also can assist adults with the same services.

### Safe OnLine Outreach Society (SOLOS)

(British Columbia): www.safeonlineoutreach.com

SOLOS educates youth, parents, professionals, and the public about online sexual exploitation, cyber-bullying, and online gang recruitment. SOLOS representatives travel throughout British Columbia speaking to youth, parents, educators, child protection, and criminal justice professionals. In particular, they explain how these activities can put young people at risk and they outline strategies for effective responses.

### Covenant House Vancouver

(Vancouver, BC): www.covenanthousebc.org

Covenant House Vancouver is a non-profit crisis intervention centre for homeless youth from sixteen to twenty-five. It's one of twenty-one Covenant House sites throughout North and Central America that assist young people to exit the dangers of street life. Covenant House runs an outreach, drop-in, temporary shelter, and transitional living program through which youth can gain the skills needed for independent living.

**ACT Alberta—Action Coalition on Human Trafficking**
(Alberta): www.actalberta.org

ACT Alberta is a coalition of government agencies, non-governmental organizations, survivors of trafficking, and the general public who help to identify and respond to human trafficking in Alberta. The coalition raises awareness of human trafficking and encourages community dialogue to develop locally relevant solutions to the problem.

**Maple Leaf Alberta Projects**
(Edmonton, AB): http://mapleleafap.wordpress.com

This organization is supporting the creation of recovery centres in Western Ukraine with Nashi, a Ukrainian NGO. The proposed residences for at-risk teens and trafficking victims will be places where they can gain vocational, language, and life skills. Maple Leaf Alberta Projects also raises awareness about human trafficking in Canada and collaborates with churches, service clubs, the media, police, and individuals.

**Manitoba Trafficked Persons Response Team**
(Winnipeg, MB): Dianna_Bussey@sacorrections.ca

This team responds to the needs of human trafficking victims in Manitoba. Members represent various organizations and agencies that can help trafficked persons both immediately and in the longer term.

**Ma Mawi Wi Chi Itata Centre, Inc.**
(Winnipeg, MB): www.mamawi.com

Directed and controlled by Aboriginals, this community-based non-profit organization provides family resource support services for Aboriginals in Winnipeg. Currently, the centre operates three community care centres (public access) in inner-city Winnipeg, four group homes for youth in the care of a child and family services agency, and one Rural Cultural Learning Centre.

### Canada Fights Human Trafficking

(Ontario): www.CanadaFightsHumanTrafficking.com

CFHT is an organization dedicated to the annihilation of all crimes associated with human trafficking, and is committed to rescuing and rehabilitating victims of human trafficking within Canada. It runs public education and awareness campaigns, legal teams, safe houses, reintegration homes, and professional services for victims.

### FCJ Refugee Centre

(Toronto, ON): lolyrico@on.aibn.com

Since 1991, the FCJ Refugee Centre has offered shelter to over one thousand women and their children. The project now operates four houses that afford refuge to twenty-five women with their children. In addition, FCJ provides counselling, advocacy, and support services to uprooted persons (i.e., refugees, people without status, and trafficked persons). Services include interpretation, referral to legal assistance, settlement and integration programs, and educational and training workshops for service providers and the public in general.

### Peel Children's Aid

(Mississauga, Brampton, Caledon, ON): lbaistrocchi@peelcas.org

Peel Children's Aid protects children and strengthens families, ensuring the safety and well-being of children in the Region of Peel in Ontario. Initiatives include caring for children under sixteen who arrive unaccompanied at Pearson International Airport.

### Toronto Police Service, Special Victims Unit

(Toronto, ON): wendy.leaver@torontopolice.on.ca

SVU is a specialized investigative unit dedicated to protecting prostituted persons from sexual predators by investigating sexual offences committed against them.

**Streetlight Support Services**

(Greater Toronto Area, ON): streetlight@live.ca

Streetlight Support Services is a community-based NGO that provides alternatives for individuals involved in sex trade activities. Streetlight uses a non-judgmental holistic approach that recognizes the interdependence of the emotional, cultural, economic, and broader social issues that affect individuals.

**Temple Committee Against Human Trafficking**

(Montreal, QB): human@templemontreal.ca

Affiliated with Temple Emanu-El-Beth Sholom in Montreal, TCAHT provides public education programs with emphasis on adolescents. The committee is part of an interfaith coalition that is represented by diverse faith-based and secular human rights groups. An additional focus is on U.S.–Canada border trafficking.

**Canadian Religious Conference—Action Committee Against Human Internal and External Trafficking**

(Trois-Rivières, Montreal, Sherbrooke, Gatineau, QC; Ottawa, ON): jbellefeuille@crc-canada.org

Formed by ten Catholic religious congregations, researchers, and a representative of the Canadian Religious Conference, the committee undertakes strategies to counter human trafficking, including raising awareness and offering education and training about human trafficking.

# METHODOLOGY

Since *Invisible Chains* is the first comprehensive book on human trafficking in Canada, it is important to briefly describe the research behind it before turning to the list of specific sources. This book is based on an empirical study that aims to support evidence-based law and policy responses to human trafficking in Canada. Research began in September 2007 and was completed in June 2010, focusing on human trafficking cases and responses since the country signed the *Palermo Protocol* in 2000.

A literature review of published research was conducted, as well as a review of other open source data, including written decisions of courts and tribunals in cases involving the criminal prosecution of alleged human traffickers or proceedings related to victims; reports by international governmental organizations, governments, and NGOs; and media accounts. In addition to recognizing potential cases, issues, and trends, this review identified potential key informants to be interviewed for this study. A "snowballing" technique was also used, wherein interview subjects recommended additional individuals to be approached.

Semi-structured expert interviews were conducted with approximately fifty individuals in governmental, law enforcement, and NGO capacities, as well as other professionals who have been directly involved in cases of human trafficking related to Canada. These interviews were conducted between May 2008 and July 2009, with one additional follow-up interview in March 2010, in accordance with protocols and procedures approved by the University of British Columbia's Behavioural Research Ethics Board (certificate of approval H08-00332). The interviews were audiotaped and conducted on an attribution basis (i.e., "on the record") unless otherwise indicated. Initial interviews took between sixty and ninety minutes, with some involving a follow-up. The majority of the interviews were conducted face to face. When this was not possible, telephone interviews were conducted. In one instance, a government department completed written responses to questions. The interview data were then coded, based on key themes that emerged across multiple interviews, in order to facilitate the identification of qualitative findings. Some interview subjects also provided written documentation.

When incidents of suspected human trafficking involving Canada as a source, destination, or transit country were disclosed during interviews, these were recorded in detail. These reported cases were later critically reviewed to determine whether they fit the definition of "trafficking in persons" in the *Palermo Protocol.* Only cases that met this definition and were found to be credible were included in this study. In many instances, cases were corroborated using court records, records released under the *Access to Information Act*, other interviews, or public accounts of the case.

An additional rich source of primary data came from over forty *Access to Information Act* filings with federal government departments and agencies (including the RCMP, Canada Border Services Agency, Citizenship and Immigration Canada, Public Safety Canada, Department of Justice, and Department of Foreign Affairs and International Trade), and provincial government departments in British Columbia, Alberta, Saskatchewan, Manitoba, Ontario, and Quebec.

For ethical reasons, and because of the perceived difficulty of locating victims often years after their cases were discovered, trafficked persons were not interviewed. However, secondary sources involving victim/survivor accounts, such as victim impact statements in court records and statements in other studies, are cited in this book to ensure that the voices of those exploited were not lost. Throughout this book, pseudonyms are used to conceal the identity of victims and survivors for their privacy and security. Exceptions to this policy are explicitly noted for victims that have commanded widespread public awareness in order to help identify the perpetrators who harmed them (i.e., Fonessa Bruyere, Hilary Wilson, and Cherisse Houle, who are deceased), to help identify their whereabouts (Jessie Edith Louise Foster), or because they are survivors who have high-profile public roles in leading NGOs (Somaly Mam and Timea Nagy). Specific information about survivors has been withheld as has detailed information about the shelters and safe houses that protect them.

# NOTES

## Epigraphs

p. vii "*Slavery is a weed*": Edmund Burke, "Speech on Moving His Resolutions for Conciliations with the Colonies" in Peter J. Stanlis, ed., *Edmund Burke: Selected Writings and Speeches* (New Jersey: Doubleday Anchor, 1963) at 220.

p. vii "*Never doubt that a*": Reproduced with permission. See Ashton Applewhite, William R. Evans III, and Andrew Frothingham, eds., *And I Quote: The Definitive Collection of Quotes, Sayings, and Jokes for the Contemporary Speechmaker* (New York: St. Martin's Press, 1992) at 71.

## Preface

p. xii "All that it takes": Various formulations of this quotation are attributed to Edmund Burke (1729–1797), although the original source has eluded historical researchers.

p. xiii Founded by Somaly Mam: Somaly Mam, *The Road of Lost Innocence: The True Story of a Cambodian Heroine* (London: Virago Press, 2008).

p. xv 30 to 35 percent: United Nations Children's Fund, *Children in Need of Special Protection* (Bangkok: UNICEF-Thailand, 2000) cited in Benjamin Perrin et al., *The Future of Southeast Asia: Challenges of Human Trafficking and Child Sex Slavery in Cambodia* (Phnom Penh: Motorola Printers, 2001) at 13, online: <http://www.thefuturegroup.org> (accessed June 8, 2010).

p. xvii "Operation Relaxation": see Chapter 1 below.

p. xviii Canada got a failing grade: The Future Group, *Falling Short of the Mark: An International Study on the Treatment of Human Trafficking Victims* (Calgary: The Future Group, 2006), online: <http://www.thefuturegroup.org> (accessed June 8, 2010).

## 1 The Renaissance of Slavery

p. 1 "Operation Relaxation": Cam Brooks, detective, Calgary Police Service, General Investigations Unit, interview with author, October 17, 2008; *R. v. Saengchanh*, [2004] A.J. No. 310 (Alta. Prov. Ct.) (Quicklaw (QL)); Mike D'Amour, "Bylaw to be massaged: Big bust prods city to review licensing structure for rubdown artists," *Calgary Sun* (November 7, 2003) (QL); "Prostitution pipeline allegedly smuggled Asian women into B.C.," *Canadian Press NewsWire* (November 9, 2003) (QL); "Human trafficking pipeline: Far-reaching sex ring," *Edmonton Sun* (November 10, 2003) (QL); "Police appeal for public help in search for sex ring boss," *Canadian Press NewsWire* (November 16, 2003) (QL); "Sex trafficking suspect turns himself in to cops," *Edmonton Sun* (December 17, 2003) (QL); "Calgary brothel boss gets two-year sentence and ticket back to Thailand," *Canadian Press NewsWire* (July 8, 2004) (QL); Daryl Slade, "Sex-slave charges dropped," *Calgary Herald* (March 18, 2006) at B2 (ProQuest).

p. 2 "We were looking at": Brooks (see above).

p. 2 "You can't let them go out": *Ibid.*

p. 3 "We see these women": "Task Force sought to halt sex slavery: Group urges co-operation to fight scourge," *Calgary Herald* (November 7, 2003) at A6.

p. 4 "This was before": Brooks (see above).

p. 5 "This is the tip of the iceberg": Canadian Press, "Alta. cops halt Asian prostitute pipeline," *Prince George Citizen* (November 7, 2003) at 14.

p. 5 Thérèse: Sherilyn Trompetter, assistant executive director, Changing Together, interview with author, September 22, 2008; Tracey Campbell, career and employment consultant, Alberta Employment and Immigration, interview with author, September 22, 2008; Citizenship and Immigration Canada, written interviews with author, December 4, 2008, and May 27, 2009 (hereafter "CIC interviews"); Claude Marchand, program adviser, Prairies and Northern Territories Region, Citizenship and Immigration Canada, "Human Trafficking Victim," April 28, 2008 (released by Citizenship and Immigration Canada under the *Access to Information Act* on December 5, 2008, File No. A-2009-01112 at 1, 398).

p. 5 "She was basically a commodity": Trompetter (see above).

p. 6 "the status or condition": *Slavery Convention*, 60 League of Nations Treaty Series (LNTS) 253, art. I(1) (entered into force March 9, 1927).

p. 7 more people are in bondage today: Kevin Bales, *Disposable People: New Slavery in the Global Economy* (Berkeley, Cal.: University of California Press, 1999).

p. 7 "Old Slavery" ... "New Slavery": *Ibid.*

p. 10 no country that is immune: CIC interviews, December 4, 2008 (see above).

## 2 Travelling Sex Offenders Fuelling Demand Abroad

p. 12 Srey Mao: *The Future of Southeast Asia* at 18–19 (see above).

p. 17 187th-poorest country: Central Intelligence Agency, "World Factbook," online: <https://www.cia.gov/library/publications/the-world-factbook/rankorder/2004rank.html> (accessed June 8, 2010).

p. 17 U.S.$300–$700: *The Future of Southeast Asia* at 16 (see above).

p. 17 "some of the missing women": Jack Christie, "Crab Park well off the city's beaten path," *Georgia Straight* (March 3, 2005), online: <http://www.straight.com> (accessed November 17, 2009).

p. 19 "that the Cambodian complainants": *R. v. Bakker*, 2005 BCPC 289, [2005] B.C.W.L.D. 5097 (Prov. Ct. B.C.); see also CTV, "Trail of a sex tourist: Canada's limited success in pursuing pedophiles," *W-FIVE* (March 7, 2009), online: <http://www.ctv.ca> (accessed November 17, 2009).

p. 20 Bakker's defence counsel, Kevin McCullough: Jennifer Wells, "Canada's offshore child sex law faces its first test," *Toronto Star* (August 29, 2004) at A2; Jane Armstrong, "Sex-tourism law faces its first challenge in B.C. case," *The Globe and Mail* (September 8, 2004) at A9.

p. 20 "moral entrepreneurship": "Prosecution of sex tourists cumbersome; Canadian's arrest spurs review of effort to fight abuses abroad," *Washington Times* (October 30, 2007), online: <http://goliath.ecnext.com/coms2/gi_0199-7124692/Prosecution-of-sex-tourists-cumbersome.html> (accessed October 20, 2009).

p. 20 "The purpose of the law": "Canada not prosecuting child-sex tourists: Lawyer," *Toronto Star* (December 18, 2007), online: <http://www.thestar.com>.

p. 20 Kenneth Klassen: *R. v. Klassen*, 2008 CarswellBC 2747, 2008 BCSC 1762 (B.C.S.C.); "B.C. police say seized child porn unspeakable," *CTV News* (September 22, 2004), online: <http://www.ctv.ca> (accessed November 17, 2009); "B.C. man pleads guilty to sex tourism charges," *CBC News* (May 21, 2010), online: <http://www.cbc.ca> (accessed June 8, 2010).

p. 23 two million children worldwide: U.S. Department of State, *Trafficking in Persons Report* (Washington, D.C.: 2008) at 14, online: <http://www.state.gov> (accessed November 17, 2009).

p. 23 (ECPAT) ... estimates: The Protection Project, *International Child Sex Tourism: Scope of the Problem and Comparative Case Studies* (Washington, D.C.: Johns Hopkins University, 2007) at 23.

p. 23 Christopher Paul Neil: Interpol, "Thai court jails pedophile arrested after INTERPOL global appeal" (August 15, 2008), online: <http://www.interpol.int> (accessed November 17, 2009); "B.C. teacher sentenced to 3 years for sexual abuse of Thai boy," *CBC News* (August 15, 2008), online: <http://www.cbc.ca> (accessed November 17, 2009); "B.C. teacher sentenced to 6 more years in Thai prison for abusing boy," *CBC News* (November 24, 2008), online: <http://www.cbc.ca> (accessed November 17, 2009).

p. 24 Rosalind Prober, president of: Rosalind Prober, president, Beyond Borders, interview with author, November 2, 2008.

p. 24 Between 1993 and 2008: "Child Molestation Cases," April 1, 2008 (released by Foreign Affairs and International Trade Canada under the *Access to Information Act* on April 24, 2008, File No. A-2007-00723 at 4-8).

p. 25 "They feel almost protected": Sabrina Sullivan, managing director, The Future Group, interview with author, August 28, 2008.

p. 25 "Scum!": "British national faces incarceration in Cambodia," *The Scotsman* (June 23, 2001).

p. 25 estimated 2 to 14 percent: International Labour Organization, "Sex as a sector: Economic incentives and hardships fuel growth," *World of Work*, No. 26 (September/October 1998), online: <http://www.ilo.org> (accessed November 17, 2009).

p. 25 "Poverty relates to the supply": UN Commission on Human Rights, *Report of the Special Rapporteur on the sale of children, child prostitution, and child pornography*, UN CHOR, 1994, U.N. Doc. E/CN.4/ 1994/ 84 at para. 6.

p. 26 Transparency International placed: Policy and Research Department, "Report on the Transparency International Global Corruption Barometer" (Berlin: Transparency International, 2007) at 4.

p. 26 In 2005, the Filipino police: Dr. Gabriella Quimson, "National Integrity Systems, Transparency International Country Study Report: Philippines 2006" (Berlin: Transparency International, 2006) at 27; Policy and Research Department, "Global Corruption Report 2007: Regional Highlights" (Berlin: Transparency International, 2007) at 1.

p. 26 after the Boxing Day tsunami: Terri Theodore, "Canada 'international pariah' for failing to prosecute child sex offenders: Lawyer," *Canadian Press* (December 18, 2007).

p. 27 Fully two-thirds of American men: *International Child Sex Tourism* at 39–41 (see above).

p. 27 "Weigh the pros and cons": Anon., "Letter to a Young Boy-Lover," *North American Man / Boy Love Association* (NAMBLA) *Bulletin* (Jan./Feb. 1993) at 30 cited in David Hechler, "Child Sex Tourism" (1995), online: Andrew Vachss <http://www.vachss.com/help_text/reports/child_sex_tourism.pdf> (accessed December 11, 2009).

## 3 International Trafficking to Canada

p. 29 "threat assessment": Marie-Claude Arsenault, sergeant, RCMP Human Trafficking National Coordination Centre, conference presentation, "Human Trafficking: A Canadian Perspective" at *Tackling Sexual Violence: 14th Sex Crimes Conference* (Toronto, Ontario: October 6, 2009).

p. 29 "[T]he number of victims": *Bi-National Assessment of Trafficking in Persons* (Government of Canada, 2006), online: <http://www.publicsafety.gc.ca/prg/le/_fl/1666i-en.pdf> (accessed June 8, 2010) at 7. Reproduced with the permission of the Minister of Public Works and Government Services Canada, 2010.

p. 30 Manuela: Loly Rico, co-director, FCJ Refugee Centre, interview with author, May 28, 2009; Lise Morjé Howard, *UN Peacekeeping in Civil Wars* (Cambridge: Cambridge University Press, 2007) at 88–89.

p. 31 "It happens most of the time": Rico (see above).

p. 32 "My boss will kill me": Wendy Leaver, detective, Toronto Police Service, Special Victims Unit, interview with author, September 22, 2008.

p. 33 "some potential victims": Melissa Gomes, senior program officer, Citizenship and Immigration Canada, "VTIP Case Monitoring.xls," February 15, 2008 (released by Citizenship and Immigration Canada under the *Access to Information Act* on December 5, 2008, File No. A-2009-01112 at 5).

p. 33 Between May 2006 and November 2008: CIC interviews (see above).

p. 34 "enabling factor": Sheldon X. Zhang, *Smuggling and Trafficking in Human Beings: All Roads Lead to America* (Westport, Conn.: Praeger, 2007) at 113–114.

p. 34 "Some enter with genuine passports": CIC interviews (see above).

p. 34 "They say there are brokers": Mark Schwartz, sergeant, Calgary Police Service, Vice Unit, interview with author, August 28, 2008.

p. 35 infiltrated the airline company: Dennis MacDonald, Canada Border Services Agency–Intelligence, Vancouver International Airport, "URGENT," November 1, 2007; Zorida Bacchus, senior program officer, Anti-Fraud and Human Trafficking, Borders Intelligence Division–Enforcement Branch, Canada Border Services Agency, "CONFIDENTIAL heads up: Possible VTIP," November 2, 2007 (both released by Citizenship and Immigration Canada under the *Access to Information Act* on December 5, 2008, File No. A-2009-01112 at 33–34).

p. 36 Luisa: Rico (see above); United Nations Office on Drugs and Crime, *World Drug Report 2009* (Vienna: UNODC, 2009) at 63–64, online: <http://www.unodc.org> (accessed September 10, 2009).

p. 39 "Operation Paladin": U.K. Border Agency Home Office, "Trafficked children missing from local authority care–U.K. Border Agency response," (May 7, 2009), online: <http://www.ukba.homeoffice.gov.uk> (accessed November 17, 2009).

p. 39 "probable trafficked child": Robin Pike, "Child Trafficking at Ports of Entry," conference presentation at *Combating Human Trafficking: Cooperating to Build Best Practices in B.C. and Beyond* (Vancouver: October 30–31, 2008).

p. 40 "In 1999, we didn't": Robin Pike, executive director, British Columbia Office to Combat Trafficking in Persons, interview with author, September 30, 2008.

p. 40 Each year in Toronto: Tat Ki Yu, service program manager, Peel Children's Aid Society, interview with author, September 29, 2008.

pp. 40–41 a representative of the Peel Children's Aid Society: *Ibid.*

p. 41 Katya: Campbell (see above).

p. 42 "Imagine you've been kidnapped": *Ibid.*

p. 42 "The humiliation experienced": Rico (see above).

p. 42 Mumbi: Deborah Isaacs, Sisters of the Good Shepherd, interview with author, November 18, 2008.

p. 43 "forced to eat, sleep": Jason Van Rassel, "Canadian authorities fighting 'global phenomenon' of human trafficking," *Canwest News Service* (September 19, 2009), online: <http://www.calgaryherald.com> (accessed September 19, 2009).

p. 44 "I have read some dancer contracts": Nina Alfaro, regional intelligence officer, Canada Revenue Agency (Niagara Falls, Ont.), "[Redacted]," March 28, 2007 (released by Citizenship and Immigration Canada under the *Access to Information Act* on December 5, 2008, File No. A-2009-01112 at 59).

p. 44 "In order to conform": Frederick Matern, second secretary (Immigration), Embassy of Canada (Bucharest, Romania), "[Redacted]," March 29, 2007 (released by Citizenship and Immigration Canada under the *Access to Information Act* on December 5, 2008, File No. A-2009-01112 at 56–58).

p. 44 "forced to do things": David Quartermain, director, Border Intelligence, Canada Border Services Agency, "Briefing Note for DG, Intelligence: Victim of Trafficking in Persons Issued Temporary Residence Permit (TRP)," September 27, 2006 (released by the Canada Border Services Agency under the *Access to Information Act* on July 2, 2008, File No. A-2008-00260).

p. 45 "When you look around": Mike Viozzi, constable, Peel Regional Police, Vice Unit, interview with author, May 27, 2008.

## 4 Across the Undefended Border

p. 47 Osoyoos: Lou Berube, human trafficking awareness coordinator, RCMP Border Integrity Program, Surrey Federal Operations Branch, interview with author, July 9, 2008; *Bi-National Assessment of Trafficking in Persons* at 21 (see above).

p. 48 "I'm absolutely convinced": Berube (see above).

p. 48 almost one hundred transit countries: See Benjamin Perrin, "Just Passing Through? International Legal Obligations and Policies of Transit Countries in Combating Trafficking in Persons" (2010) 7(1) *European Journal of Criminology* 11–27 at 11.

p. 49 14,500 to 17,500 victims: *Bi-National Assessment of Trafficking in Persons* at 7 (see above).

p. 49 "There seems to be a": Analyst, U.S. Department of State, interview with author, October 1, 2008 (unattributed per U.S. Government policy).

p. 49 "Despite activity in both": Criminal Intelligence Service Canada, *2008 Report on Organized Crime* (Ottawa: CISC, 2008) at 30, online: <http://www.cisc.gc.ca> (accessed June 8, 2010), ©(2008) HER MAJESTY THE QUEEN IN RIGHT OF CANADA as represented by Criminal Intelligence Service Canada. Reproduced with the permission of Criminal Intelligence Service Canada.

p. 50 In July 2004, eleven women: Royal Canadian Mounted Police—Headquarters, "Occurrence Summary: 2008387125 Immigration and Refugee Protection Act—Enter by False Means @ 2008/04/11 13:18 MDT," May 13, 2008 (released by the RCMP under the *Access to Information Act* on October 12, 2008, File No. GA-3951-3-01397/08 at 655-657).

p. 50 Criminal networks have long operated: Benjamin Perrin, "Trafficking in Persons and Transit Countries: A Canada–U.S. Case Study in Global Perspective," *Metropolis B.C. Working Paper* 10-05 (2010), online: <http://riim.metropolis.net> (accessed June 8, 2010).

p. 51 "She was extremely nervous": Steve Richardson, sergeant, RCMP, Windsor Immigration and Passport Section, "Possible HT file," May 25, 2007 (released by Citizenship and Immigration Canada under the *Access to Information Act* on December 5, 2008, File No. A-2008-01112 at 125; see also 121–124).

p. 51 Also in 2007 ... Tasha: Zorida Bacchus, senior program officer—anti-fraud and human trafficking, Borders Intelligence Division—Enforcement Branch, Canada Border Services Agency, "Heads Up: TIP investigation underway," November 7, 2007 (released by Citizenship and Immigration Canada under the *Access to Information Act* on December 5, 2008, File No. A-2009-01112 at 29).

p. 51 In February 2001, the Vancouver Police: *Bi-National Assessment of Trafficking in Persons* at 21 (see above).

p. 52 Castana: Michelle Miller, executive director, REED (Resist Exploitation, Embrace Dignity), interview with author, February 19, 2009.

p. 53 "work in the commercial sex business": Royal Canadian Mounted Police—Headquarters, "Occurrence Summary: 2008236390 Assistance to US Police Agency (except FBI) @ 2008/03/05 12:52," May 13, 2008 (released by the RCMP under the

*Access to Information Act* on October 12, 2008, File No. GA-3951-3-01397/08 at 1, 283-284).

p. 53 forty prostituted women ... "flipped": John Fenn, executive director, Streetlight Support Services, interview with author, May 28, 2008.

p. 53 the Edmonton Police Service: Andrew Hanon, "Social networking sites used for human-trafficking: Hundreds of Albertans get targeted each year," *Edmonton Sun* (November 11, 2007).

p. 53 "lured from Edmonton": Royal Canadian Mounted Police—Headquarters, "Occurrence Summary: 2005705522 Immigration and Refugee Protection Act—Trafficking in Persons @ 2005/09/09 00:00 MMDT," May 13, 2008 (document released by the RCMP under the *Access to Information Act* on October 12, 2008, File No. GA-3951-3-01397/08 at 38).

p. 53 "Canadian females being lured": Criminal Intelligence Service Canada, *Organized Crime and Domestic Trafficking in Persons in Canada* (August 2008) at 3, 5, online: <http://www.cisc.gc.ca> (accessed November 17, 2009), ©(2008) HER MAJESTY THE QUEEN IN RIGHT OF CANADA as represented by Criminal Intelligence Service Canada. Reproduced with the permission of Criminal Intelligence Service Canada.

p. 54 Jessie Edith Louise Foster: See numerous news articles on the Jessie Foster website <http://www.jessiefoster.ca>; "Jessica Edith Louise Foster: Free-spirited young woman disappears from Vegas home," *America's Most Wanted*, online: <http://www.amw.com> (accessed December 12, 2009); Daphne Bramham, "B.C. Mother believes missing daughter trafficking victim," *Vancouver Sun* (October 30, 2008).

p. 55 "My sweet, dear, wonderful Jessie": Glendene Grant, "Letter to Jessie," (August 2007), online: <http://www.jessiefoster.ca/index_files/Page8680.htm> (accessed December 12, 2009). This excerpt has been edited for length. A complete copy is available online. Reproduced with the permission of Glendene Grant.

## 5 Buying Local—Canadian Victims

p. 58 "That's it. That's human trafficking": Leaver (see above).

p. 58 "They were sold for drug debt": Schwartz (see above).

p. 59 Detective Jim Kenney: Jim Kenney, detective, Vancouver Police Department, Vice Unit, interview with author, October 23, 2008.

p. 59 Genevieve: *R. v. Jacques Leonard-St. Vil* (November 10, 2008), Brampton (Sup. Ct. J.), Durno J. (unreported), transcript on file with author.

p. 61 "love bombing": Michel Dorais and Patrice Corriveau, *Gangs and Girls: Understanding Juvenile Prostitution* (Montreal & Kingston: McGill-Queen's University Press, 2009) at xvii. Reproduced with permission.

p. 62 "gang bangs": *Ibid.* at 30–33.

p. 64 International Association of Chiefs of Police: Adapted from International Association of Chiefs of Police, *The Crime of Human Trafficking: A Law Enforcement Guide to Identification and Investigation* (Alexandria, Virginia: 2006) at 4, online: <http://www.theiacp.org> (accessed December 29, 2009).

p. 67 "I owe five hundred dollars": Anick Gagnon, Projet intervention prostitution de Québec, interview with author, June 10, 2008.

p. 67 "You'll start to dress her": Mickey Royal, *The Pimp Game ... Instructional Guide* (Los Angeles: Sharif Publishing, 1998), cited by Melissa Snow, project director, Shared Hope International, interview with author, October 3, 2008; as well as Kristine Arnold, constable, Peel Regional Police, Vice Unit, interview with author, May 27, 2008; and Viozzi (see above).

## 6 The New Technology of Trafficking

p. 69 "You can buy a used lawnmower": Viozzi (see above).

p. 69 "I cannot believe": Arnold (see above).

p. 70 "I'll fuck you up": *R. v. Imani Nakpangi* (June 24, 2008), Brampton (Ont. Ct. J.), Atwood J. (unreported decision) at 2, transcript on file with author.

p. 71 more than three-quarters: Ipsos Reid, "Canadian teens flock to social networking sites," *Digital Home* (June 23, 2009), online: <http://www.digitalhome.ca/content/view/3809/280/> (accessed November 17, 2009).

p. 71 Sarah: Canwest News Service, "Prostitution sting nets six arrests," *Times-Colonist* (Victoria) (November 11, 2008), online: <http://www.timescolonist.com/> (accessed December 10, 2008); Canwest News Service, "Child prostitute alleges she was lured to Victoria," *Times-Colonist* (Victoria) (November 18, 2008); Canwest News Service, "Child pornography added to list of charges," *Times-Colonist* (Victoria) (December 24, 2008); Joanne Hatherly, "Psychiatric assessment for man who beat sex worker," *Times-Colonist* (Victoria) (April 25, 2009).

p. 72 A survey by Microsoft Canada: Microsoft Canada and Youthography, "Fact sheet: Microsoft Canada and Youthography internet safety survey" (January 2009), online: <http://news.microsoft.ca/corporate/archive/2009/02/25/fact-sheet-microsoft-canada-and-youthography-internet-safety-survey.aspx> (accessed November 17, 2009).

p. 72 twenty-nine thousand registered sex offenders: Gary D. Robertson, "MySpace: 29,000 sex offenders have profiles," *Associated Press* (July 24, 2007), online: <http://www.msnbc.msn.com> (accessed December 11, 2009).

p. 72 over three thousand five hundred: Office of the Attorney General (New York), "Attorney General Cuomo announces thousands of sex offenders purged from Facebook and MySpace in first sweep under State's new 'E-Stop' law," *Press Release*

(December 1, 2009), online: <http://www.oag.state.ny.us> (accessed December 11, 2009).

p. 73 "They may post sexual images": Kevin Poulsen, "Pimps go online to lure kids into prostitution," *Wired.com* (February 25, 2009), online: <http://www.wired.com> (accessed November 17, 2009).

p. 73 "one of the most": James Weldon, "North Vancouver teens advertising sex for sale on Craigslist: RCMP," *North Shore News* (June 29, 2009).

p. 73 "Many of these at-risk youths": RCMP, "North Vancouver–North Vancouver RCMP working to help teenage sex trade workers," *Press Release* (June 16, 2009), online: <http://bc.rcmp.ca> (accessed November 17, 2009).

p. 74 "Parents have to be": Weldon (see above).

p. 74 In August 2007, the parents: Sergeant Mark L. Schwartz, Calgary Police Service, Vice Unit, *Expert Report: www.Cragislist.org* (2009) at 2 (on file with author).

p. 75 "the medium of choice": *Ibid.*

p. 75 "cruising through the listings": *Ibid.*

p. 76 Craigslist took further action: Craigslist, "Joint Statement with Attorneys General and NCMEC," November 6, 2008, online: <http://blog.craigslist.org/2008/11/joint-statement-with-attorneys-general-ncmec/> (accessed January 3, 2010); Tamara Cherry, "Experts hope Canadian site will follow U.S. lead: American Craigslist drops section advertising 'adult services'," *Toronto Sun* (May 15, 2009), online: <http://www.torontosun.com > (accessed January 3, 2010).

p. 76 Vytautas Vilutis: Documentation provided by Arnold (see above), April 16, 2009.

## 7 Breaking the Bonds That Enslave Victims

p. 78 The Criminal Intelligence Service Canada: *Organized Crime and Domestic Trafficking in Persons in Canada* (see above).

p. 78 "Nobody can get into": Viozzi (see above).

p. 79 "I ran away once": *Gangs and Girls* at 50 (see above).

p. 79 definitions of torture: Documentation provided by Snow (see above), reproduced with the permission of Shared Hope International; see also *Domestic Sex Trafficking: The Criminal Operations of the American Pimp* (Polaris Project, 2006).

p. 80 "Part of the psychology": Mary Pichette, executive director, Servants Anonymous Society, interview with author, February 27, 2009.

p. 80 "It's unreal the hold": Winn Blackman, Sister/Pastoral counsellor, Salvation Army, interview with author, February 17, 2009.

p. 81 "The Rules": Viozzi (see above).

p. 81 "The bottom line is": *Ibid.*

p. 82 "were under the control": *Gangs and Girls* at 45, 58 (see above).

p. 82 lack of control over schedule: Adapted from Kevin Bales & Ron Soodalter, *The Slave Next Door: Human Trafficking and Slavery in America Today* (Berkeley, Cal.: University of California Press, 2009) at 164; RCMP Press Release (June 16, 2009) (see above); Snow (see above).

p. 83 "He does it because": Chantal Fredette, Le Centre jeunesse de Montréal—Institut universitaire, interview with author, June 11, 2008.

p. 84 "a certain dysfunctional attachment": Dr. Patrick J. Carnes, *The Betrayal Bond: Breaking Free from Exploitative Relationships* (Deerfield Beach, Fl: HCI Publisher, 1997) at 29 cited in Linda A. Smith et al., *The National Report on Domestic Sex Trafficking: America's Prostituted Children* (Arlington, Va.: Shared Hope International, 2009) at 43.

p. 84 "cleaned up": Jackie Anderson, children-in-care coordinator, and Diane Redsky, acting executive director, Ma Mawi Wi Chi Itata Centre, interviews with author, November 3, 2008.

p. 84 "Limos would pull up": Brenda Wootten, Salvation Army, Florence Booth House, interview with author, May 29, 2008.

p. 85 a female victim was assaulted: Kenney (see above).

p. 85 "Do you have a boyfriend?": Snow (see above).

p. 85 overcoming the trauma bonds: Documentation provided by Snow (see above), reproduced with the permission of Shared Hope International.

p. 86 "She wanted out": Leaver (see above).

p. 87 "They may have come here": Employee, U.S. Department of Justice, interview with author, October 6, 2008 (unattributed per U.S. Government policy).

p. 87 Joyeuse: Sam Pazzano, "Alleged pimp wooed young mom," *Toronto Sun* (April 30, 2009), online: <http://cnews.canoe.ca>; Melissa Leong, "Girl, 3, used as pawn to force Mom into prostitution: Police," *National Post* (April 30, 2009), online: <http://www.nationalpost.com>; Tamara Cherry, "Pimps guilty of trafficking: Prof," *Toronto Sun* (April 30, 2009), online: <http://www.torontosun.com> (all accessed November 17, 2009).

p. 88 Laura Emerson: Laura Payton, "Ottawa woman gets seven years in teen-luring case," *Ottawa Citizen* (April 10, 2009) at A1; "Corrections," *Ottawa Citizen* (April 16, 2009), online <http://www.ottawacitizen.com> (both accessed April 20, 2009); "Woman faces human trafficking charge in forced prostitution case," *CBC News* (August 12, 2008), online: <http://www.cbc.ca> (accessed November 17, 2009); "Gatineau couple charged in teen prostitution ring in court," *Montreal Gazette*

(August 7, 2008), online <http://www.canada.com/montrealgazette> (accessed December 26, 2009).

p. 89 "Don't testify": *Ottawa Citizen*, April 10, 2009 (see above).

p. 89 "Members of the LBC": Vince Bevan, "Gang Issues in Ottawa," *Ottawa Police Service Report*, May 10, 2004, online: City of Ottawa <http://www.ottawa.ca/calendar/ottawa/citycouncil/opsb/2004/05-17/item2.htm> (accessed December 26, 2009).

p. 91 "I have three of them": Louis-Denis Ebacher, "J'en ai trois sur ma liste—Gordon Kingsbury," *Le Droit* (December 16, 2009) (translated).

## 8 First Nations, Last Chance

p. 93 "As we got outside": Anderson (see above).

p. 94 "At the end of the day": Redsky (see above).

p. 95 According to Dianna Bussey: Dianna Bussey, director, Salvation Army's Anti–Human Trafficking Network, interview with author, September 17, 2008.

p. 95 A 2001 study: Assistant Deputy Ministers' Committee on Prostitution and the Sexual Exploitation of Youth, *Sexual Exploitation of Youth in British Columbia* (Victoria: Ministry of Attorney General, Ministry for Children and Families, and Ministry of Health, 2001) at I.5.

p. 95 75 percent of Aboriginal girls: S.D. McIvor, & T. A. Nahanee, "Aboriginal Women: Invisible Victims of Violence," in K. Bonnycastle & G.S. Rigakos, eds., *Unsettling Truths: Battered Women, Policy, Politics, and Contemporary Research in Canada* (Vancouver: Collective Press, 1998) at 63–69 cited in Anupriya Sethi, "Domestic Sex Trafficking of Aboriginal Girls in Canada: Issues and Implications" (2007) 3:3 *First Peoples Child & Family Review* 57–71 at 59.

p. 95 "very young girls": Lee Lakeman, Vancouver Rape Relief, interview with author, February 20, 2009.

p. 96 At least five hundred First Nations girls: Sethi at 57 (see above).

p. 96 "Aboriginal girls are being hunted": "No Legalized Brothels for the Olympics 2010," *Aboriginal Women's Action Network Statement on Prostitution* (December 2007), online: <http://sisyphe.org/article.php3?id_article=2823> (accessed December 11, 2007).

p. 96 "Men see Aboriginal women": Redsky (see above).

p. 96 A landmark study in 2007: Sethi (see above).

p. 97 Fonessa Bruyere: Anderson (see above).

p. 97 "Police were notified but": "Winnipeg's murdered women deserve task force, say aboriginal groups," *CBC News* (September 6, 2007), online: <http://www.cbc.ca> (accessed May 21, 2009).

## 9 Falling Through the Cracks

p. 100 "We were concerned": Documentation provided by Janet Dench, executive director, Canadian Council for Refugees, interview with author, September 25, 2008.

p. 100 Tasha: Zorida Bacchus, senior program officer—anti-fraud and human trafficking, Borders Intelligence Division—Enforcement Branch, Canada Border Services Agency, "Heads Up: TIP investigation underway," November 7, 2007, & Debra Masters, Citizenship and Immigration Canada, Redacted Subject Line Email, November 21, 2007 (released by Citizenship and Immigration Canada under the *Access to Information Act* on December 5, 2008, File No. A-2009-01112 at 26-29).

p. 101 "I don't think anything": Mike Hamel, detective sergeant, Toronto Police Service, Sex Crimes Unit, interview with author, May 28, 2008.

p. 101 "We have very little": Leaver (see above).

p. 102 "We need money for": Arnold (see above).

p. 102 Timea Nagy: To read her story, see Timea E. Nagy, *Memoirs of a Sex Slave Survivor* (Communication Dynamics, 2010).

p. 102 "federal issues ... They're immigration": Antonella Artuso, "Sex slaves snubbed: Tory MPP cites Sun article," *Toronto Sun* (November 27, 2009), online: <http://www.torontosun.com> (accessed December 23, 2009).

p. 103 Svetlana and Dina: Wendy Quirion, regional program adviser, Ontario Region, Citizenship and Immigration Canada, "3 TIP cases—Toronto," May 2, 2008 (released by Citizenship and Immigration Canada under the *Access to Information Act* on December 5, 2008, File No. A-2009-01112 at 2).

p. 104 "been charged with": Rachel James, immigration enforcement officer, Pacific Region Enforcement Center, Citizenship and Immigration Canada, "[Redacted Email Subject]," January 22, 2007 (released by Citizenship and Immigration Canada under the *Access to Information Act* on December 5, 2008, File No. A-2009-01112 at 72-73).

p. 105 "When it comes to the tattoo": Tamara Cherry, "The story of Eve," *Toronto Sun* (November 2, 2009), online: <http://www.torontosun.com> (accessed December 27, 2009).

p. 106 Between May 2006 and November 2008: CIC interviews (see above)

p. 107 In March 2009: Pike (see above), interview with author, July 3, 2009.

p. 108 raid of massage parlours in December 2006: Pichette, Miller, and Isaacs (see above).

p. 108 An internal RCMP review: Corporal Norm Massie, human trafficking awareness coordinator, RCMP, "Continuation Report: Lower Mainland execution of 17 search warrants—bawdy houses," 2007-01-03 (documents released by the RCMP under the *Access to Information Act* on October 12, 2008, File No. GA-3951-3-01397/08 at 423).

p. 109 "... don't question them": Trompetter (see above).

p. 109 "There were huge pitfalls": *Ibid.*

## 10 Homegrown Human Traffickers

p. 111 $280,000 annually: *Organized Crime and Domestic Trafficking in Persons in Canada* (see above).

p. 112 Estimated Revenue of a Domestic Sex Trafficking Network: *Ibid.*

p. 114 "Our bars were rampant": Viozzi (see above).

p. 114 "North Preston's Finest and the Haitian gangs": *Ibid.*

p. 114 "You don't put a woman": Schwartz, interview with author (see above).

p. 115 "I've never met a juvenile": Documentation from Snow (see above).

p. 115 "These pimps say": Viozzi (see above).

p. 115 "These guys are psychology majors": Arnold (see above).

p. 115 "One girl was on the bottom floor": *Ibid.*

p. 116 "Many girls say": Dominic Montchamp, detective sergeant, Montreal Police Service, interview with author, June 11, 2008.

p. 117 "If you want to leave": Viozzi (see above).

## 11 Justice Too Often Denied

p. 118 In 2008 alone: Data compiled from U.S. Department of State, *Trafficking in Persons Report* (Washington, D.C.: 2009), online: <http://www.state.gov> (accessed November 17, 2009).

p. 119 On November 25, 2005: *Criminal Code*, R.S.C. 1985, c. C-46, s. 279.01.

p. 119 "causing the victim to provide": *Ibid.*, s. 279.04.

p. 120 "No person shall knowingly": *Immigration and Refugee Protection Act*, S.C. 2001, c. 27, s. 118.

p. 122 Prairie provinces: Colin Lock, corporal, RCMP, Northwest Region Immigration and Passport Section, interview with author, August 28, 2008; see Chapter 14.

p. 123 "I asked her what": Arnold (see above).

p. 124 "Careless, indeed, is": Case details and quotes from *R. v. Nakpangi* (see above).

p. 126 "the range of appropriate sentencing": Case details and quotes from *R. v. Jacques Leonard St. Vil* (see above).

p. 127 "You feel like it's your fault": Tamara Cherry, "Canada's 'troubling picture': Authorities fight losing battle against sale of human beings," *Toronto Sun* (November 13, 2008), online: <http://www.torontosun.com > (accessed January 3, 2010).

p. 127 Michael Lennox Mark: *R. v. Michael Lennox Mark* (November 10, 2008), Coupal J. (unreported decision) (audio-file of sentencing hearing on file with author); Montchamp (see above), interview with author, November 20, 2008.

p. 127 Vytautas Vilutis: Documentation provided by Arnold (see above), April 16, 2009; Tamara Cherry, "Pimp guilty of human trafficking," *Sun Media* (April 18, 2009), online: <http://cnews.canoe.ca> (accessed November 17, 2009); John Stewart, "Man charged under new human trafficking law," *The Mississauga News* (November 13, 2008), online: <http://www.mississauga.com> (accessed November 17, 2009).

p. 127 "respect for the law": *Criminal Code*, s. 718 (see above).

p. 129 Tyrel Henwood: sources cited in Chapter 6 for Sarah (see above)

p. 130 "They didn't want this": Leaver (see above).

p. 130 "trafficking-related" cases: Department of Justice, "Trafficking-related cases by Criminal Law Policy Section (Justice Canada)," May 11, 2008 (on file with author).

p. 132 Wai Chi (Michael) Ng case: Case details and quotes from *R. v. Ng*, [2007] B.C.J. No. 1388, 2007 BCPC 204 per MacLean Prov. Ct. J.

p. 134 "All the offences committed": *R. v. Ng*, 2008 BCCA 535 per Low J.A., para. 23.

p. 134 In January 2008, an Eastern European woman: Leaver (see above).

p. 134 "Credibility, sometimes, can be": Hamel (see above).

## 12 Ending Impunity, Offering Hope

p. 139 The Criminal Intelligence Service Canada warns: *Organized Crime and Domestic Trafficking in Persons in Canada* (see above).

p. 139 "Human trafficking?": Tamara Cherry, "Pimps guilty of trafficking: Prof," *Toronto Sun* (April 30, 2009), online: <http://www.torontosun.com> (accessed November 17, 2009); see also Joyeuse in Chapter 7.

p. 140 "[w]hen we investigated massage parlours": Montchamp (see above), interview with author, June 11, 2008.

p. 140 "The Special Victims Unit": Hamel (see above).

p. 140 $250,000 and entailed: Standing Committee on the Status of Women, *Turning Outrage into Action to Address Trafficking for the Purpose of Sexual Exploitation in Canada*, 39th Parl., 1st Sess. (February 2007) at 43.

p. 142 NGO representatives like Loly Rico: Rico (see above).

p. 142 "If you were a betting individual": Dr. Scharie Tavcer, Calgary Network on Prostitution and Mount Royal University, Department of Justice Studies, interview with author, September 8, 2008.

p. 143 "escape the influence of traffickers": Citizenship and Immigration Canada, *IP1: Temporary Resident Permits* (June 19, 2007) at 26, online: <http://www.cic.gc.ca/english/resources/manuals/ip/ip01-eng.pdf> (accessed June 8, 2010). Reproduced with the permission of the Minister of Public Works and Government Services, 2010.

p. 144 From May 2006 to November 2008: CIC interviews (see above).

p. 145 The RCMP believed the individuals were: Documents released by Citizenship and Immigration Canada under the *Access to Information Act* on December 5, 2008, File No. A-2009-01112 at 36-39, 46–49.

p. 145 "The dilemma for me": Pike (see above), interview with author, September 30, 2008.

p. 145 "miscommunication was a problem": Documents released by CIC, File No. A-2009-01112 at 111 (see above).

p. 146 In June 2007, the RCMP: *Ibid.*

p. 146 provide his or her own interpreter: *Ibid.* at 42.

p. 147 "the claimant has been victimized": *D.J.P. (Re)*, [1999] C.R.D.D. No. 155, No. T98-06446, para. 12 (IRB) per José Andrés Sotto and Raza Naqvi (concurring).

p. 147 "While some victims": CIC interviews (see above).

p. 147 six separate cases: Rico (see above).

p. 148 Protection services: Adapted from *Protocol to Prevent, Suppress and Punish Trafficking in Persons, Supplementing the United Nations Convention Against Transnational Organized Crime*, UN Doc. A/55/383 at 25 (2000); UN Doc. A/RES/55/25 at 4 (2001); 40 ILM 335 (2001) (entered into force December 25, 2003) ("Palermo Protocol"); Laura Barnett, "Trafficking in Persons" (Ottawa: Library of Parliament, revised July 18, 2008) at 16–17, online: Parliament of Canada <http://www.parl.gc.ca> (accessed November 17, 2009).

p. 149 One young woman controlled by: Viozzi (see above).

p. 149 "We have to keep the pimp": *Ibid.*

p. 149 "The victim witness protection program": Hamel (see above).

p. 150 … 'urgent and essential': *IP 1 Temporary Resident Permits* at 28 (see above).

p. 152 just 7 percent of foreign trafficking: CIC interviews (see above).

p. 152 eligible to receive income support: Alberta, Employment and Immigration, "Expected to Work/Not Expected to Work Policy & Procedures, 04 Special Groups, Victims of Human Trafficking," *Alberta Works Policy Manual* (July 4, 2008).

p. 153 British Columbia also extended: Order in Council 219, *B.C. Regulations Bulletin No. 11* (April 11, 2008).

p. 153 "age out": Anderson and Redsky (see above).

## 13 From Average Joes to Average Johns

p. 154 Sean's request to the escort agency: Case details and quotes from Hamel (see above).

p. 156 "When you look at all those ads": *Ibid.*

p. 157 "hundreds" of foreign women: Jeff Danroth, sergeant, Vancouver Police Department, interview with author, October 23, 2008.

p. 157 "[i]nternational women formerly in": Janice G. Raymond & Donna M. Hughes, *Sex Trafficking of Women in the United States: International and Domestic Trends* (March 2001) at 46, online: <http://www.ncjrs.gov/pdffiles1/nij/grants/187774.pdf> (accessed November 17, 2009).

p. 157 "Indentured sex trade workers": Rosie DiManno, "Sex slave 'victims' weren't captives chained to beds," *Toronto Star* (September 12, 1997) at A7.

p. 158 "Our approach to these women": Hamel (see above).

p. 158 Jennifer suspected that her husband: Fenn (see above).

p. 159 "Why is there tolerance": Shared Hope International, *Demand.: A Comparative Examination of Sex Tourism and Trafficking in Jamaica, Japan, the Netherlands, and the United States* (Shared Hope International, 2007) at 14.

p. 159 "They go for whatever": Fenn (see above).

p. 159 "whether or not the woman": Donna Hughes, *Best Practices to Address the Demand Side of Sex Trafficking* (August 2004) at 3–4.

p. 160 "If nobody knows about": Fenn (see above).

p. 160 "I have low self-esteem": *R. v. Nakpangi* at 3–4 (see above).

p. 160 purchasers of sex acts generally do not believe: Steven Sawyer et al., "A Brief Psychoeducational Program for Men Who Patronize Prostitutes" (1998) 26:3 *Journal of Offender Rehabilitation* 111 at 120.

p. 160 human beings are not born wishing: Bridget Anderson & Julia O'Connell Davidson, *Is Trafficking in Human Beings Demand Driven? A Multi-Country Pilot Study* (Switzerland: IOM, 2003) at 41.

p. 161 David Ramsay: Unless otherwise noted below, all quotes are from *R. v. Ramsay*, 2004 BCSC 756. See also "Former B.C. judge gets 7 years for sex assaults," *CTV News* (June 2, 2004), online: <http://www.ctv.ca>; "No parole for former judge

Ramsay," *The Vancouver Province* (September 12, 2007), online: <http://www.canada.com/theprovince> (both accessed November 17, 2009).

p. 165 "no meaningful attempt": Frank Peebles, "Ramsay dies in custody," *The Prince George Citizen* (January 21, 2008), online: <http://www.princegeorgecitizen.com> (accessed November 17, 2009).

p. 165 "the average client is": Stephen Grubman-Black, "Deconstructing John," presented at *Demand Dynamics: The Forces of Demand in Global Sex Trafficking* (Chicago, Illinois: October 17–18, 2003) at 23.

p. 165 A 1988 Gallup poll: "Prostitution not a problem, 58% tell Gallup," *Toronto Star* (March 9, 1992) cited in John Weitzer, *Sex for Sale: Prostitution, Pornography, and the Sex Industry* (Routledge, 1999) at 265.

p. 165 "the tip of the iceberg": Michel Greene, prosecutor, Government of Quebec, interview with author, June 9, 2008. See also Clifford Krauss, "Quebec journal: Still stinging from scandal, quiet city cries out in pain," *The New York Times* (December 22, 2003) at A4; Alexander Panetta, "Girls in sex ring recruited at malls and schools: Police," *Toronto Star* (December 19, 2002) at A34.

p. 166 potential bosses were former "clients": Fredette (see above).

p. 166 60 to 72 percent: M. Alexis Kennedy et al., *Men Who Solicit Prostitutes: A Demographic Profile of Participants in the Vancouver Police Department's Prostitution Offender Program* (February 2004) at 3, online: <http://www.popcenter.org>; Martin A. Monto, *Focusing on the Clients of Street Prostitutes: A Creative Approach to Reducing Violence Against Women—Final Report* (June 9, 2000) at 29, online: <http://www.ncjrs.gov> (both accessed November 17, 2009).

p. 166 over seven thousand men: Fenn (see above).

p. 166 50 percent ... were fathers: Rose Dufour, *Je vous salue ...* (MultiMondes: Quebec, 2005) cited in *Gangs and Girls* (see above) at 69; see also *Focusing on the Clients* at 30 (see above); Sawyer at 122–123 (see above).

p. 166 between twenty-four and twenty-seven: *Focusing on the Clients* at 32 (see above); *Men Who Solicit* at 7 (see above).

p. 166 forty-two paid encounters: *Men Who Solicit* at 7 (see above).

p. 166 "deeply troubled ... suffer from": Sven-Axel Månsson, "Men's Practices in Prostitution and Their Implications for Social Work" in Sven-Axel Månsson & Clotilde Proveyer Cervantes, eds., *Social Work in Cuba and Sweden: Achievements and Prospects* (Göteborg and Havana: Göteborg University and University of Havana, 2005) at 9, online: <http://www.caase.org/pdf/resources-research/26.pdf> (accessed June 9, 2010).

p. 167 "McSex": Blanchard (1994) cited in *Focusing on the Clients* at 34 (see above).

p. 167 "Some of them fall in love": Fenn (see above).

p. 167 "forcing sex acts that": Grubman-Black (see above).

p. 167 "[H]e tells you that": Excerpt from Aboriginal Women's Action Network, written statement of speech delivered on June 17, 2009, at "Buying Sex Is Not a Sport" (co-sponsored with the Langara Dialogues at the Vancouver Public Library) ("Terri-Lynn" is a pseudonym).

p. 168 people who wouldn't otherwise: Janelle Bird, corporal, RCMP, Internet Child Exploitation Unit, interview with author, November 4, 2008; *Focusing on the Clients* (see above).

p. 169 Studies in the United States: Kanouse et al., "Markers for HIV-1 hepatitis B and syphilis in a probability sample of street prostitutes in Los Angeles County, California" (1992, International Conference on AIDS/III STD World Congress, Amsterdam) and Hoffman et al., "The high HIV incidence in New York City streetwalkers may have peaked in 1990" (1992 International Conference on AIDS/ III STD World Congress, Amsterdam) cited in *Focusing on the Clients* (see above).

p. 169 prostituted females in Vancouver: Collin W. McInnes et al., "HIV/AIDS in Vancouver, British Columbia: A growing epidemic" (2009) 6:5 *Harm Reduction Journal* at 3.

p. 169 "At the height of my addiction": Laurie Monsebraaten, "A design on social change," *Toronto Star* (February 23, 2003) cited in *Best Practices to Address the Demand Side* at 38 (see above).

## 14 Doing the Dirty Work: Forced Labour

p. 171 "You can see when you": Rico (see above).

p. 171 twenty-eight complaints: Lock (see above). Conditions of complainants described in RCMP–Headquarters, "Occurrence Summary: 2008387125 Immigration and Refugee Protection Act—Enter by False Means @ 2008/04/11 13:18 MDT," May 13, 2008 (document released by the RCMP under the *Access to Information Act* on October 12, 2008, File No. GA-3951-3-01397/08 at 16).

p. 172 "3D work": International Labour Conference, *Towards a Fair Deal for Migrant Workers in the Global Economy* (Report IV), ILO, 92nd sess. (2004) at 11.

p. 172 "work or service which": *Convention Concerning Forced or Compulsory Labour* (May 1, 1932), 39 U.N.T.S. 55, art. 2.

p. 172 Shaughnessy ... two Filipina women: Lakeman (see above).

p. 173 abandoned in an emergency room: Richard B. Fadden, deputy minister, Citizenship and Immigration Canada, "Memorandum to the Minister's Office: Trafficking in Persons in Canada," June 29, 2007, at 3 (released by Citizenship and Immigration Canada under the *Access to Information Act* on January 5, 2009, File No. A-2008-01134 at 112).

p. 173 "They'd taken her papers": Isaacs (see above).

p. 174 Senait Tafesse Manaye: "Que. couple faces human trafficking charges," *CTV News* (May 18, 2007), online: <http://www.ctv.ca>; Canadian Press, "Montreal couple face human trafficking charge," *Toronto Star* (May 18, 2007), online: <http://www.thestar.com>; Canadian Press, "'Human trafficking' couple say they are innocent," *CTV News* (May 20, 2007), online: <http://www.ctv.ca>; Sue Montgomery, "RCMP's human trafficking case falls apart," *Montreal Gazette* (December 7, 2007), online: <http://www2.canada.com/montrealgazette> (all accessed November 17, 2009); "Quebec couple sues Crown, RCMP and Police over bogus human-slavery charge," *Canadian Press* (May 21, 2008).

p. 175 Elmvale 11: Dale Brazao, "Exploited workers Canada's 'slave trade': Skilled Filipino workers packed into filthy house, denied pay, threatened with deportation," *Toronto Star* (August 30, 2008), online: <http://www.thestar.com> (accessed June 9, 2010).

p. 175 "Inside there was mud": *Ibid.*

p. 176 "This was a chain gang": *Ibid.*

p. 176 "The way exploitation is phrased": *Ibid.*

p. 176 "[i]mproving the integrity": CIC interviews (see above).

p. 177 "will increase program integrity": *Ibid.*

p. 177 "a more rigorous assessment": Citizenship and Immigration Canada, "Minister Kenney proposes improvements to the Temporary Foreign Worker Program," *News Release*, October 9, 2009, online: CIC <http://www.cic.gc.ca/english/department/media/releases/2009/2009-10-09a.asp> (accessed October 19, 2009). Reproduced with the permission of the Minister of Public Works and Government Services, 2010.

## 15 Battling Trafficking Across Canada

p. 179 "emphasize the sacredness": Kookum Gaa Na Da Ma Waad Abinoojiig Council (Grandmothers Protecting Our Children) *Children Are Sacred Newsletter*, (September 2008); Jen Skerritt, "Grandmothers walk to stop child abuse: Aboriginal elders say exploitation must stop," *Winnipeg Free Press* (September 22, 2008), online: <http://www.winnipegfreepress.com> (accessed November 19, 2009).

p. 180 Cinderella's Silence: Le Centre jeunesse de Montréal—Institut universitaire, "Companion Guide to Cinderella's Silence—A Story of Gang Prostitution" (Montreal: 2002).

p. 180 Coordinator Anick Gagnon: Gagnon (see above).

p. 181 Most sexually exploited youth in Winnipeg: Stop Sex with Kids, online: <http://www.stopsexwithkids.ca> (accessed November 17, 2009) citing *Transition, Education, and Resources for Females (TERF) Mentor and Youth Program Evaluation*

*Reports 2005; 2006 Prostitutes and Other Women for Equal Rights (POWER) Evaluation Report*, Campbell and Heinrich, 1995.

p. 183 Unmanned aerial "drones": Phil Couvrette, "New patrol to monitor Quebec-U.S. border," *Canwest News Service* (February 4, 2009), online: <http://www.financialpost.com> (accessed June 9, 2010).

p. 183 only 30 percent of inadmissible persons: Alain Jolicoeur, president, CBSA, "Briefing Note for the Minister: Canada Border Services Agency Activities Against Trafficking in Persons" (undated) at 3 (released by the Canada Border Services Agency under the *Access to Information Act* on July 2, 2008, File No. A-2008-00261).

p. 184 "We are in a constant race": Government of Manitoba, "StreetReach offers protective hand to sexually exploited youth: Mackintosh," *Press Release* (October 6, 2009), online: <http://news.gov.mb.ca> (accessed December 9, 2009).

p. 185 "We were seizing their cars": Viozzi (see above).

p. 186 "The registered owner": Arnold (see above).

p. 186 In November 2009: Chris Kitching, "Thirty Winnipeg males arrested in prostitution sting," *Winnipeg Sun* (November 17, 2009), online: <http://www.winnipegsun.com> (accessed December 9, 2009).

p. 187 "may act as a deterrent": *Men Who Solicit* (see above).

p. 187–88 "If they don't get the point": Joe Parker, Lola Greene Baldwin Foundation, (Portland, March 23, 2004), cited in *Best Practices to Address the Demand Side* at 36 (see above).

p. 188 "Here's a guy who": Fenn (see above).

p. 188 "to scare the bejesus out": *Ibid.*

p. 189 The Vancouver Prostitution Offender Program: *Men Who Solicit* (see above).

p. 190 fewer than 2 percent: Fenn (see above).

p. 191 "Why are they getting diverted?": Lakeman (see above).

p. 193 *Canadian Criminal Law Review*: Benjamin Perrin, "Taking a Vacation from the Law? Extraterritorial Criminal Jurisdiction and Section 7(4.1) of the Criminal Code" (2009) 13 *Canadian Criminal Law Review* at 175–209.

p. 193 From 1995 to 2007: Australian Federal Police, "Inquiry into Crimes Legislation Amendment (Child Sex Tourism Offences and Related Measures) Bill 2007," submission to the Senate Standing Committee on Legal and Constitutional Affairs at 1 (September 20, 2007), online: <http://www.aph.gov.au> (accessed November 17, 2009).

p. 193 Between 2003 and early 2008: U.S. Immigrations and Customs Enforcement, "Operation Predator: Child Exploitation and Sex Crimes," November 19, 2008, online: <http://www.ice.gov> (accessed November 17, 2009).

p. 194 "Unfortunately, we are totally": Mary Vallis, "Canadian John Wrenshall pleads guilty to running brothels for pedophiles in Thailand," *National Post* (May 6, 2010), online: <http://news.nationalpost.com> (accessed June 9, 2010); see *United States of America v. John Wrenshall*, Indictment and News Release (December 15, 2008), online: <http://justice.gov/usao/nj/press/2008releases.html> (accessed October 20, 2009).

p. 194 "Internationally, we've got": Camille Baines, "At least 146 Canadians charged overseas for child sexual abuse: Justice Dept.," *Canadian Press* (April 1, 2008).

p. 195 "I don't understand why": Matt McClure, "Alleged pedophile ran free, Suspect lived 11 years in India; Canadian authorities fumbled extradition while executive stayed at large in India," *Toronto Star* (June 3, 2007), online: <http://www.thestar.com> (accessed June 9, 2010).

## 16 Dealing with Trafficking on a Global Basis

p. 198 In 2007, the Belgian government reported: *Trafficking in Persons Report* (2009) at 78 (see above).

p. 199 Of 495 adults referred: *Ibid.*

p. 200 889 unaccompanied minors: Ilse Derluyn & Eric Broekaert, "On the Way to a Better Future: Belgium as Transit Country for Trafficking and Smuggling of Unaccompanied Minors" (2005) 43(4) *International Migration* at 31–32.

p. 200 "the result of a compromise": Federal Public Service Foreign Affairs Belgium, Kingdom of Belgium, *The Fight Against Trafficking and Smuggling in Human Beings: Policy and Approach* (Brussels: 2008) at 3.23, online: <http://www.diplomatie.be/en/pdf/mensenhandelen.pdf> (accessed November 28, 2009).

p. 201 five hundred police specialists: Centre for Equal Opportunities and Opposition to Racism (CEOOR) Belgium, *Trafficking and Smuggling of Human Beings: Preface & Part I: An integral evaluation of policy in the fight against trafficking in human beings, Report 2007* (May 2008) at 46.

p. 202 In 2008, U.S.$9.41 million: *Trafficking in Persons Report* (2009) at 168 (see above).

p. 202 "On the Road": Danish Red Cross, *Good Practices in Response to Trafficking in Human Beings—Cooperation Between Civil Society and Law Enforcement in Europe* (Danish Red Cross, 2005) at 101–102.

p. 203 literacy courses for 588 victims: *Trafficking in Persons Report* (2008) at 148 (see above).

p. 203 issued 1009 residence permits: *Ibid.*

p. 203 Between 2003 and 2006: United Nations Office on Drugs and Crime, *Global Report on Trafficking in Persons* (February 2009) at 260, online: <http://www.unodc.org> (accessed June 9, 2010).

p. 203 "cultural mediator": Humantrafficking.org, "News & Updates—Italian Group Uses 'Street Units' to Protect Victims of Sex Trafficking" (September 2005), online: <http://www.humantrafficking.org/updates/310> (accessed June 9, 2010).

p. 204 "[T]he trafficked women want": Anti-Slavery International interview with COLCE (Cooperativa Lotta Contro L'Emarginazione) (Varese, 30 January 2002) cited in *Anti-Slavery International*, "Human traffic, human rights: Redefining victim protection" (2002) at 145, online: <http://www.antislavery.org> (accessed June 9, 2010).

p. 205 "Sadly, there are thousands": U.S. Attorney General, *Attorney General's Annual Report to Congress and Assessment of U.S. Government Activities to Combat Trafficking in Persons Fiscal Year 2008* (June 2009) at 1, online: <http://www.state.gov> (accessed November 28, 2009).

p. 206 assistance for 1696 foreign trafficking victims: *Ibid.*

p. 206 2300 T-visas were: *Ibid.*

p. 206 "the subtle means of coercion": Department of Health and Human Services, *Trafficking Victims Protection Act of 2000: Fact Sheet* at 2.

p. 207 prosecuted 531 alleged human traffickers: *Attorney General's Annual Report* at 42–43 (see above).

p. 208 A 2008 study by Northeastern University: Northeastern University Institute on Race and Justice, "Executive Summary–Understanding and Improving Law Enforcement Responses to Human Trafficking" (June 2008) at 8.

p. 208 Office of the Inspector General: *Attorney General's Annual Report* at 24 (see above).

p. 208 In Boston, the police: Northeastern University Institute on Race and Justice at 9 (see above).

p. 208 In Dallas, Texas, police: *The National Report on Domestic Sex Trafficking* at 66 (see above).

p. 208 Innocence Lost Initiative: *Attorney General's Annual Report* at 36–37, 42 (see above).

p. 209 National Human Trafficking Resource Center: *Ibid.* at 22; online: <http://nhtrc.polarisproject.org> (accessed November 28, 2009).

p. 210 Swedish model: See Arthur Gould, "The Criminalization of Buying Sex: The Politics of Prostitution in Sweden" (2001) 30:03 *Journal of Social Policy* at 427.

p. 211 Sweden allocated 213 million Krona: Ministry of Integration and Gender Equality (Sweden), *Info Sheet: Action Plan Against Prostitution and Human Trafficking for Sexual Purposes* (2008), online: <http://www.sweden.gov.se/content/1c6/11/06/29/fcd261a4.pdf> (accessed November 30, 2009).

p. 211 Initiatives include: Ministry of Integration and Gender Equality (Sweden), *Against Prostitution and Human Trafficking for Sexual Purposes* (Stockholm) at 10, online: <http://www.sweden.gov.se/content/1/c6/13/36/71/ae076495.pdf> (accessed November 30, 2009).

p. 212 From 1998 to 1999: Sweden, Socialstyrelsen, *Prostitution in 2003: Knowledge, Beliefs & Attitudes of Key Informants* (National Board of Health and Welfare Report, 2004) at 23, online: <http://www.childcentre.info/projects/exploitation/sweden/dbaFile11751.pdf > (accessed June 9, 2009).

p. 212 over 500 men had: Rachel Williams, "How making the customers the criminals cut street prostitution: Sweden's law against buying sex views women involved as victims of male violence," *The Guardian* (January 5, 2008), online: <http://www.guardian.co.uk/politics/2008/jan/05/uk.world> (accessed June 9, 2010).

p. 212 dropped by 40 percent: Karl Ritter, "World takes notice of Swedish prostitute laws," *The Independent* (March 17, 2008), online: <http://www.independent.co.uk/news/world/europe/world-takes-notice-of-swedish-prostitute-laws-796793.html> (accessed June 9, 2010).

p. 212 between 105 and 130 women: André Anwar, "Prostitution ban huge success in Sweden," *Der Spiegel* (August 11, 2007), online: <http://www.spiegel.de/international/europe/0,1518,516030,00.html> (accessed June 9, 2010).

p. 212 A 2005 study commissioned: Andrea Di Nicola et al., *Study on National Legislation on Prostitution and the Trafficking in Women and Children* (Brussels: European Parliament, August 2005), IPOL/C/FEMM/ST/2004-05 at ix, 102–103, online: <http://transcrime.cs.unitn.it/tc/412.php> (accessed November 29, 2009); see also Gunilla Ekberg, "The Swedish Law that Prohibits the Purchase of Sexual Services: Best Practices for Prevention of Prostitution and Trafficking in Human Beings" (2004) 10:10 *Violence Against Women* 1187 at 1200.

p. 212 "They can only run": Williams, *The Guardian* (see above).

p. 212 Swedish National Police also believe: Sweden, National Criminal Police: Criminal Intelligence and Investigation Division, *Trafficking in Human Beings for Sexual Purposes: Situation Report No. 8* (Rikskriminalpolisen, 2006), online: <http://www.osce.org/documents/cthb/2007/05/24548_en.pdf> (accessed June 9, 2010).

p. 212 80 percent of the population: Ekberg at 1204 (see above).

p. 213 "[W]ithout significant investment": John Picarelli & Anna Jonsson, "Fostering Imagination in Fighting Trafficking: Comparing Strategies and Policies to Fight Sex Trafficking in the U.S. and Sweden" (National Institute for Justice, May 2008) at 56, online: <www.ncjrs.gov> (accessed June 9, 2010).

p. 214 "I argue that any society": "Address by the Swedish Deputy Prime Minister, Margareta Winberg, at the Third Joint Seminar of the Nordic and Baltic Countries"

(November 28, 2002), online: <http://www.regeringen.se/sb/d/1105/a/6848> (accessed November 30, 2009).

p. 214 "Prolonged and repeated trauma": Melissa Farley, "Prostitution Is Sexual Violence" in Louise Gerdes, ed., *Prostitution and Sex Trafficking: Opposing Viewpoints* (New York: Thomson Gale, 2006) 101 at 103.

p. 214 In Australia's state of Victoria: *Prostitution Control Act 1994*, No. 102 of 1994, Version No. 65 (Australia, State of Victoria), ss. 19–20, online: <http://www.legislation.vic.gov.au> (accessed November 29, 2009); Consumer Affairs Victoria, *A Guide to the Prostitution Control Regulations 2006 for Licensees and Approved Brothel Managers* (May 2007) at 3, online: <http://www.bla.vic.gov.au> (accessed November 29, 2009).

p. 215 "a clear and close connection": Parliament of Victoria, Drugs and Crime Prevention Committee, *Inquiry into People Trafficking for Sex Work*, No. 312 Session 2006–2010 (Melbourne: June 2010) at v, 3, online: <http://www.parliament.vic.gov.au> (accessed June 9, 2010).

p. 215 "When legal barriers disappear": Janice G. Raymond, "Ten Reasons for Not Legalizing Prostitution and a Legal Response to the Demand for Prostitution" (2004) 2:3 *Journal of Trauma Practice* 315 at 322.

p. 215 more than eighty violent pimps: "Amsterdam draws curtain on sex industry as red light windows close," *Daily Mail* (U.K.) (September 21, 2007), online: <http://www.dailymail.co.uk>; David Charter, "Half of Amsterdam's red-light windows close," *The Times* (U.K.) (December 27, 2008), online: <http://www.timesonline.co.uk> (both accessed November 30, 2009); A.L. Daalder, *Prostitution in the Netherlands Since the Lifting of the Brothel Ban* (The Hague: WODC, 2006) at 95.

p. 215 results in *higher* levels of violence: *Study on National Legislation on Prostitution and the Trafficking in Women and Children* at x (see above).

p. 215 "unpredictable client behaviour": *A Guide to the Prostitution Control Regulations* at 3 (see above).

p. 215 In New Zealand: Ministry of Justice, *New Zealand Prostitution Law Review Committee* (Wellington: May 2008) at 17, 157, online: <http://www.justice.govt.nz/> (accessed November 30, 2009).

p. 216 "a broad and progressive": OBJECT, "Position on Prostitution," online: <http://www.object.org.uk/index.php/the-prostitution-facts> (accessed June 9, 2010).

## 17 Building a New Underground Railroad

p. 217 "I'm on my way to Canada": Cited in "Canadian Confederation: Influence of the American Civil War," online: <http://collectionscanada.ca/confederation/023001-2050-e.html> (accessed November 6, 2009).

p. 218 *A Federal Strategy on Trafficking in Persons*: "Draft #3: Federal Strategy on Trafficking in Persons (DRAFT—For Discussion Purposes Only—Not for Distribution," January 20, 2005 (released by the Department of Foreign Affairs under the *Access to Information Act* on May 25, 2009, File No. A-2007-00724/BD).

p. 218 Standing Committee on the Status of Women: House of Commons Standing Committee on the Status of Women, "Eleventh Report: A Comprehensive Strategy to Combat Human Trafficking in Canada," 39th Parl., 1st Sess., online: <http://www2.parl.gc.ca> (accessed June 9, 2010).

p. 218 In 2007, the entire House of Commons: M-153. *Trafficking in persons (human trafficking), combatting* (Smith), House of Commons, 39th Parl., 1st Sess. (February 22, 2007), agreed to, Journal No. 116 at 1061.

p. 222 recommended that Canada adopt the Swedish: *Turning Outrage into Action* at 15 (see above).

p. 223 Victims of crime should be treated: Department of Justice, *Canadian Statement of Basic Principles of Justice for Victims of Crime* (2003), online: <http://www.justice.gc.ca/eng/pi/pcvi-cpcv/pub/03/princ.html> (accessed November 27, 2009). Reproduced with the permission of the Minister of Public Works and Government Services Canada, 2010.

p. 226 counter–human trafficking police units: *Turning Outrage into Action* at 44 (see above).

p. 229 In Canada, local police forces should: Adapted from *The Crime of Human Trafficking* at 9 (see above).

p. 232 a total of 947 companies: The Code, "List of travel and tourism companies signatories of the Child-Protection Code of Conduct" (November 3, 2009), online: <http://www.thecode.org> (accessed November 27, 2009).

p. 233 top five risks to Canadian children: Cybertip.ca, "Top 5 Risks to Canadian Children on the Internet," online: <http://www.kidsintheknow.ca/PDFS/internet_risk_eng.pdf> (accessed November 26, 2009).

p. 234 In January 2010, four Filipina: Pike, interview with author, March 9, 2010 (see above).

p. 236 *A 2009 report by the U.S. Department of Labor*: U.S. Department of Labor, Office of Child Labor, Forced Labor and Human Trafficking, *The Department of Labor's List of Goods Produced by Child Labor or Forced Labor* (2009) at 21–28, online: <http://www.dol.gov> (accessed November 27, 2009).

p. 238 "*Deep in our history*": *Conscience for Change* (CBC Learning Systems, 1967) cited in McGill Faculty of Law, online: <http://www.mcgill.ca/maritimelaw/history/kingjr> (accessed June 7, 2010).

p. 238 "collection of the facts": Martin Luther King, Jr., *Letter from Burmingham Jail* (April 16, 1963), online: <http://abacus.bates.edu/admin/offices/dos/mlk/letter.html> (accessed November 27, 2009).

p. 238 "snug little house and garden": Adam Hochschild, *Bury the Chains: Prophets and Rebels in the Fight to Free an Empire's Slaves* (New York: Houghton Mifflin Company, 2005) at 230.

p. 239 "I just normally hear": Sam Pazzano, "Alleged pimp wooed young mom," *Toronto Sun* (April 30, 2009), online: <http://cnews.canoe.ca> (accessed November 27, 2009).

p. 240 "*Having heard all*": William Wilberforce, speech to Parliament (May 12, 1789); see Eric Metaxas, *Amazing Grace: William Wilberforce and the Heroic Campaign to End Slavery* (New York: Harper, 2007).

# ACKNOWLEDGMENTS

It is humbling to be the author of a book that so many dedicated people helped make happen. I want to thank The Maytree Foundation for confronting modern-day slavery in Canada by generously supporting this project. Alan Broadbent and Ratna Omidvar recognized the need for this book at our very first meeting in August 2007, and I'm grateful for their advice and encouragement ever since. Mary Anne Bobinski, Peter Dauvergne, and Julie Wagemakers also placed their confidence in this project and ensured the full institutional support of the University of British Columbia (UBC) Faculty of Law and Liu Institute for Global Issues.

The individuals whom I interviewed for this book have helped shine a bright light in some very dark places of our country—I'm indebted to them for sharing their expertise and continue to be inspired by the strength of their commitment to end human trafficking. I want particularly to thank Kristine Arnold with the Peel Regional Police for helping me understand the systematic nature of sex trafficking; Robin Pike with the B.C. Office to Combat Trafficking in Persons for our candid discussions about the challenges of addressing human trafficking; Diane Redsky and Jackie Anderson at the Ma Mawi Wi Chi Itata Centre for opening my eyes to the plight of sexually exploited Aboriginal girls and the healing that is possible when their community responds; and Marie-Claude Arsenault with the RCMP for always being accessible and willing to consider new ideas in the fight against human trafficking. I also want to recognize Matthew Taylor at Justice Canada and David Batstone with the Not for Sale Campaign who both shared documentation about several cases.

An enthusiastic group of UBC law students was instrumental at each stage of the research and writing of this book. The thousands of hours they spent on this challenging project, and the insightful ideas they contributed, made me proud to be one of their professors. All of my research assistants made notable contributions and are starting promising careers, including Jody Barber, Sarah Galeski, Bruno Godin, Fleur Heck, Rose Higgins, Dan Loutfi, Erica Olmstead, Kari Schroeder, Bethany Tapp, and Yichuan Wang. An outstanding group of volunteer student researchers with the UBC Human Trafficking Working Group met weekly to present their research findings and brainstorm ideas to overcome challenges we were facing. Thanks to Rebecca Aleem, Sarah Bishop, Erin Frew, Arielle Furneaux, Jodie Gauthier, Polly Grace, Alicia Hubbard, Katherine Hegarty, D.J. Larkin, Samuel Loeb, Colleen McLeod, Masao Morinaga, Paige Morrow, Lisa Nevens, Jennifer Nyland, Emily Pitcher, Karen Slaughter, and Jennifer Winstanley.

I'm grateful to my colleague Joel Bakan for helping open the door at Penguin Group (Canada) and for his advice about the project. The publishing team, including Diane Turbide, Justin Stoller, Sandra Tooze, Barbara Bower, and Sharon Kirsch, have helped the call to action in this book reach you, and for that I thank them. The book's manuscript was greatly improved because of the experienced feedback and editorial assistance of John Lawrence Reynolds, who helped me tell this story in a way that would reach a broader audience. I cannot thank Claudia Ho Lem enough for her invaluable comments from the first draft of the proposal all the way through to the final proofs. Her indispensable feedback helped ensure the voice of victims was more strongly heard, recommendations were streamlined, and ideas presented more clearly. I also want to thank Andrew Perrin for taking time away from his own research endeavours to suggest improvements to the book proposal and for helpful observations on early drafts of several chapters.

I am fortunate to have been able to work with some exceptional people over the last decade on this issue, including Monte Solberg, Shuvaloy Majumdar, and Sabrina Sullivan, to name but a few. While this book was still being written, I began to work with others to address some of the pressing problems that it identifies. MP Joy Smith has been a national leader in fighting human trafficking in Canada. She quickly took up the task of courageously spearheading Bill C-268, a private member's bill to toughen sentences for child trafficking. Joel Oosterman, her chief of staff, and Senator Yonah Martin (who sponsored the bill in the Senate) helped build a remarkable coalition both in Parliament and among average Canadians in support of this legislation. The way they cut through the politics of Ottawa to have this important law enacted has kept my idealism alive.

At times, this project was very personally difficult. Investigating the cruelty and injustice of human trafficking on a daily basis was heartbreaking and, occasionally, paralyzing. Reading Gary Haugen's book *Good News About Injustice* helped me come to terms with the suffering that I was witnessing and the struggle to overcome it. Regular hikes in the peaceful mountains of Vancouver's North Shore with Richard, Maxime, Marvin, and Skip brought welcome moments of respite. I have leaned heavily on my supportive parents, family, and close friends, as well as Pastor Owen—all of you have helped me so much without even realizing it. Above all, I want to thank my wife for her unwavering support throughout this journey. She has been there at every step of the way through the late nights, early mornings, and weeks apart. Her patience, understanding, and compassion were so much more than I could have ever asked anyone to give.

# INDEX

## S